Discovering Our Past

DISCOVERING OUR PAST

A Brief Introduction to Archaeology

SECOND EDITION

Wendy Ashmore
Robert J. Sharer
University of Pennsylvania

MAYFIELD PUBLISHING COMPANY
Mountain View, California
London • Toronto

Library of Congress Cataloging-in-Publication Data

Ashmore, Wendy
Discovering our past: a brief introduction to archaeology
/ Wendy Ashmore, Robert J. Sharer. — 2nd ed.
p. cm.
Includes bibliographical references (p.) and index.
ISBN 1-55934-521-7
1. Archaeology. I. Sharer, Robert J. II. Title.
CC75.A74 1995
930.1— dc20   95-3683
                                                  CIP

Manufactured in the United States of America
10 9 8 7 6 5 4 3

Mayfield Publishing Company
1280 Villa Street
Mountain View, CA 94041

Sponsoring editor, Janet M. Beatty; *production editor,* Julianna Scott Fein; *manuscript editor,* Dale Anderson; *art director,* Jeanne M. Schreiber; *text and cover designer,* Susan Breitbard; *manufacturing manager,* Randy Hurst. The text was set in 10/12 Janson and printed on 50# Finch Opaque by Malloy Lithographing, Inc.

Cover image: DeWitt Jones/Tony Stone Images.

For Mary Grow

 Preface

As children, many of us learn to associate archaeologists with adventurous exploits and searches for long-lost civilizations in exotic places. As adults, our associations of archaeology with adventure are often strengthened when we see and hear stories in the media about fantastic archaeological finds. But what is it that archaeologists actually *do* on a normal work day in the field? This book corrects some of the popular myths about archaeologists and archaeology and explains what archaeologists really do, and how they do it.

We begin with a brief overview of archaeology, how it grew over the past few centuries, and how archaeologists today use various means to attempt to discover the past. The remainder of the book is organized to follow the steps of actual archaeological research. Beginning with the formulation of questions that define the goals of each research effort, we then look at the methods used to gather and analyze archaeological evidence, how archaeologists interpret this evidence, and how they present results to other archaeologists and the public. The book closes with a discussion of the challenges faced by archeologists—how to reconcile the needs of archaeologists and other concerned groups who have an interest in the past.

The book is written specifically for introductory archaeology courses, especially surveys of human prehistory that include an introduction to archaeological method and theory. It derives from our more comprehensive text, *Archaeology: Discovering Our Past* (Second edition, Mayfield 1993). Both texts follow the same basic organization and share the same underlying philosophy—that archaeology is part of the broader field of anthropology with its concern for investigating all aspects of the human experience. Both books are also based on the premise that the evidence sought by archaeologists in their study of the past represents a nonrenewable resource. This resource is fragile and especially precious, for archaeological evidence is the only means for us to discover most of our past. This doesn't mean that there is only one way to view our past—often there are several ways to study the evidence from the past. There is no single way for doing archaeology, and the best archaeology is that which uses the best methods available in each research situation.

NEW TO THIS EDITION

We have updated the text throughout to reflect the latest developments in archaeology. New coverage includes expanded discussions of Native American reburials (Chapters 1 and 10) and the issues involved in human skeletal analysis (Chapter 6). Dating methods and other laboratory analyses (Chapter 7) now include uranium series age determination and electron spin resonance. We have added new sections on Geographic Information Systems (GIS) to Chapter 5. To underscore the importance of conserving archaeological sites, we introduce the tragic case of Slack Farm in Kentucky in Chapter 1 alongside the dramatic ongoing work at the Sipan tomb in Peru. Pseudoarchaeology and looting are included now in Chapter 1 so that readers can become more quickly aware of contemporary challenges to archaeological research.

The treatment of theoretical frameworks has been moved much earlier in the book (Chapter 3) and now includes a discussion of contextualism; the comparison of the approaches of culture history, cultural process, and contextualism should help readers understand the value of integrating them in archaeological research.

In addition to the extensive glossary and index, we've introduced several learning aids. To help readers better orient themselves, we have added maps of archaeological sites discussed in the text to the front of the book. For those readers who want more information on specific chapter topics, each chapter now ends with a guide to further reading, which is keyed to the bibliography at the end of the book.

ACKNOWLEDGMENTS

In preparing this book we have been helped by many people. We are especially grateful to our colleagues who reviewed the manuscript and made many helpful suggestions for improvement: Kathryn Cruz-Uribe, Northern Arizona University; Paul Farnsworth, Louisiana State University; John W. Olsen, University of Arizona; Susan Riches, Fort Lewis College; and William A. Turnbaugh, University of Rhode Island.

The staff of Mayfield Publishing Company was both kind and helpful to us in all stages of preparing this book for publication. Jan Beatty was once again the spark that kindled the development of the book, and we add that her friendship is as important to us as is her expertise and professionalism. The essential copyediting was done by Dale Anderson, and Julianna Scott Fein oversaw the final production. We are very grateful to everyone for their time and effort.

Wendy Ashmore

Robert J. Sharer

 Contents

8

RECONSTRUCTING THE PAST   164

9

UNDERSTANDING THE PAST   196

10

ARCHAEOLOGY TODAY   218

Arctic Ocean

Cape Krusenstern

Bering Strait

Pacific Ocean

Big Horn Medicine Wheel

Powers Fort

Lindenmeier
Olsen-Chubbuck

Cahokia

Plimouth Plantation

Colonial Pennsylvania
Plantation

China Lake

1.
3 • Folsom
• Fort Craig
2

Slack Farm,
Savage Cave

Williamsburg,
Martin's Hundred

Chaco Canyon

Mimbres area

1. Oraibi
2. Sunset Crater
3. Point of Pines

Teotihuacan

Atlantic Ocean

Tenochtitlan

Tehuacán

Caribbean Sea

Archaeological Areas in North America and Mexico

Palenque

Port Royal

Tikal, Uaxactún, Jimbal

Copán,
Gualjoqueto,
Tencon

Altar de Sacrificios
El Porton, Las Tunas
Chalchuapa, Ceren

Caribbean Sea

Atlantic Ocean

Chan Chan, Moche
Virú Valley

Machu Picchu
Ayacucho

Pacific Ocean

Tiwanaku

Easter Island

Archaeological Areas in Central and South America

Archaeological Areas in Europe and North Africa

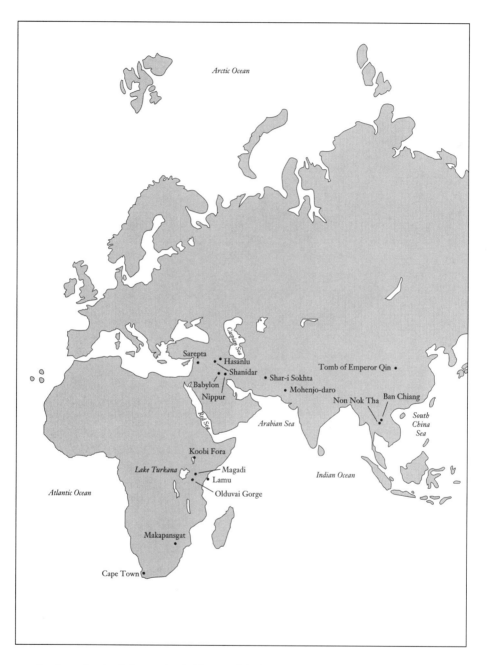

Archaeological Areas in Africa and Asia

1

Introduction

For many generations the Slack family worked their farm in Kentucky. But long before any European set foot in the Americas, this land had been the setting for a sizable Native American town. The name of this settlement has been lost, but we know that it was occupied for some two centuries, beginning about 1450. We also know that these Native Americans were part of a great tradition, now known as the Mississippian culture, that dominated southeastern North America from about A.D. 900 to the time these people (and all other Native Americans) were overwhelmed by European colonists.

In size, the settlement we now call the Slack Farm site was similar to other Mississippian towns, with a population estimated at 300 to 500. Like other towns of this culture, the settlement was composed of houses and other buildings used by its living inhabitants and places of burial for the dead. Most of the houses were occupied by farming families, but there were also large earthen platforms that supported the more elaborate houses of powerful families, those of the chiefs. Other earthen platforms supported the temples that housed the gods worshipped by these agricultural people.

We know these things about the Slack Farm site because of what archaeologists have learned from careful excavation of other Mississippian settlements. But although archaeologists had known for decades that the remains of this Native American town existed on Slack Farm, it had never been excavated. Thanks to the care of the Slack family, this site had been preserved. This preservation was all the more remarkable since most other Mississippian sites, along with those of other Native American cultures, have been badly damaged or destroyed. Some of this destruction has been accidental—mostly due to

1

FIGURE I.I

This aerial view of Slack Farm illustrates dramatically the destruction
wrought by looters: in just two months, ten men reduced this Native
American site to a pitted wasteland, littered with pottery fragments and
shattered human remains. (Kenny Barkley, Morganfield, Kentucky.)

European colonization and the expansion of modern society. But a great deal of
destruction of Native American sites, and archaeological sites all over the
world, is intentional. These sites are destroyed by looters who churn through
the ground in their search for objects that have value—everything from sou-
venirs to treasure that can be sold for thousands or even hundreds of thousands
of dollars.

The Slack Farm site was the largest known Mississippian site that had
escaped devastation by looters. All that changed in 1987, when the farm was
sold out of the family. Its new owners immediately leased artifact-mining rights

FIGURE 1.2

Archaeologists and volunteers from Kentucky and Indiana investigated the looters' holes and dirt piles at Slack Farm to document damage and to salvage information about this important habitation and mortuary site. (Courtesy of David Pollak, Kentucky Heritage Council, and Cheryl Ann Munson, Indiana University, Bloomington.)

to a small group of looters, pocketing $10,000 from the deal. Within two months, the looters had transformed this preserved monument of Native American culture into a pock-marked wasteland. The site looked like a moonscape, littered with bits of pottery and human bone thrown out of more than 450 craters dug to find whatever few remains might prove valuable enough to repay the looters' investment (Fig. 1.1).

Once archaeologists learned of the destruction, they moved rapidly to salvage what they could (Fig. 1.2). But by that time the greater part of the site was demolished. Destroyed with the site were all the remains, once preserved beneath the ground, that could have told us about the lives of the people who lived there. True to form, the looters wantonly desecrated the burials of the people who had once lived there, destroying the human remains in at least 650 graves and callously offending their living descendants. (Human burials are prized targets for looters because they often contain objects with tremendous appeal to collectors of art and antiquities.)

Neither the Slack Farm site, nor any other archaeological site, can tell us about all aspects of an ancient society. Because peoples the world over have *working w/ living* (handwritten in left margin)

buried their dead with objects reflecting their roles in life, burials offer invaluable insights into the past. But as we shall see later (Chapter 10), the excavation of human burials also raises important ethical issues. Many Native Americans do not want the remains of their ancestors disturbed in any way, and museums in the United States are returning previously excavated human remains to their living descendants. Most archaeologists want to work with Native Americans and other concerned ethnic groups to preserve the remains of the past. In some cases this means ensuring that archaeological sites are set aside as undisturbed cultural preserves. In other cases, this means archaeologists and Native Americans or other ethnic groups work together to create well-planned and careful excavations to recover and preserve invaluable information about the past.

Looters are the real enemies of all people who want to preserve the past. All over the world, archaeologists who want to understand the human past are in a constant race with looters who destroy the past for personal gain. Why do people look for remains of the past at all, and once found, what is done with these materials? The objective for looters is obvious—to find valuable objects that can be sold for profit. The objectives for archaeologists are to preserve and to learn.

ARCHAEOLOGISTS AND ARCHAEOLOGY

It is obvious that archaeologists are people who are interested in the past, but their interest is defined by specific questions they seek to answer. These questions involve our origins as human beings, the origins of specific cultures, how societies develop through time, and the relationship between the past and the present. Ultimately, archaeologists seek to better define who we are and understand why we behave as we do. What we are today, the way we behave, our customs, our beliefs, our entire civilization, are all the result of what happened in the past—an incredibly long and complex chain of human accomplishments that extends over millions of years. Thus, if we want to understand ourselves and our world today, we must try to understand our past.

The desire to understand ourselves motivates many people to careers in fields such as psychology, sociology, economics, and other social sciences. These fields study different aspects of humanity, but they are all limited to the present—to today's behavior and today's society. Others seek knowledge about humanity in the biological sciences, medicine, molecular biology, and related fields, but these fields also study what we are today, in the present. To understand ourselves as fully as possible, we also must understand where we came from and how we developed over time. Of course, history also studies the past, but its scope is limited to the last few thousand years of our past—the era of written documents. Archaeology is the only field that explores and reveals the full extent of our past, from the most remote origins of human characteristics

FIGURE 1.3

Excavating the tomb of the "Lord of Sipán" required great care to recover
the well-preserved but fragile remains. Here archaeologists have just
removed the skeleton of this Moche lord, revealing lavish gold and feather
ornaments on which he had lain. Whereas looters would have been concerned only with profit from selling the sumptuous offerings, archaeologists aim to recover the insights the tomb and its occupant, as well as the
offerings, can give us about life and death in the Moche world. (Martha
Cooper, © 1988 National Geographic Society.)

to the recent past. In this work, archaeologists encounter both the greatest
achievements and greatest failures of human history.

   This book is about archaeology and how archaeologists conduct their work
to better understand the past. Archaeology fascinates many people. Some people become archaeologists because of an interest that began when they were
children. Certainly to many children and adults alike, archaeology may seem to
promise a life of adventure, travel to exotic lands, and discovery of lost civilizations. This romantic image can be found in books, on television, and in
motion pictures—best represented by the adventures of Indiana Jones. Fiction
aside, this image of archaeology is reinforced by the occasional reports of real
discoveries, such as the first unlooted Moche royal tomb in Peru (Fig. 1.3) or

FIGURE I.4

Chinese archaeologists clear one of hundreds of clay soldiers, part of
the effigy army created to protect the tomb of Qin Shi Huang, the first
emperor of China, excavated from a collapsed underground vault near
the village of Xiyang, Shaanxi Province, China. (Courtesy of Beijing
Photo Studio.)

the spectacular ceramic army of China's first emperor (Fig. 1.4). Even a discovery made over seventy years ago—Howard Carter's opening of the tomb of
the Egyptian Pharaoh Tut-ankh-amun (Fig. 1.5)—continues to excite the public imagination.

In truth, discoveries such as these are very rare. Most archaeologists never
find spectacular tombs or lost civilizations. It is far more usual for archaeologists to spend long periods of time doing spectacularly tedious research, apparently rewarded only by dramatically uncomfortable living conditions, bad food,
pests, and diseases! Clearly then, most archaeologists cannot be motivated by
the prospect of a life of thrilling discovery or adventure. More importantly,
they are not driven by the prospect of finding treasure or anything for its monetary or aesthetic value. The actual motivation of archaeologists is far more
mundane: to recover information that will increase our understanding of the
past. Although finding that information may be tedious and uncomfortable at
times, the rewards are great, for archaeologists have the privilege of being time
travelers who can discover for themselves and educate others about parts of our
past that otherwise would be lost forever.

FIGURE 1.5

Howard Carter opening the inner doors of the tomb of Tut-ankh-amun. (Griffith Institute, Ashmolean Museum, Oxford.)

Archaeology and Pseudoarchaeology

Archaeologists have other competitors besides looters: those who create descriptions of the past based not on evidence, but on what is calculated to sell tabloids, magazines, books, and films. These accounts of the past are often appealing, for they describe dramatic mysteries and baffling paradoxes supposedly found in the archaeological record. But they are not archaeology, they are pseudoarchaeology. Looters destroy precious evidence before it can be used to understand the past. People who promote pseudoarchaeology ignore the evidence and spread misinformation, some of which is so fantastic only a small lunatic fringe gives it any credence ("Monster Aliens from Krypton Gave Us Civilization"). Other accounts are more subtle and lead people into believing things about our past that are not only untrue, but can even be harmful.

Pseudoarchaeologists claim to build their accounts from evidence, but in fact they do not. Examples include many of the accounts dealing with the supposed lost civilizations of Atlantis and Mu, imaginary continents inhabited by amazingly sophisticated peoples that supposedly gave rise to the known early civilizations throughout the world before disappearing beneath the waves of the Atlantic and Pacific oceans. Every so often reports of finding lost hieroglyphs or symbols revive the speculation about the mysterious origins of some

FIGURE I.6

Rubbing made from the sculptured
sarcophagus lid found in the tomb
beneath the Temple of the Inscriptions
at Palenque, Mexico, representing the
dead ruler surrounded by Maya supernatural symbols. (Rubbing, permission
of Merle Greene.)

famous civilization, usually with the added punch that, once again, all the so-
called experts were wrong.

Money is the usual motive for pseudoarchaeology. Pitchmen peddling
bogus accounts keep proving P. T. Barnum correct: there *is* a sucker born every
minute. Many millions of dollars have gone into the pockets of unscrupulous
authors who sell millions of pseudoarchaeology books in many languages all
over the world. These have also spawned television programs, movies, and
numerous imitations by people anxious to get in on this lucrative scam. Over
the years the most successful of these pseudoarchaeological writers has been
Erich von Däniken, who has updated the old Atlantis and Mu stories by trying
to show that the world's civilizations stem from ancient visits by alien beings.
As one of his alleged proofs, von Däniken describes the sculptured scene on the
sarcophagus lid from a famous tomb at the Maya site of Palenque, Mexico, as
representing an ancient astronaut at the controls of his rocket (Fig. 1.6). In
making this claim, von Däniken ignores a vast amount of evidence from Maya
art, symbolism, and inscriptions, all of which identify the sculptured figure as
the ruler buried in the sarcophagus, shown falling into the underworld at his
death. In this and other examples of pseudoarchaeology, carefully selected
items are used to support the case being made, while all other evidence is
ignored. In this case, a mere superficial resemblance between an astronaut's
launch position and the carved portrait of a dead Maya ruler is treated as if it
were positive evidence for the ancient space visitor theory.

One might argue that such fantasy is harmless, no matter how lucrative pseudoarchaeology is for its creators, but sometimes pseudoarchaeology is used for political motives, as when nationalistic or racist doctrines are supported by falsified reconstructions of the past. The most tragic case of this kind was promoted by Nazi Germany. The German prehistorian Gustav Kossinna (1858–1931) manipulated archaeological evidence to build a false and racist reconstruction of the past. Kossinna was interested in showing the superiority of Germany above other nations. By exaggeration and falsification, he produced a prehistoric reconstruction that claimed everything of importance had begun in Germany before spreading to surrounding allegedly inferior nations.

This pseudoarchaeological view of the past was used by Adolf Hitler in his book, *Mein Kampf*, to help justify the doctrine of German racial superiority. In this case, therefore, what began as a nationalistic pseudoarchaeological reconstruction ended up as part of the rationale for Nazi German military expansion, leading to World War II in Europe and, ultimately, to the slaughter of millions of innocent people.

The terrible experience of Nazism provides a bitter lesson about the impact of racist doctrine. While the harmful effects of such blatantly racist pseudoarchaeology are obvious, fictional accounts that claim past civilizations were founded by survivors of Atlantis or by space aliens are a subtler but still insidious form of racism. Such pseudoarchaeology assumes that the actual builders of these civilizations could not have succeeded without outside help. Inherent in von Däniken's version of the past is the assumption that the ancient Egyptians, Maya, or Inca did not themselves possess the ability to build their great monuments. In fact, the accomplishments of these civilizations did not require superhuman skills or knowledge. Ancient Egyptians, and all other early civilizations, were quite able to move huge and heavy stones from quarries to their building sites by either water or land.

The peoples of the past were certainly capable of more artistic, engineering, and intellectual achievements than the purveyors of pseudoarchaeology are willing to admit. Tales of extraterrestrial visits make exciting science fiction, but we should keep these imaginative stories in the realm of fantasy where they belong. As a science seeking to understand the human past, archaeology has a responsibility to ensure our ancestors get credit for their accomplishments.

Archaeology Defined

Archaeology is the study of the human past through its material remains. During the past few hundred years archaeology has grown from an amateur's pastime to a scientifically based profession. In that time, it has emerged as the field that uses recovered physical remains to order and describe ancient events, to explain the human behavior behind those events, and to understand the meaning of the past. To study the past, archaeologists have developed a series of methods by which they discover, recover, preserve, describe, and analyze the remains from the past. These remains are referred to as the **archaeological**

record. To make sense of this record, archaeologists are guided by a body of theory. Ultimately, theory provides the means to interpret archaeological evidence and allows description, explanation, and understanding of the past. This book will explore both the methods (Chapters 4–7) and the theory (Chapters 8–9) used by archaeologists.

Archaeology has four principal goals in studying the past. The first is to reveal the **form** of the past: the description and classification of the physical evidence that is recovered. Analysis of form allows archaeologists to outline the distribution of remains of ancient societies in both time and space. The second goal is to discover **function.** By analyzing the form and interrelationships of recovered evidence, archaeologists attempt to determine the purposes of the objects found. The determination of function leads to reconstructing past activities. The third goal is to understand cultural processes by using the remains of ancient cultures to explain how and why they changed through time. Finally, the fourth goal is to understand the meaning of culture for people in the past and learn from the past things that may be of use to us today.

ARCHAEOLOGY AS A SCIENCE

Science is concerned with gaining knowledge about the natural world by observation. Science is not concerned with things that cannot be observed or examined; these are the subjects of theology, philosophy, the occult, or pseudoscience. To do its job, science systematically describes phenomena, classifies observations, and reaches conclusions. This often involves controlled and repeatable laboratory experiments, such as those in chemistry or psychology, but it may also consist of detailed observation *without* experiment. Some fields cannot rely on experiments; these are called *historical sciences*. Examples include geology, evolutionary biology, and archaeology. All deal with long-ago events that no longer can be directly observed, although the evidence left behind can be studied to reconstruct what took place.

Some scientists follow a uniform set of formal procedures in an effort to be as objective as possible. Many scholars, however, question whether any scientific study can be truly objective and unbiased, regardless of the procedures used. They argue that all scientists have inherent biases based on their own cultural and personal background and that these biases affect objectivity. For example, most archaeologists are the products of modern Western society and may perpetuate views of the past that are biased by that society's view of itself. This implies that there are many ways of viewing the past, and that the meaning of the past (goal four, mentioned above) may vary with the viewpoint of each individual archaeologist.

To be as unbiased and objective as possible, science uses an approach to acquiring knowledge that is continuously self-correcting, so that the conclusions reached in earlier research are subject to repeated testing and refinement.

This self-correcting set of procedures for gaining and testing our knowledge of the observable world is called the **scientific method.**

Science discovers facts about the natural world by observing objects or events. A scientist may draw conclusions by observing the real world and then test those conclusions by seeing if they hold true in other circumstances or cases. This involves starting from specific observations and proceeding to a generalization based on those observations. You can also do the opposite, deriving specific propositions from a generalization. For instance, if prerecorded cassette tapes from the Whizbang Company frequently went bad after only a few playings, you might generalize that Whizbang's products were unreliable. If the same company started issuing videotapes, you might reason that the quality of these products is also suspect. You could then *test* your conclusion about Whizbang's general manufacturing quality standards by buying and playing some of the new products.

To see how these reasoning processes work within archaeology, let us look at an example. Julian Steward, an anthropologist of great importance to archaeology, conducted extensive fieldwork in the Great Basin of the western United States in the 1920s and 1930s, studying the Native American Shoshonean peoples living in this region. From this work with living groups, he developed a generalization to describe the distribution of earlier, prehistoric Shoshonean activities and campsites, relating their locations to the changing seasonal cycle of food procurement. That is, Steward presented his data as a **model,** a summary description of the patterns and regularities in the behavior of the ancient Shoshonean people as they moved from place to place to acquire food.

In the 1960s David Hurst Thomas took Steward's model of shifting settlement in the Great Basin and derived from it a series of propositions or **hypotheses** (statements of relationships based on a set of assumptions). As Thomas phrased it, "if the late prehistoric Shoshoneans behaved in the fashion suggested by Steward, how would the artifacts have fallen on the ground?" (Thomas, 1973). If Steward's model of shifting settlement and seasonal exploitation of food resources in different locations were true, Thomas could expect to find the tools associated with specific food activities in predictable locations. For example, more hunting tools and butchering knives should be found in the sagebrush zones where, according to the model, hunting was more important.

Thomas's archaeological research supported more than 75 percent of the hypotheses derived from Steward's model. As a result, the model was refined, and new hypotheses were generated, which in turn allowed further improvement of our understanding of the ancient Shoshone. This sequence of generating and testing hypotheses could be continued indefinitely.

The contrast between this approach to understanding the past and pseudoarchaeology could not be stronger. Instead of systematically collecting and evaluating all available evidence and using this to develop and test hypotheses to produce the most reasonable reconstruction of the past, writers of pseudoarchaeology dismiss much of what has been learned about the past, choosing instead to select only those bits of information that can be made to fit their preconceived theories.

It is important to note that the scientific method does not attempt to prove one hypothesis correct. Rather, the testing of a series of contrasting hypotheses tries to eliminate those that are incorrect and isolate the one hypothesis that best fits the observed phenomena. Thus, there is no *proof* in science, only elimination or disproof of inadequate hypotheses. Science advances by disproof, promoting what are the most adequate propositions of the moment, knowing that new data and better explanations will come along in the future. Scientists, therefore, often disagree with each other, presenting alternative interpretations for consideration.

Like other scientists, archaeologists apply the scientific method to a specified class of phenomena: the material remains of past human activity. Like other scientists, archaeologists attempt to isolate, classify, and explain the relationships among pieces of evidence—in this case, among the variables of form, function, time, and space. Archaeologists can observe the variables of form and space directly to determine the composition, size, and shape of each piece of evidence and its location. The variables of function and time must be inferred, to determine the purpose and age of each piece of evidence. Once these relationships are established, the archaeologist uses the evidence to infer past human behavior and, by combining many such examples, begins to reconstruct past human societies.

Because of the sheer volume of the evidence that archaeologists deal with, and the need to quantify and statistically manipulate these data, computers have become virtually indispensable for archaeological research. Computers and statistics are tools to aid research, but these should not be equated with the scientific method. It is the underlying philosophy and procedures governing the search for knowledge that define the scientific method.

The scientific method requires that archaeologists carefully state the assumptions under which they work and clearly formulate the questions they attempt to answer about the past. To answer those questions, archaeologists present their data and hypotheses and explain how these hypotheses were tested. It is important to remember, however, that although archaeologists, like other scientists, try to be completely objective in their search for knowledge, they can never escape their cultural and personal experiences. While complete objectivity remains the goal, all scientific research is shaped to some degree by cultural factors.

ARCHAEOLOGY AND HISTORY

Archaeology and history are related by their common concern with human events in the past. The major difference between the two disciplines is their sources of information. **History** works with written accounts from the past; archaeology works with the material remains of the past. These material remains are mute; their significance depends entirely on the inferences made by trained archaeologists. In contrast, historical records are direct communications from the past, although their significance is also subject to interpretation by trained historians.

By definition, history focuses on societies with writing, Moreover, since relatively more documents deal with the richest and most powerful people in those societies, it tends to emphasize the royal and priestly elite. Archaeology is less partial to rich or learned folk. Everyone eats, makes things, discards trash, and dies, so everyone contributes to the archaeological record. Archaeology, far more than history, deals with the whole range of humanity, regardless of social standing. Because of these contrasts, history and archaeology often complement each other, together providing a more complete record of the past than either can furnish alone. While archaeology considers all aspects of the past, there are always some things that leave no material traces, and these activities may be described in historical documents. Archaeology, in turn, by finding evidence of the daily lives of common people in earlier societies, can enrich the view that historians hold.

For these reasons, archaeology and history are closely allied in fields where the methods of both disciplines are applied to the study of a particular era. For instance, the field of classical archaeology combines the methods of archaeology with the use of historical sources to document the classical civilizations of Greece and Rome. Classical archaeology is also allied to the field of art history, which provides another route—the analysis of art styles and themes—to understanding the past.

Most archaeologists, however, are concerned with aspects of the past that cannot be directly supplemented by historical studies. History is limited to a relatively recent era of human development, beginning with the invention and use of writing systems. This era extends at most some 5000 years into the past, in southwestern Asia, the area with the earliest examples of writing. When compared with about 2.5 million years of human cultural development, the era of history represents less than 1 percent of the total (Fig. 1.7). Historical studies are even more limited in time outside Southwest Asia, and they are not possible in areas where writing systems never developed.

The contrasts between history and archaeology distinguish **historical archaeology,** or archaeology combined with analysis of written records, from **prehistoric archaeology,** or research on societies and time periods that lack written records. The latter seeks to understand the full sweep of human development on earth, from its earliest traces to its most remote variations. Of course, both historical and archaeological data are fragmentary; neither can provide a complete reconstruction of the past. Even when historical records are available, archaeological information can add to our understanding of that past era. A good example in which history was illuminated by archaeology is the excavation of Martin's Hundred, where archaeologist Ivor Noël Hume and his associates have unearthed the fragile remnants of one of the earliest British colonial settlements of tidewater Virginia. Originally the team had been seeking traces of the 18th-century Carter's Grove plantation. Illustrating that

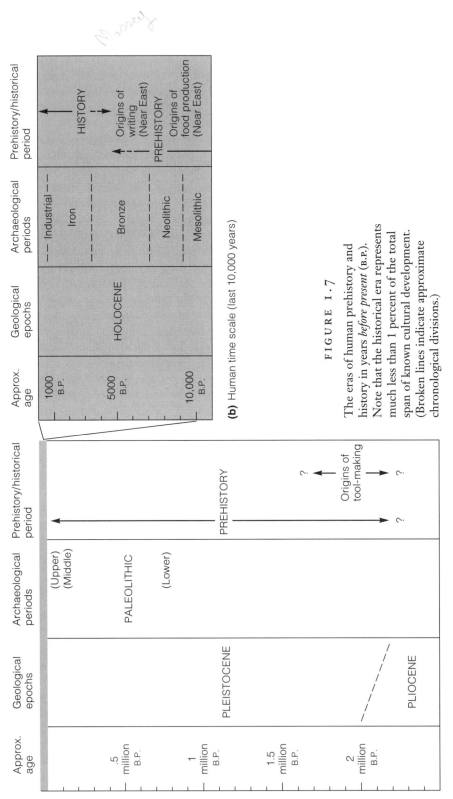

Massey

(b) Human time scale (last 10,000 years)

Approx. age	Geological epochs	Archaeological periods	Prehistory/historical period
1000 B.P.		— — Industrial — —	
	HOLOCENE	Iron	HISTORY
5000 B.P.		— — — — — — Bronze	Origins of writing (Near East)
		— — — — — Neolithic	PREHISTORY
10,000 B.P.		— — — — Mesolithic	Origins of food production (Near East)

FIGURE 1.7

The eras of human prehistory and history in years *before present* (B.P.). Note that the historical era represents much less than 1 percent of the total span of known cultural development. (Broken lines indicate approximate chronological divisions.)

Approx. age	Geological epochs	Archaeological periods	Prehistory/historical period
.5 million B.P.		(Upper) (Middle)	
1 million B.P.	PLEISTOCENE	PALEOLITHIC (Lower)	PREHISTORY
1.5 million B.P.			Origins of tool-making
2 million B.P.	PLIOCENE		?

(a) Human time scale (last 2.5 million years)

archaeology often discovers the unexpected, they found instead remains from the early 1600s, virtually all that was left of what historical records refer to as Wolstenholme Towne in a tract known as Martin's Hundred. The tract was established in 1619 by fewer than 200 English settlers, who faced disease, hunger, and the unknowns of living in North America. In 1622, the town was attacked and burned and some inhabitants killed by local Native Americans. Although Martin's Hundred was reoccupied, Wolstenholme Towne was subsequently all but forgotten.

Noël Hume's excavations in the 1970s rediscovered the settlement and documented the drama of the massacre. Ash and other traces of the fires were abundant, and several human skeletons attested to a violent end (one bore evidence of scalping) and hasty burial. As dramatic as these findings are, however, the deeper impact of these excavations is what could be learned about daily life in early colonial Virginia. The products and discards of a resident potter reveal local manufacturing, while the discovery of imported helmets and other pieces of armor are the earliest such pieces known for colonial America. The traces of a wooden fort, the oldest example of its kind yet recovered, testify to the well-founded insecurity of the settlers. While the town was small, its sometimes poignant traces have yielded important glimpses of life and death in what Noël Hume calls "the teething years of American colonial history" (1979).

Both archaeology and history have contributed to our knowledge of Martin's Hundred. For most of the human past, however, archaeology lacks any sort of historical record to supplement its studies. Nevertheless, prehistoric archaeology can draw on the resources and results of allied fields, including history, historical archaeology, cultural anthropology, and geography. Both historical and prehistoric archaeology have usually allied themselves most closely to anthropology. Through the concept of culture, anthropology provides a variety of frameworks for archaeology to describe, explain, and better understand the past.

ARCHAEOLOGY AND ANTHROPOLOGY

In its broadest sense, **anthropology** is the comprehensive science of humankind—the study of human beings both as biological organisms and as culture-bearing creatures. It also studies human society from two perspectives: a **diachronic** view that stresses development through time and a **synchronic** view that emphasizes the contemporary state of human societies with little or no time depth.

Anthropology is divided into four major subdisciplines, biological (or physical) anthropology, cultural anthropology, linguistic anthropology, and archaeology (Fig. 1.8). Each of these subdisciplines incorporates numerous specialties. Biological anthropology studies the human species as a biological organism, including our evolution (a diachronic aspect) and our contemporary

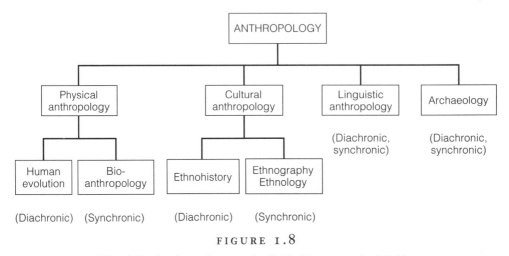

FIGURE I.8

The field of anthropology can be divided into several subfields.

biological characteristics and variations (a synchronic aspect). Cultural anthropology studies the human species as a cultural organism, including two synchronic approaches to the study of living societies. The first, **ethnography,** studies individual cultures throughout the world. The second, **ethnology,** uses a comparative and generalizing perspective to understand the way all cultures work. Ethnohistory takes a diachronic approach within cultural anthropology, using records and oral history to reconstruct the past. Linguistic anthropology specializes in the study of human languages throughout the world, individually and comparatively (a synchronic aspect) and developmentally how languages change and evolve through time (a diachronic aspect). The subject of our book, archaeology, studies the human past from a variety of perspectives. It often emphasizes a diachronic view, to describe and understand the development of societies through time, but archaeology may also emphasize a synchronic view, as in the study of a society at a particular moment in the past. As we have already seen, archaeology can be divided into the fields of historical and prehistoric archaeology.

This description of anthropology is a simplified view of a complex field. The pursuits of anthropological research must be as diverse as the varieties of human behavior and the complexities of culture. The concept of culture is what unifies all the subfields of anthropology. The term **culture** has both a general and a specific meaning. In its general sense, *culture* refers to the uniquely human addition to the biological and social dimensions we share with other life forms. It is in this general sense that we will be concerned with culture and will define it below. But we must also realize that the term may also be used in a specific sense to refer to the particular and unique cultural systems of individual human societies, as when we speak of the "culture of the Shoshone."

The concept of culture in the general sense is much too complex to define comprehensively in a few paragraphs, encompassing as it does some 2.5 million years of human evolution, as well as hundreds of unique and varied contemporary societies throughout the world. One of the most often cited definitions, written more than 120 years ago by Edward Tylor (1871), remains useful today:

> That complex whole which includes knowledge, belief, art, morals, law, custom, and any other capabilities and habits acquired by [a person] as a member of society.

Today many archaeologists prefer to emphasize culture as the primary means by which human societies adjust or adapt to their environment, in contrast to the genetic (biological) adaptations of our own and other life forms. According to this view, culture comprises the cumulative resources of human societies, perpetuated by language, that provide the primary means for nongenetic adaptation to the environment by regulating behavior on three levels: the technological (relationships with the environment), the social (organizational systems), and the ideational (belief systems).

We will return to this concept later in this book, when we discuss the various views of culture that have developed along with the field of anthropology.

Archaeology has benefited as well from the contributions of many other fields. In pursuing their goals, archaeologists often make use of the expertise of specialists in the other subfields of anthropology, as well as those in disciplines like art history, geography, history, biology, astronomy, physics, geology, and computer science, among others. These fields enrich the mix of scientific and humanistic perspectives that characterize modern archaeology. They also contribute both to the refinement of archaeological methods and to the development of archaeological theory by which the evidence of the past is interpreted.

ARCHAEOLOGY AS A PROFESSION

Because archaeology is both fascinating and important—it is the only bridge to our entire past heritage—many people are interested in the prospects for a career in archaeology. As we have seen, archaeology is a diverse field, so there are many different career opportunities for all kinds of interests.

Formal academic training is not a requirement for participating in archaeological research. Many people begin their experiences in discovering the past by joining an archaeological dig or by volunteering their time to help a museum preserve or study archaeological collections. Some individuals who are employed full-time in other jobs continue to follow their interest in archaeology as volunteers, working on weekends or during their vacations. To one interested in pursuing archaeology as a profession, however, some sort of formal academic training is necessary.

Training in archaeology usually begins in the classroom, where methods and theory can be introduced by lectures and discussions, but archaeology cannot be learned solely in a traditional academic setting. Archaeological training must also include time spent in the field—participating in research at archaeological sites and in the field laboratory—so that coursework can be put into practice. In most cases, archaeological field schools are where students learn the practical application of research methods. After such training, students may take more advanced courses (in data analysis and theory, among other fields) leading to a degree. Most archaeological training in the United States is offered within anthropology programs, and the resulting degrees, both undergraduate and graduate, are in anthropology, not archaeology.

Most archaeologists subscribe to the definitions and goals outlined earlier in this chapter. Yet when it comes to the actual application of method and theory to meet these goals, a considerable diversity becomes apparent. There is more variation in the standards by which archaeological sites are excavated and the results recorded than there should be. In some extreme cases, unfortunately, the lack of proper standards leads to an irreparable loss of information about the past, rather than a gain in knowledge. For example, Kent Flannery describes the following scene at a site in Mexico:

> Four stalks of river cane, stuck loosely in the ground, defined a quadrilateral (though not necessarily rectangular) area in which two *peones* [laborers] picked and shoveled to varying depths, heaving the dirt to one side. On the backdirt pile stood the archeologist himself, armed with his most delicate tool—a three-pronged garden cultivator of the type used by elderly British ladies to weed rhododendrons. Combing through every shovelful of dirt, he carefully picked out each figurine head and placed it in a brown paper shopping bag nearby—the only other bit of equipment in evidence. This individual was armed with an excavation permit that had been granted because, in the honest words of one official, "he appeared to be no better or worse than any other archeologist who had worked in the area." When questioned, our colleague descended from the backdirt pile and revealed that his underlying research goal was to define the nature of the "Olmec presence" in that particular drainage basin; his initial results, he said, predicted total success.
>
> As [we] rattled back along the highway in our jeep, each of us in his own way sat marveling at the elegance of a research strategy in which one could define the nature of a foreign presence in a distant drainage basin from just seven fragmentary figurine heads in the bottom of a supermarket sack.
>
> (FLANNERY 1976:1–2)

At first this case strikes us as humorous, until we realize that it is based on an actual incident, and that, unfortunately, similar situations continue in the name of archaeology throughout the world. Due in part to this problem, the Society of Professional Archeologists (SOPA) has attempted to define as specifically as possible the professional qualifications and standards for archaeologists. These include the following criteria for education, training, and experience:

1. Education and Training
   a. A professional archaeologist must have received a graduate degree in archaeology, anthropology, history, classics, or another pertinent discipline with a specialization in archaeology;
   b. A professional archaeologist must have supervised experience in basic archaeological field research consisting of at least 12 weeks of field training and 4 weeks of laboratory analysis or curating;
   c. A professional archaeologist must have designed and executed archaeological research, as evidenced by a Master of Arts or Master of Science thesis or an equivalent research report.

2. Experience
   A professional archaeologist must have at least one year of experience in one or more of the following:
   a. Field and laboratory situations under supervision of a professional archaeologist, with a minimum of 6 months as a supervisor
   b. Analytic study of archaeological collections
   c. Theoretical, library, or archival research
   d. Administration of archaeological research
   e. Management of cultural resources
   f. Museum work
   g. Teaching
   h. Marine survey archaeology.

In the United States there are seven national professional archaeological societies, some of which are listed in Table 1.1. Several of these have regular publication series, and the Archaeological Institute of America also publishes annual listings of field schools and excavation opportunities. There are also numerous regional and state archaeological societies throughout the country. Further information about these and other archaeological organizations in your area can be found by contacting the office of your state archaeologist or the State Historic Preservation Office (SHPO) in your state capital.

Traditionally, most archaeologists have academic appointments in universities or museums, where they teach archaeology as well as conduct fieldwork. Today, however, growing numbers of archaeologists are employed by private or governmental agencies, such as the National Park Service, where they engage in **cultural resource management** (or CRM). CRM is concerned with the identification and evaluation of archaeological sites to protect them from disturbance or destruction and the investigation of those that cannot be saved. CRM is the fastest-growing segment in archaeology and now accounts for more than half of all professional archaeologists employed in the United States.

TABLE I.I

Professional Archaeological Organizations

American Anthropological Association
4350 North Fairfax Drive, Suite 640
Arlington, VA 22203

Archaeological Institute of America
675 Commonwealth Avenue
Boston, MA 02215

Society for American Archaeology
900 Second Street, NE, Suite 12
Washington, DC 20002

Society for Historical Archaeology
P.O. Box 30446
Tucson, AZ 85751

The growth of CRM is the result of an increasing concern over the destruction of archaeological sites in this country and throughout the world. In the United States, as in many other countries, legislation has been enacted to protect our cultural heritage. This development is part of the larger concern about the destruction of our environment (natural as well as cultural resources). Like many natural resources, past cultural remains are a nonrenewable resource. Unlike natural resources, however, each archaeological site is a fragile and unique representative of our human heritage. As we learned in the case of Slack Farm, once an archaeological site has been destroyed, that portion of our past is lost forever.

SUMMARY

Archaeology is both a popular and fascinating subject, and it often captures considerable public attention, especially when dramatic discoveries are made. Such discoveries, along with the appeal of exotic adventures, are certainly part of the reason for the popular fascination with archaeology. But a deeper attraction is generated by the substance of archaeology itself—the study of the past—and by the realization that the reconstruction of the past mirrors our present lives.

Archaeology is the one field that studies the full range of our human past. This work is threatened by the alarming number of archaeological sites being destroyed by looting. In contrast to looters, who care only for objects with monetary value, archaeologists try to recover and analyze the full range of surviving material remains to reconstruct the past.

The goals of archaeology are to describe the form of archaeological evidence and its distribution in time and space; to determine the function of these remains and thereby reconstruct past behavior; to define the processes of culture to determine how and why cultures change through time; and to use the archaeological record to understand the meaning of culture in the past and its relevance to the present.

The purpose and goals of archaeology stand opposed to those of pseudoarchaeology—fictitious reconstructions of the past that ignore facts and instead cater to human desires for fantasy and mystery. Archaeology, like any scientific discipline, involves a search for knowledge based on making careful observations and following a logical and consistent method, all guided by a body of theory. Archaeology is allied to several other disciplines. These include history, the study of the past from the written record, and anthropology, the study of human society, past and present, from both cultural and biological perspectives. The span of history divides the realm of archaeology into historical and prehistoric archaeology. In the United States, both historical and prehistoric archaeology are part of the broader discipline of anthropology. Anthropology, history, and related fields provide the theories that guide prehistoric archaeology in reconstructing the past from material remains.

The training of professional archaeologists usually combines classroom, laboratory, and field experiences at both the undergraduate and graduate level. Professional standards for archaeological research have been defined, but considerable variation in their application still exists.

FOR FURTHER READING

Following is a list of sources organized by chapter heading, followed by a more inclusive set of sources for further background reading ("additional sources"). A similar list can be found at the end of each chapter. Complete titles and publication information can be found in the bibliography.

INTRODUCTION
Arden 1989; Cleere 1989; Fagan 1975, 1988; McBryde 1985; Smith and Ehrenhard 1991

ARCHAEOLOGISTS AND ARCHAEOLOGY
Alva 1990; Cottrell 1981; Feder 1990; Layton 1989a, 1989b; Topping 1978; Trigger 1970; Veit 1989; Wauchope 1962; Wheeler 1954; White 1974; Williams 1991

ARCHAEOLOGY AS A SCIENCE
Binford 1983a, 1983b, 1989; Clarke 1972a; Flannery, 1986; Salmon 1982; Shennan 1988; Steward 1955; Thomas 1973; Watson, LeBlanc, and Redman 1984

ARCHAEOLOGY AND HISTORY
Deetz 1977; Falk 1991; Noël Hume 1969, 1979; Schuyler 1978; South 1977

ARCHAEOLOGY AND ANTHROPOLOGY
Binford 1962; Gibbon 1984; Hodder 1982; Taylor (1948) 1967; Tylor 1871

ARCHAEOLOGY AS A PROFESSION
Flannery 1976; Gathercole and Lowenthal 1989; McBryde 1985; Pearce 1990; Society of Professional Archeologists 1978; Stone and MacKenzie 1989; Stuart 1976

ADDITIONAL SOURCES
Bass 1966; Binford 1972, 1983a, 1983b; Butzer 1982; Champe et al. 1961; Champion 1980; Charleton 1981; Chippendale 1986; Coggins 1972; Davis 1982; Dunnell 1982; Fagan 1985; Gould 1985, 1986; Hamilton and Woodward 1984; Haviland 1985; Hester, Heizer, and Graham 1975; Isbell 1978; Johnstone 1980; Joukowsky 1980; King 1983; LeBlanc 1983; Lipe 1974, 1984; McGimsey 1972; McKusick 1984; Meltzer, Fowler, and Sabloff 1986; Miller 1980; Numbers 1982; Pulak and Frey 1985; Rathje 1978; Sabloff 1982; Schliemann (1881) 1968; Wilson 1982; Wiseman 1984

2

Archaeology's Past

THE DEVELOPMENT OF SCIENCE is one of the hallmarks of Western civilization. Although their origins can be traced several thousand years into the
past, science and the scientific method have taken their modern form in the 500
years since the European Renaissance. Archaeology is a relative newcomer
among sciences, since it emerged as a distinct field only in the 19th century.
But archaeology has followed a developmental course similar to other scientific
disciplines, and by briefly describing its history we can better understand its
present characteristics.

Many scientific fields, including archaeology, originated with the work of
amateur collectors. These individuals, often part-time hobbyists, pursued their
interests because they valued the objects collected, often as things of beauty or
curiosity. For example, the modern field of biology took root with European
collectors of local plant and animal life, including many 17th- and 18th-
century English country parsons and other gentlemen of leisure. Amassing a
collection leads naturally to attempts to bring order to the assembled material.
These often result in efforts at **classification**, dividing a collection into groups
that share one or more traits. The earliest classifications were usually based on
the most obvious characteristics, such as appearance or form.

Attempts to classify collections often led further, to questions concerning
the meaning of both similarities and differences seen in the things being studied. The desire to know more about a collection leads to questions about its
origins, its purpose, or the relationship of one category in a classification to
another. Such questions were often answered initially with pure speculation,
but at times firmer conclusions emerged that were based on systematic

23

observation. More often than not, however, the first answers to such questions have long since been replaced by more firmly grounded explanations.

In time, amateur collectors increasingly gave way to individuals committed to discovering the meaning behind the assembled facts. First, the full range of forms might be defined and broken down into classes. This might be followed by attempts to infer purpose from physical appearance and discover the underlying organizing principles inherent in the classification. In other words, a concern with function and meaning replaced concern with simple form. With this step, the first professionals within a given discipline can often be discerned. The amateur never disappears completely, and of course nonprofessionals in many fields continue to make important discoveries even today. But in every scientific discipline, the emergence of true professionalism corresponds to the rise of full-time specialists interested in understanding rather than merely collecting.

As attention shifts more to questions of function and explanation, it becomes obvious that descriptive classifications based solely on isolated traits cannot provide sophisticated answers about the origins and significance of a set of observable phenomena. The next step toward understanding any phenomenon is the attempt to comprehend the processes of its development—to explain the causes of change.

THE ORIGINS OF ARCHAEOLOGY

These trends of scientific development are visible in the emergence of archaeology as a professional discipline. Archaeology did not spring forth fully developed, but emerged gradually from diverse origins. As with other fields of inquiry, its roots lie in the work of amateur collectors and speculators; such individuals interested in the human past are often called **antiquarians.** But archaeology did not begin to develop as a separate discipline until its practitioners went beyond the mere collecting of ancient remains and developed the means to use these materials as evidence for a reasonable reconstruction of the past.

Countless individuals have encountered remains of the past, often accidentally or, in the case of looters, as the result of treasure seeking. As the number of discoveries accumulated, some individuals began to realize that these remains had an importance beyond curiosity or monetary value—they were, in fact, direct clues to the understanding of entire societies that had long since disappeared.

Examples of interest in the past can be found among the earliest known historical accounts, including those of China, India, and Egypt. For example, Thutmose IV, pharaoh of Egypt in the 15th century B.C., ordered the excavation of the Great Sphinx at Giza, then already centuries old and nearly buried by sand. He left a record of his work inscribed on a stone tablet between the paws of the sphinx. Nearly a thousand years later, in the mid-6th century B.C.,

FIGURE 2.1

A street in the Roman city of Pompeii, Italy, after excavation and partial
reconstruction. (Courtesy of Elizabeth K. Ralph.)

the Babylonian king Nabonidus sponsored excavations in the ruined cities of
his Sumerian predecessors and exhibited the artifacts that were found. These
early examples of interest in the past illustrate several things that would eventually become part of archaeological research—excavating to reveal ancient
remains, recording the work, and preserving the finds.

The later Romans were also interested in the past, but usually for personal gain. Wealthy Romans often systematically looted many sites of the
Mediterranean area for sculpture and other works of art to decorate their
palaces and gardens, but they seemed to have little concern for using these
finds to understand the past.

It wasn't until the Renaissance of the 14th to 17th centuries, an era of
reawakened interest in the arts, literature, science, and learning in general, that
the study of the past began to flourish. Excavation and direct recovery of
antiquities became increasingly popular in Italy as Roman ruins were probed in
search of artifacts and art. In 1594, the construction of a water channel near
Naples led accidentally to the most famous discovery of the period, that of the
lost Roman city of Pompeii (Fig. 2.1). Archaeological excavation has continued
at this site to the present day. Discoveries such as these stimulated a general
frenzy of digging, often resembling looting more than archaeological inquiry,

FIGURE 2.2

The ancient function of Stonehenge, located on the Salisbury Plain of England, remains a subject of popular speculation—regardless of the archaeological evidence.

not only in Italy, but also throughout the Mediterranean world and beyond. Although this resulted in much destruction of important evidence, some knowledge was gained, monuments and works of art were saved, and excavation techniques began to improve.

Even as looting and destruction of antiquities became more common, some individuals stood out not only as notable collectors, but as people interested in learning about the past through classification and study of material remains. One of the earliest of these was William Camden. In 1587, he produced *Britannia*, the first compilation of all archaeological sites and artifacts then known in England, a work that marks the beginning of serious interest in British prehistory. Two other British antiquarians of the 17th and 18th centuries, John Aubrey and William Stukeley, are notable for their pioneering but speculative attempts to interpret the purposes of the great stone enclosures of Avebury and Stonehenge (Fig. 2.2).

Elsewhere in Europe, other individuals were also beginning to probe their local prehistoric past. In 16th- and 17th-century Scandinavia, for example, royally commissioned antiquarians such as Ole Worm of Denmark and Johan Bure of Sweden were recording ancient runic inscriptions (Fig. 2.3), excavating early burial sites, and compiling inventories of national antiquities. Interestingly, centuries earlier, their Viking ancestors seem to have conducted the first archaeological work in North America, excavating a prehistoric site near their settlement on Greenland.

Speculative interpretation of European prehistory gradually gave way to firmer reconstructions as the archaeological evidence accumulated. The first problem to be solved was the recognition of the earliest products of human activity, usually tools made of stone. William Dugdale, a 17th-century British

FIGURE 2.3

Runic inscriptions were used as early as the 16th and 17th centuries to aid archaeological investigation in Scandinavia. (By permission of the British Library.)

prehistorian, identified ancient stone handaxes as "weapons used by the Britons before the art of making arms of brass or iron was known." This essentially correct interpretation was a revolutionary advance over the prevailing view, that these artifacts were the work of elves or other mythical beings. Another two centuries would pass, however, before the implications of these discoveries for human prehistory would be generally accepted. The initial reaction to such discoveries was to ignore or reject them, since they conflicted with the dominant view, based on the version of the creation given in the Old Testament. This belief held that human existence was confined to a mere 6000 years since the earth's creation.

Once these earliest artifacts were recognized as products of human manufacture, determination of their true age became a pressing concern. The best indication of the antiquity of human presence in Europe came from a growing inventory of human bones and tools found associated with the bones of extinct animals. For example, in 1797 John Frere described the discovery of chipped flint artifacts in association with bones of extinct animals from 12 feet below the earth's surface at the English site of Hoxne, sealed in place by three higher and therefore, as he realized, later deposits. Frere concluded that these remains belonged "to a very remote period indeed; even beyond that of the present world." In the mid-19th century, a French customs inspector named Boucher de Perthes found a group of stone handaxes and extinct animal bones among the gravels of the Somme River. By this time the fossilized remains of the earliest inhabitants of Europe had begun to appear, one of the first being the discovery in 1856 of bones from the Neander Valley in Germany. This find is now well known as an example of the ancient Neanderthal people, but at the time the ancient anatomical attributes of these bones were explained away as coming from a pathological modern individual.

After bitter and heated debate, the tide of scientific opinion finally turned in the mid-19th century. By this time, geologists such as Charles Lyell had demonstrated the considerable antiquity of the earth and proposed that the processes responsible for its current form were the same in the past as today—a position known as uniformitarianism. (The opposing view, catastrophism, held that the earth's features were shaped by violent cataclysmic events.) They had also shown that many of the human tools discovered with extinct animal bones were indeed so ancient that the literal interpretation of the book of Genesis was clearly contradicted. In 1859 the publication of Charles Darwin's *On the Origin of Species* provided a systematic scientific theory to account for the evolution of all life that was in harmony with the geological evidence pointing to the earth's great antiquity. All in all, by the mid-19th century the combination of archaeological, geological, and biological evidence was able to challenge successfully the theological position regarding prehistoric human development in the Old World.

Still unresolved, however, was the central issue of New World prehistory—who had built the now-abandoned cities of the Americas? The many ruined mounds, temples, sculptures, and tombs found in North, Central, and South America offered a new mystery whose solution was first sought in wild speculation. European bias saw Old World immigrants as the most likely sources for the ruins of sophisticated societies being discovered in the Americas, variously crediting ancient Egyptians, Hebrews, Phoenicians, Hindus, Chinese, and even the mythical inhabitants of Atlantis and Mu with these accomplishments. Native Americans were usually dismissed as incapable of such achievements. Even such a sober scientist as Benjamin Franklin attributed the construction of the monumental mounds of the Mississippi Valley to the early Spanish explorer Hernando de Soto!

The growing weight of archaeological data, however, including a pioneering mound excavation in Virginia by Thomas Jefferson, eventually established rightful credit for the ancient New World sites. Jefferson's excavation of an earthen mound in Virginia established that it had been built by Native Americans. Jefferson was also a pioneer in systematic excavation, accurate recording, and the use of **stratigraphy** (see Chapter 4), by observing that the sequence of earthen layers (or **strata**) reflected the passage of time.

In 1841 and 1843, John Lloyd Stephens and Frederick Catherwood published their accounts of the discovery of spectacular ruins of the Maya civilization in the jungles of Mexico and Central America. Stephens and Catherwood's books revealed the wonders of ancient Maya culture to the populace of England and the United States (Fig. 2.4). Publicity of this kind helped spur the often romantic and destructive search for other so-called lost civilizations, not only in the New World, but in Africa and Asia as well. But Stephens's appraisal of the source of Maya civilization stands in marked contrast to the speculations popular at the time: "We are not warranted in going back to any ancient nation

FIGURE 2.4

Publication of drawings by Frederick Catherwood sparked public interest
in ancient New World civilizations in the mid-19th century. (From an
original print, courtesy of the University of Pennsylvania Museum.)

of the Old World for the builders of these cities. . . . There are strong reasons
to believe them the creations of the same races who inhabited the country at
the time of the Spanish Conquest."

In 1848, E. G. Squier and E. H. Davis published the results of their
research into the mounds of the Mississippi and Ohio Valleys, providing one of
the first classifications to distinguish burial mounds, temple platforms, and effigy mounds, inferring that these different types of mounds served different
functions. But in trying to identify the ancient occupants of these sites, they
lapsed into pure speculation, refusing to believe that Native Americans—or
their ancestors—could be the builders. In contrast, Samuel F. Haven's sober
appraisal of Native American prehistory—*Archaeology of the United States*, published in 1856—used available archaeological evidence to dismiss many fantastic theories about the origins of the Native Americans and concluded that the
prehistoric monuments in the United States were built by the ancestors of living tribal groups. Further research reinforced this conclusion, so that by the
end of the 19th century the weight of archaeological evidence required recognition of a complex past for Native American societies without the need to
resort to pseudoarchaeological tales of Old World visits or other influences.

Also by this time, archaeology was gaining recognition as a separate field of endeavor and a legitimate scholarly pursuit in both the Old and New Worlds. Unfortunately, at the same time, other forces led to an increase in looting and the destruction of archaeological sites. In particular, as European and American colonial expansion moved more deeply into Asia, Africa, and Latin America, proprietary claims were staked over newly discovered areas, including archaeological sites, which were often mined like mineral deposits. For instance, from 1802 to 1821, Claudius Rich, a British consular agent in Baghdad, collected and removed thousands of antiquities and sent them to England. The extraordinary Italian, Giovanni Belzoni, working for the British government, systematically looted Egyptian tombs, even using battering rams to enter the ancient burial chambers. And Thomas Bruce, the seventh earl of Elgin, spent several years at the beginning of the 19th century removing a series of sculptures, now called the Elgin Marbles, from the Parthenon in Athens to their present location in the British Museum, sparking a dispute that continues today.

As destructive as many of these activities were by today's standards, many important discoveries were made. Prominent among these was the unearthing of the Rosetta Stone in Egypt, which allowed Jean François Champollion to decipher Egyptian hieroglyphs in 1822. Similar discoveries of inscribed clay tablets in Mesopotamia led to the decipherment of cuneiform writing soon thereafter. As a result of these two breakthroughs, historical records from two of the world's earliest civilizations were suddenly available to scholars and public alike.

THE EMERGENCE OF MODERN ARCHAEOLOGY

As the discoveries continued, archaeology became recognized as a distinct professional discipline. Professional archaeology emerged in the 19th century as many of its practitioners became full-time specialists (rather than part-time hobbyists) and as interpretations of the past relied more on evidence than on speculation. By this time, the impact of the accumulating evidence of the human past was impressive. And the increase in finds was accompanied by a gradual refinement of methods of recovery and classification, which served to make the record even stronger. But what did all this new information mean? How could it be interpreted?

The problem was immense. Depending upon the particular circumstance, archaeologists usually have only scattered remnants of past cultures to work with. One way to visualize the problem is to imagine what could survive from our own civilization for archaeologists to ponder some 5000 or 10,000 years from now. What could they reconstruct of our way of life on the basis of scattered soft-drink bottles, porcelain toilets, plastic containers, spark plugs, reinforced concrete structures, and other nonbiodegradable products of our civilization? In approaching the problem of interpreting the past, the archaeologist needs a framework to help in putting the puzzle together. Imagine an incredibly complex three-dimensional jigsaw puzzle. If we knew nothing about its size, form, or subject matter, the puzzle would be impossible to reconstruct. But if we proposed a scheme that accounted for the puzzle's size, form, and subject, we could use this scheme to attempt to put it together. If one scheme failed to work, we could propose another in its stead, until we succeeded.

Today, the interpretive frameworks used by professional archaeologists and other scientists are generally called **models.** A model is essentially a form of hypothesis that describes the subject of investigation in a simplified way; it is constructed and tested according to the scientific method (see Chapter 1).

The earliest archaeological interpretations were based on historical models. The first historical scheme widely used by archaeologists was the **three-age technological sequence,** which held that prehistoric society developed progressively through ages of stone, bronze, and iron technology. While the idea behind this model can be traced to writings from several ancient civilizations, including those of Greece, Rome, and China, credit for promulgating the three-age sequence for European prehistory is generally given to two early 19th-century Danish scholars. Christian Thomsen organized the collections in the Danish National Museum of Antiquities according to this scheme, not only as a convenience but also because it seemed to reflect chronological stages of human progress. His colleague, Jens Worsaae, conducted excavations in burial mounds, thereby verifying that stone tools underlay (and were thus earlier than) those of bronze, which underlay the still later tools of iron.

With further research, the sequence grew more detailed. In 1865 Sir John Lubbock distinguished an earlier technology in which stones were chipped to make points (Paleolithic or "Old Stone Age") from a later technology in which stones were ground (Neolithic or "New Stone Age"). In 1871, Heinrich Schliemann used quasi-historical sources—Homer's *Iliad*—to discover the site of Bronze Age Troy, thereby linking the study of prehistoric societies with the later classical civilizations known to history (Fig. 2.5). Also in the 19th century, archaeological method was refined to near-modern precision by the work of the Englishman General A. L. Pitt-Rivers.

Thus by the end of the 19th century, European archaeology was based on a well-developed chronological framework that followed a historical model. To this day, many European archaeologists regard their discipline as allied more closely to history than to any other field.

By the early 20th century, archaeologists in America were borrowing the excavation methods developed largely in the Old World but taking a rather different path from their Old World counterparts in their attempts to interpret the past. The difference was due largely to contrasting circumstances. For one thing, the New World, unlike many areas of the Old World, appeared to lack historical records. In addition, cultural development in the Americas did not seem to have the time depth found in the Old World; the earliest migration in the New World appeared to be relatively recent, taking place during the last glacial epoch. This meant that the historical (or historically based) schemes used in the Old World could not be meaningfully applied in the New.

FIGURE 2.5

A contemporary view of Heinrich Schliemann's excavations at Troy. (From Schliemann 1881.)

Since the connection with history was not so immediately apparent in the New World, archaeologists turned to anthropology to interpret the remains that were being discovered. They compared contemporary Native American artifacts with those recovered archaeologically, using those artifacts of known use to infer uses for artifacts from the past. As a result, for New World archaeologists, anthropology, with its unifying concept of culture, ultimately became the main source of interpretive models, replacing history. Indeed, many anthropologists of this period, such as F. H. Cushing in the Pueblo area of the American Southwest, did archaeological as well as ethnographic and linguistic fieldwork.

In both Europe and America, several related interpretive currents fused into a broad interpretive model referred to as **cultural evolution.** The previously discussed three-age system was one contributing factor to the idea of cultural evolution. So too was a general belief that all cultural change, in technology and other customs, was progressive, from simple to complex and from primitive to civilized. Development of evolutionary theory in biology followed a parallel trend and supported acceptance of cultural evolution. These notions were coupled with the recognition of tremendous diversity among living societies, documented in the course of European colonial expansion, plus the need to explain (and thereby justify) the political and economic dominance of 19th-century Europeans over many other societies. The result was a model of **unilinear cultural evolution.**

The unilinear theory of cultural evolution, as developed by Herbert Spencer, Lewis Henry Morgan, Edward B. Tylor, and others, was based on comparisons among societies. Data from any source—ethnographic, archaeological, or whatever—were accepted in assessing a society's evolutionary status.

Above all, cultures were compared in order to determine their relative positions on a single scale of development or success. The assumption that all human cultures develop along a single or unilinear path is perhaps best expressed by Morgan's evolutionary stages: savagery, barbarism, and civilization. The inflexibility of this scheme stands out as both the principal hallmark and the greatest weakness of 19th-century cultural evolutionary theory.

The errors of the unilinear evolutionists are readily apparent to us, with the benefit of more than 100 years of hindsight. Above all, these 19th-century theorists were **ethnocentric**—their assessment of the developmental stages of other societies was heavily biased by their assumption that contemporary Western culture represented the pinnacle of evolutionary achievement.

Of course, the idea that human behavior does change and that societies and cultures do evolve remains an important aspect of modern anthropological theory. But by the turn of the 20th century it was evident that the weaknesses in the unilinear view of cultural evolution outweighed its strong points. As a consequence, attempts to write a universal history of human culture were either cast aside or altered to remove the inherent problems of unilinear schemes.

The emergence of modern anthropology and archaeology took a somewhat different turn in America, through the influence of Franz Boas and his students. These individuals rejected attempts to apply a universal developmental scheme via uncritical cultural comparisons. Instead, they saw a need for accumulation of great amounts of well-controlled and documented empirical data—archaeological, ethnographic, and linguistic—for a single society. These data would then be used to reconstruct the unique cultural history of each society.

While rigorous collection of data with a localized geographic focus originated with Boasian anthropology, this emphasis persisted and dominated American archaeology until the middle of the 20th century. As a result, archaeological research was directed to the establishment of specific cultural histories, usually concentrating on tracing form, style, and technological changes in particular artifacts, such as pottery. For the most part, however, cultural historians in America shied away from attempting broader comparative statements concerning developmental parallels and contrasts in the prehistoric record.

Beginning in the mid-20th century, comparative approaches regained popularity in American archaeology as part of a growing interest in understanding the processes of change and stability in prehistoric cultures. The study of artifact styles and reconstruction of localized cultural historical sequences have remained useful, especially in previously unstudied regions. At the same time, more sophisticated questions are now being asked of archaeological data, such as how a given culture was organized internally—how it functioned—at particular points in time. Cultural evolution has again become an acceptable interpretive model, but now in a version recognizing that cultures do not develop according to some predetermined plan. Each society's development is conditioned by the natural ecological setting in which it occurs, the neighboring societies with which it interacts, and its own traditions. Therefore, the specific courses of evolutionary change must be expected to be **multilinear** rather than following a single universal or unilinear path. And as we shall see in Chapter 3, archaeology is going beyond evolutionary questions and exploring questions of meaning and symbolism that can be gained from the archaeological record.

SUMMARY

Like many other branches of science, archaeology has its roots in the work of amateur collectors of long ago. As the number of antiquities collected grew, attempts were made to bring order to collections by classification. This search for meaning led to the first attempts at understanding the prehistoric past, but such explanations were largely speculative. In the Old World prehistoric archaeology emerged from attempts to understand human origins and evolution, while in America, the central issue was the antiquity of human populations in the New World.

The emergence of archaeology as a professional, scientific discipline was marked by the rise of full-time specialists committed to understanding the patterns and diversity in the physical remains from the past. This commitment to understanding required adopting models or interpretive frameworks that could be tested against the evidence. Models developed in the Old World, such as the three-age system, were initially derived mainly from history. In the New World, where most native cultures lacked written histories, archaeology became closely allied with anthropology. For both areas at the time the dominant framework was unilinear cultural evolution, defining the same broad stages for all societies. In the early 20th century the weaknesses in this scheme led to more rigorous descriptive approaches. More recently multilinear evolutionary models have emerged, focusing research on the process of culture change and the individual developmental career of each society.

FOR FURTHER READING

THE ORIGINS OF ARCHAEOLOGY
   Christenson 1989; Daniel 1967, 1981; Daniel and Chippendale 1989; Fagan 1978; Willey and Sabloff 1980; Wood 1985

THE EMERGENCE OF MODERN ARCHAEOLOGY
   Brew 1968; Harris 1968; Trigger 1989; Willey and Sabloff 1980

ADDITIONAL SOURCES
   Fagan 1975, 1985; Flannery 1967; Meltzer, Fowler, and Sabloff 1986; Schliemann (1881) 1968; Trigger 1984; Willey 1974; Wilson 1982

3

Contemporary Approaches to Archaeology

ARCHAEOLOGY IN THIS CENTURY has developed increasingly diverse and sophisticated approaches. The earliest of these, the cultural history approach, is based on a description of the archaeological record and the ordering of past events in time and space. The emphasis in cultural history is *what, when,* and *where* events took place in the past. In the 1960s, the cultural process approach emerged, seeking to explain the events of the past and identify the general processes of cultural change. Cultural process focuses on *how* and *why* past events took place. A third approach that emerged in the 1980s, contextual archaeology, attempts to understand the meaning of the past. Contextual archaeologists also aim at the *why* of past events, but emphasize the perspective of the ancient people involved—to gain an insider's understanding, rather than an outsider's explanation, of the past.

Taken together, these approaches address all four of the basic goals of archaeology outlined in Chapter 1—the form, function, process, and meaning of the past. Thus they all contribute to the field of archaeology as practiced today. But each approach also asks different questions, and doing so, uses different definitions of culture, distinct ways of conducting research, and different frameworks for reconstructing the past. We will consider each of these topics separately, but we should remember that many archaeologists combine various aspects from all of these approaches to best suit their particular needs.

35

THE CULTURAL HISTORY APPROACH

The cultural history approach dominated archaeology during the first half of the 20th century. Its aims of defining the sequence and spatial distribution of past events by studying patterns of material remains is still the foundation for most archaeology done today. Because it leads to an outline of the general trends of both cultural change and continuity, it often serves as the starting point for all other kinds of research.

The Normative Model of Culture

The **cultural history approach** reconstructs the past by using a normative model of culture. The normative model holds that a culture is a set of rules or **norms** that govern behavior in a particular society. These rules are passed from one generation to the next; each new generation learns the norms of behavior within the family (parent to child), schools (teacher to student), occupations (master to apprentice), peer groups, and similar situations. Because the learning of rules of behavior is not perfect, a degree of change in the normative system is inevitable. Some behavior, of course, is idiosyncratic—unique to the individual— and may not be perpetuated. In any given culture, a range of behaviors is tolerated for each situation; what the norms specify are the ranges and their limits.

The archaeologist often makes use of this model of culture to describe and reconstruct behavior in the past. Those who take this view assume that the material remains of ancient cultures represent past behavioral norms. For instance, pottery is a good indicator of culturally controlled behavior. Although the methods for making and decorating pottery are many and varied, each society uses only a few of these techniques, learned by each potter as an apprentice. Departures from these manufacturing norms are usually discouraged by social and economic sanctions. Archaeologists, therefore, can infer the ancient rules governing pottery making by studying shared characteristics in the surviving ceramics.

Within this conceptual framework, the cultural history approach emphasizes the goal of outlining the sequence (time dimension) and geographical distribution (space dimension) of past cultural norms. Once this is done, interpretation proceeds to apply descriptive models, usually drawn from ethnography and history, that describe the mechanisms most likely to have been involved in stability and change. The culmination of the interpretive process is thus a chronicle of events and general trends of cultural change and continuity in the prehistoric past. In fact, a cultural history approach is well suited to outlining the temporal, spatial, and even functional dimensions of prehistory. It is less suitable, however, for analyzing the causal factors operating in cultural development and change.

Cultural History Research

Typical cultural history research begins with specific data from individual sites, combining these in increasing degrees of generalization and synthesis. The spe-

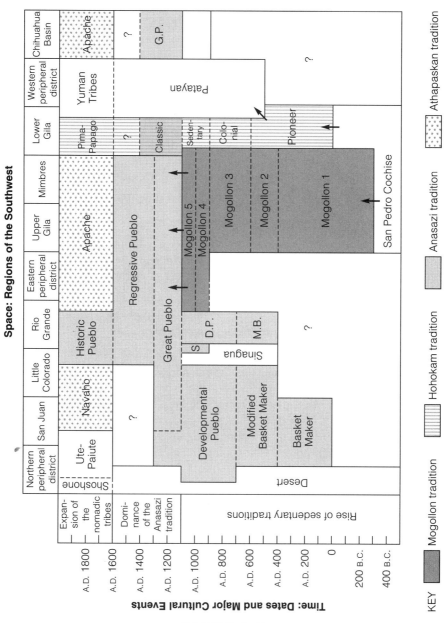

FIGURE 3.1

The cultural history approach leads to the development of time-space grids, like this one for the southwestern United States, to summarize ancient events and cultural relationships. (After Rouse 1962.)

cific techniques used to collect, process, and analyze archaeological data will be discussed later on. Here we will briefly describe how archaeological research leads to the application of cultural history frameworks for reconstructing the past.

The choice of an area of archaeological research is made by weighing a variety of factors (discussed in Chapter 4). In most cases, a reconnaissance program identifies archaeological sites, and a surface survey provides the initial round of data collection. The archaeologist selects the material cultural traits that seem most sensitive to temporal change and that will therefore best allow a collection to be arranged in a tentative chronological sequence. Depending on the kind of archaeological site being investigated, these chronologies may be based on traits seen in stone tools, pottery, architecture, or other remains.

Once the preliminary chronological scheme is proposed, excavations are undertaken to test the sequence and to provide further data to refine the sequences. Other goals may also be pursued in excavation, but the first goal in the cultural history approach is usually the discovery and investigation of stratified deposits that enable the archaeologist to perfect or further document the tentative time scheme.

Cultural History Frameworks

Cultural history begins with chronology. By correlating all of the sequences of data, the archaeologist defines chronological **periods** or phases for the site as a whole. The next step in the procedure is to expand the chronology beyond the individual site to encompass wider geographical areas. This enlargement of scope is accomplished by investigating sites adjacent to those already studied. Newly acquired data can be compared to extant sequences. In this way, not only is the cultural chronology refined, but the archaeologist can also begin to plot the spatial distributions of data. As more and more sites are investigated and the number of known prehistoric cultural sequences grows, the temporal and spatial coverage expands over ever widening areas. These larger temporal and spatial frameworks are called **time-space grids** (Fig. 3.1).

As a rule, the largest time-space grid used in cultural history research is the **culture area,** a geographical region based on ethnographically defined cultural similarities (Fig. 3.2). Archaeologists working within a given culture area usually help their investigations by using common terminology and concepts to make information from different sites comparable. The first cultural history synthesis of an entire culture area in the Americas was defined for the American Southwest. Since that time, other prehistoric culture area syntheses have been worked out, both in the Old World and throughout the Americas.

As cultural history research began to create broader and more general syntheses in the Americas, it became increasingly obvious that some kind of overriding interpretive model would be necessary. Such a framework was worked out in the mid-20th century; it represents a temporal-spatial synthesis for all the Americas (Fig. 3.3). The terminology is distinct from that used in the Old World, where such frameworks were usually based on unilinear cultural evolution (Chapter 2). Yet the resulting framework in the Americas does suggest

FIGURE 3.2

Cultural attributes combined with geographical factors are used to define culture areas, in this case, those of North America.

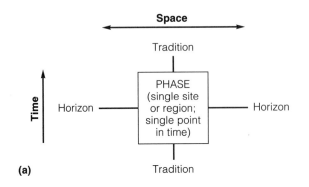

(a)

DEVELOPMENTAL STAGES	ATTRIBUTES		
	Technological	*Social*	*Ideological*
Postclassic	Metallurgy	Complex urbanism, militarism	Secularization of society
Classic	Craft specialization, beginnings of metallurgy	Large ceremonial centers, beginnings of urbanism	Developed theocracies
Formative	Pottery, weaving, developed food production	Permanent villages and towns; first ceremonial centers	Beginnings of priest class (theocracy)
Archaic	Diversified tools, ground stone utensils, beginnings of food production	Beginnings of permanent villages	?
Lithic (or Paleo-Indian)	Chipped stone tools	Nonsettled hunters and gatherers	?

(b)

FIGURE 3.3

Willey and Phillips comprehensively outlined New World cultural history by (a) integrating the dimensions of time and space through the concepts of tradition and horizon (a *phase* represents the form or content of a particular tradition on a particular horizon) and (b) summarizing the inductively documented course of cultural development through five generalized stages. (After Willey and Phillips 1958; part (a) copyright 1958 by The University of Chicago Press.)

a course of cultural development from simple to complex that, although certainly not identical, was clearly parallel to the course of Old World prehistory.

The model for the Americas was developed by Gordon R. Willey and Philip Phillips based on the complementary concepts of tradition and horizon. Tradition refers to cultural continuity through time; horizon deals with ties and uniformity across space at a single point in time (Fig. 3.3). Applying these concepts to data from all areas of the Americas, Willey and Phillips defined a series of five developmental stages or, as they have been more commonly treated, chronological periods. The exact temporal boundaries for each stage differ from area to area, but overall, Willey and Phillips's scheme represents a cultural history synthesis for the entire New World that remains useful today.

THE CULTURAL PROCESS APPROACH

The second major approach to reconstructing the past is by using **cultural process interpretation.** Cultural process refers both to how the component parts of a culture function as a system at one point in time and to how cultures change through time. It seeks to explain the processes of culture by discovering the causes of change at both points—within the internal workings of specific cultures, and from the broader perspectives of cross-cultural interaction in space and cultural change through time.

Ecological and Materialist Models of Culture

The cultural process (or simply *processual*) approach is based on two complementary models of culture. The ecological model emphasizes a synchronic view of culture; the materialist model emphasizes a diachronic or evolutionary view of culture.

The ecological model portrays culture, and especially technology, as the primary means by which human societies adapt to their environment. Whereas the normative model emphasizes regularities and rules, the ecological model highlights the variation evident in cultural forms (for example, spearpoints used in hunting or horticultural implements used to cultivate different crops), seeing the range and variety as potential clues to how the society in question dealt with its environment as a whole. Change stems from alteration of this adaptive relationship between culture and environment, as reflected archaeologically in new forms or new frequencies of particular material remains.

The ecological model has an analog in biology, where scientists study how each species adapts to a set of environmental conditions, but archaeologists must take into account additional factors. Animal species adapt to both a physical environment (geography, climate, and so on) and a biological environment (other species of plant and animal life). Human societies adapt to these same environments but also to a cultural environment (neighboring groups or societies). Moreover, in biology physical and behavioral traits are transmitted genetically, from parent to offspring, leaving the ability of a species to adapt to environmental change relatively limited and inflexible. Human societies, however, also have culture as a mechanism for the transmission of behavior (see the discussion of the normative model of culture on page 36). Because culture is learned, changes need not wait for new generations to be born before they spread. This does not mean that all cultures are constantly undergoing rapid changes. But culture gives human societies the *potential* for speedy and flexible responses when a change in the environment occurs.

It must be stressed that this ecological model does not imply that the environment determines the form of a culture. Indeed, the contrary is true; through time and on a global scale, our physical and biological environments have become increasingly determined by human culture. We need only look around us to see the changes our culture has wrought—altering the landscape and the very composition of the water we drink, the food we eat, and the air we breathe.

The ecological model does see the culture's mode of adapting to the environment as significant, though. The environment provides the opportunities for human exploitation. Each technology exploits a different part of the environment. Since each technology is different, the organizational and ideological aspects of each culture, which follow the technological adaptation, will also be unique. Also, certain environments offer more alternatives—and more fruitful choices—than others. Finally, in another parallel with biology, societies that are less specialized in their environmental adaptations tend to be less vulnerable to changes in their environment than more specialized societies.

One benefit of the cultural process approach is an increased understanding of causality. By viewing the archaeological record from an ecological perspective, the archaeologist may detect shifts in adaptation that suggest causes and consequences of change, rather than merely describing changes in norms.

As mentioned, the processual approach also relies on a materialist model of culture. Cultural materialism holds that there are biological and psychological needs common to all humans, such as hunger, sex, protection, and so forth. How these shared needs are met in different societies provides a means for evaluating each society's adaptive efficiency by measuring input, output, costs, and benefits. Human needs are satisfied most directly by a culture's infrastructure, composed of technology, economy, and demography (the size and composition of its human population). The infrastructure is the main focus of change as it responds to changing human needs and environmental conditions by optimizing benefits relative to costs for each society. Changes in the infrastructure also foster change in the culture's social, political, and ideological systems.

These factors are illustrated in one of the most basic materialist models, advanced by anthropologist Leslie White and his students. It focuses on increases in harnessing energy and organizing human labor as the key to the relative efficiency of evolving human societies. Critical changes occurred when *energy sources* [handwritten marginal note]

people increased their productive potential by increasing their energy output, at first by using animals to serve as beasts of burden. This allowed the same number of people to do more work and increase production while using less time. Other transitions took place with the advent of water, steam, and oil as energy sources.

Cultural Process Research

How does the processual approach attempt to identify the causes of change and thereby explain cultural processes? It begins with hypotheses that specify, at the outset of research, the working model of change (or interaction) and the kinds of data that will support or refute each hypothesis. Competing hypotheses are then tested against the archaeological data in order to eliminate those not supported by the evidence. Hypotheses that are supported in the first test are retested and refined by further research in order to isolate the factors involved in a given situation of prehistoric cultural change. An example of this is David Hurst Thomas's tests of Steward's model of Great Basin culture, discussed in Chapter 1. In the processual approach, then, interpretation refers to the selection and refinement of hypotheses that best delineate cultural processes.

Of course the processual approach is rooted, either directly or indirectly, in cultural history reconstructions. A direct link may be apparent when the hypotheses have been derived from cultural history research. In an indirect way, however, *all* processual interpretation is built on a cultural history foundation, since cultural history provides the temporal and spatial frameworks of prehistory. These frameworks furnish the foundations without which cultural processes cannot be discerned.

For example, in studying the ancient society of the Ulua valley around Santa Bárbara, in west-central Honduras, initial cultural history research suggested that two adjacent valley pockets had quite different developmental sequences. Gualjoquito supported a small local capital between about A.D. 200 and 900, but seemed to lack earlier or later evidence of localized leaders. Tencoa yielded a comparable center, but one that pertained to an earlier period, probably 400 B.C.–A.D. 200. Tencoa has better agricultural resources, but Gualjoquito occupies an obvious crossroad position (which Tencoa does not). Also, Gualjoquito's period of peak development seemed to coincide with the florescence of the major Maya city of Copán, to the southwest along one of the routes linked by the crossroads.

From these data, several models were proposed to be tested against new data. One linked Gualjoquito's rise and fall to the importance of external alliances, specifically to ties with Copán. Since the valley pockets are small, the model included the further hypothesis that, when the crossroads was not in active use, the pocket with more natural subsistence resources (Tencoa) would be the seat of local power. If the model were correct, further survey should reveal no further elite centers in the two periods cited, and should yield evidence of a return to power in Tencoa after A.D. 900. Survey and excavation should also turn up more imports, especially those likely to be owned by society's leaders, in Gualjoquito, and the homes and possessions of those same leaders should show strong links with the culture and styles of Copán.

The next step in the processual approach involves assembling all the data relevant to rigorous testing of hypotheses under consideration. Hypothesis testing in archaeology, as in any scientific discipline, must follow an explicit, fully documented procedure. As discussed in Chapter 1, many sciences test hypotheses by conducting controlled and repeatable experiments. For example, the hypothesis that explains how a barometer works holds that the weight of the earth's atmosphere—atmospheric pressure—supports the column of mercury. An experiment to test this hypothesis would involve moving one barometer to a new altitude while a second remained at the first altitude, as a check against change in weather conditions. This experiment is controlled, in that it rules out interference by other factors (in this case, weather). It is also repeatable: it can be performed any number of times.

In some cases, as in the experimental archaeology examples discussed later in Chapter 8, archaeologists do use controlled experiments to test specific findings. But generally archaeologists cannot rely upon controlled, repeatable experiments to test hypotheses. The archaeological record already exists, and those who study it cannot return to the past to manipulate situations to test their reconstructions. This observation highlights a fundamental distinction between the physical sciences (such as physics and chemistry) and the historical sciences (evolutionary biology, geology, and archaeology). In the words of Stephen Jay Gould, "historical sciences are different, not lesser. Their methods are comparative, not always experimental; they explain, but do not usually try to predict; they recognize the irreducible quirkiness that history entails" (1985:18). Archaeologists and other historical scientists can, however, test their reconstructions by explicitly and clearly stating the conditions and expectations of their hypotheses and then collecting and analyzing the data specified by the expectations.

The testing procedure for archaeological hypotheses actually begins at the outset of research, with the formulation of multiple hypotheses that make mutually exclusive predictions about the data. The use of **multiple working hypotheses** means that as many explanatory alternatives as possible are considered. This minimizes the opportunity for explanatory bias on the part of the investigator and maximizes the chance of finding the best available explanation. In the example cited earlier, archaeologists working in the Santa Bárbara area set forth at least two mutually exclusive hypotheses. If Copán and the crossroads were the key to Gualjoquito's prosperity, the predictions outlined above should be met. If, however, other resources underlay its leaders' successes, the data would match predictions from models other than the one described here. Three years of subsequent data collection and analysis supported the link to Copán.

In this and other situations, the goal is to invalidate all but one hypothesis. The surviving hypothesis may then be advanced, not as proven, but as the best possible explanation given the present state of knowledge. All science involves the assumption that contemporary explanations will eventually be modified or replaced as new data become available.

Cultural Process Frameworks

Two interrelated frameworks underlie most process research: cultural systems and multilinear cultural evolution. Following from the ecological model, cultural process research is concerned with reconstructing past societies as integrated cultural systems. A **system** is a complex entity made up of interrelated components. The relationships among these components are as important as the components themselves. Each human society is actually composed of many subsystems that function together. For example, all societies have a means for acquiring food (see Fig. 3.4), a subsystem composed of all the activities involved in ensuring that members of the society have enough to eat. The components of this subsystem include the ways of collecting or growing food and of processing, storing, distributing, and preparing food. Changes in one component would create changes in other components because all are interrelated. As a result of one change, therefore, the entire system would change.

Archaeologists use the ecological model of culture to identify as many components of a past cultural system as possible. If the system can be reconstructed and a change in one of its components identified, then the consequences of that change for other components can be traced. For instance, a change in weapons technology may lead to successes against enemy societies, increased wealth, and perhaps an increase in population. This might then change the economic and political system, perhaps resulting in a more authoritarian power structure. Eventually, changes in the belief system could follow, such as increased importance of worship of deities for war and political authority.

By viewing the archaeological record this way, the archaeologist can move from a well established synchronic base to a diachronic perspective. Thus, the ecological culture model and a systems framework lead together to finding the causes and consequences of change instead of merely describing the appearance of new weapons, new status goods, and new images of deities. In other words, rather than merely describing what has changed, the archaeologist begins to unravel the process of change.

This brings us to the second framework of processual archaeology, multilinear cultural evolution. This framework is actually based on both ecological and cultural materialist models of culture. The ecological model shows that cultural systems do not evolve according to a single uniform sequence. Rather, cultural evolution is a many-channeled process, governed by each society's ecological adaptation within its own environmental setting. The materialist model holds that each human society adapts to its environment primarily via its technology and secondarily through its organizational and ideational subsystems. When viewed over the long term, changes in each individual culture result

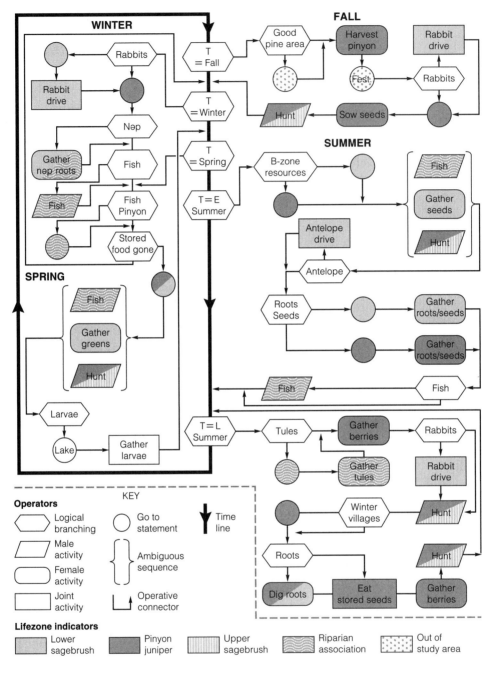

WINTER

FALL

SUMMER

SPRING

KEY

Operators

Logical branching

Male activity

Female activity

Joint activity

Go to statement

Ambiguous sequence

Operative connector

Time line

Lifezone indicators

Lower sagebrush

Pinyon juniper

Upper sagebrush

Riparian association

Out of study area

FIGURE 3.4

An example of a cultural system, in this case made up of the related activities (components) of food acquisition used by the Shoshonean people of the Great Basin in the western U.S. (After Thomas, reproduced by permission of The Society for American Archaeology, adapted from *American Antiquity* 38:159, 1973.)

from the accumulation of all of its specific adaptive responses. What suits one society to one environment won't necessarily be adaptive elsewhere.

Beyond the particular instances of adaptation and change stressed by the ecological model, multilinear evolution emphasizes the degree of success or efficiency of each system from a materialist perspective. This leads to the measurement of the efficiency of cultural development by how it survives over time or, if appropriate, how it becomes extinct. A particular society may be well adapted to its environment so that it achieves a stable balance or equilibrium, in which change is minimal and survival is the measure of adaptive efficiency. In other cases, human societies become involved in growth cycles. For example, changes originating either from the environment or from within the society may trigger changes in the technological system—and as a result in the organizational and ideational systems. If these technological changes result in increases in food production and if the organizational and ideational changes allow for increases in population size, a process of growth may begin. Continued growth will eventually place new strains on technology (the amount of food produced), organization (management of people), and ideology (beliefs justifying the other two systems). This pressure may trigger further changes in the society—technological innovations to increase food production further or new forms of social and political organization to mobilize the population—and the cycle may continue. Such a growth spiral is evident in the archaeological record of the development of civilization in both the Old and New Worlds.

The frameworks of cultural systems and multilinear evolution allow prehistoric archaeologists to explore the patterns and dynamics of growth within human societies. While cultural history reconstruction emphasizes identification of cultural interaction and change through description of a sequence of events, cultural process reconstruction is concerned with discovering the causes of interactions and change. That is, the processual approach seeks not only to identify and describe similarities and differences across time and space, but also to explain the observed distributions.

THE CONTEXTUAL APPROACH

The contextual approach emerged from the perceived shortcomings of processual archaeology. Whereas cultural process archaeologists treat culture as adaptation and portray cultural change as a response to shifts in one or another aspect of the environment, some archaeologists began to argue for a more humanistic approach that would recognize the importance of nonmaterialist factors in people's lives. These archaeologists contend that changes in behavior have to be understood in the context of each culture's particular values, attitudes, and other beliefs that give the world meaning. Thus the name **contextual archaeology**—a view of the past that is dependent on the specific conditions and perspectives of the society being investigated.

More broadly, there are at least four ways in which the contextual approach complements both the cultural history and cultural process perspectives. First, believing that the normative, ecological, and materialist cultural models present people as passive, contextual archaeologists call for a more active or dynamic model of culture. This model focuses on the human ability to create and modify idea systems as an important source of how societies operate and change. Second, rather than dealing with time in large undivided blocks, contextual archaeologists treat time more like the continuous flow in which people actually live their lives. Third, where both cultural history and cultural process are concerned with collective behavior at the level of entire societies, contextual archaeologists attempt to get at the smallest-scale behaviors, such as those of the individual, family, or ethnic groups. Fourth, while cultural history and cultural process interpret the archaeological record from an outside scientist's point of view, contextual archaeologists aim at an insider's perspective, trying to see how the people who created the material remains saw their own world.

This goal of achieving an internal perspective reflects changes in studies of human culture, a cycle alternating between knowledge gained from formal objective science and from subjective insight. For process archaeologists, the goal of objective science is explanation—the definition of components, relationships, and points of change within past cultural systems. For contextual archaeologists, the goal of subjective insight is understanding—determining the meaning of past events within their own cultural contexts. This has brought the fourth goal of archaeology, the determination of meaning (see Chapter 1) to the forefront.

The Cognitive Model of Culture

As we have seen, the models for culture used in the cultural history and process approaches emphasize people as collective and passive participants rather than individual and active agents. For contextual archaeologists, the key characteristic of culture is that it is the vehicle for each person to define and interpret his or her world. This is a cognitive model of culture, one that sees culture as the set of meanings (categories and relationships) people construct for making sense of their lives. People, therefore, are active agents, individually reworking learned norms and traditions to fit the contexts of their own lives. Because culture is seen as perpetually changing, even on a short-term basis, this model of culture is diachronic. Contextual archaeologists try to address spans of time between the moment and the long term, which they feel earlier archaeologists have ignored.

The cognitive model incorporates notions of culture as a set of durable systems of norms. Here we authors have deliberately adopted terms from the other models of culture to suggest common ground. But with the cognitive model, norms do not determine human behavior; instead, they define options available to each individual to use and adapt to suit their needs. In this way, culture is seen as constantly in flux and as redefined in each situation. Also, the available norms within each culture are seen as variant and unique expressions of deep-seated and highly structured patterns that underlie all cultures. Material remains are to be read as if they were texts, expressing these unique patterns based on common and familiar themes. In another major difference, where traditional cultural history and cultural process archaeology often assumed a male-oriented perspective, contextual archaeology also seeks to discover the particular aspects of the archaeological record that reflect female activities to provide a more balanced view of the past.

Let us contrast how the three approaches view pottery. Cultural historians see pottery decorations as idealized traits that allow identification of cultures and their variations in time or space. Processual archaeologists see the same decorations as a means of defining social groups and changing through time in response to shifts in those boundaries. Contextual archaeologists look at not only the decoration, but the context in which it occurs, to see how it relates to other expressions within the specific culture. In many (but not all) cases potters are women, so that pottery may reflect a particular gender-related outlook within the ancient society. This can be done by attempting to decipher the message being conveyed by the choice of particular pottery styles and by the choice of pottery vessels as the medium for their expression.

Contextual Research

As we have mentioned, a central tenet in contextual archaeology is to gain meaning from the archaeological record by using material culture to reconstruct an internal view of an ancient symbol system. While ethnographers may interact with living people of other cultures to gain this insider's view, doing so with an extinct prehistoric society is obviously much more difficult. Under some circumstances, historical or ethnohistoric documentation may provide clues. Archaeologists must rely on the deep common themes that underlie all human societies to reconstruct the meanings of specific aspects of the archaeological record.

The means for generating and testing propositions used by contextual archaeologists differ little from those used by other archaeologists. For example, the archaeological record is examined for regularities and patterns, and these patterns are interpreted by propositions that can be tested by data from subsequent research.

Archaeologists schooled in the hypothesis-testing procedures of the scientific method wonder how to derive and test a proposition describing an ancient symbol system that once existed in the minds of long-dead people. Contextual archaeologists do not deny the difficulty or even impossibility of using the formal scientific method to this end; rather, they conclude that traditional science is simply inappropriate for the task, since it represents a perspective inherently bound to a Western cultural tradition. Instead, when archaeological data are linked by cultural continuity to specific and known ethnic groups, meanings of specific cultural values, gained from ethnographic or ethnohistorical accounts, may be used as the basis for understanding similar patterns in past situations.

In cases without such links to the past, a far more speculative method has been suggested. This is aimed at reconstructing ancient meanings of material remains using the so-called reenactment method. This attempts to place the archaeologist in the role of a person in the past society being studied. To do so, the archaeologist must obtain as much information as possible about conditions, motives, techniques, and other aspects of the study subject. The goal is to use this information to determine the most consistent proposition describing the past situation. A proposition derived from this method could even be tested by more rigorous scientific procedures, as in the use of multiple hypotheses.

Contextual Frameworks

Contextual archaeologists seek meaning beyond the technological, environmental, and social dimensions on which archaeologists have traditionally relied. A basic framework of contextual archaeology is that the archaeological record should be viewed from multiple perspectives and seen as possessing multiple meanings. These different levels of meaning should not be seen as mutually exclusive. Although these multiple dimensions may be difficult to reconstruct, it is important to attempt to understand as many aspects of past human behavior as possible.

These multiple levels of meaning can be seen in specific artifacts and features known from the archaeological record. For example, an implement such as the atlatl, or spear thrower, is usually seen as a weapon, but it also has social and ideological meanings in native North American societies. In North America the atlatl was replaced by a more efficient weapon, the bow and arrow, by about A.D. 500. Instead of disappearing, the ancient atlatl continued to survive, transformed over time into the calumet or "peace pipe," thus becoming an important social and religious symbol (Fig. 3.5). Socially it became an emblem for kin groups, such as clans. Ritually, it became a symbol of peace or friendship celebrated between adversaries. In this way, a former weapon evolved into a symbol used in meetings between potential enemies, much as our handshake derives from a gesture to demonstrate that no weapon is being held in the hand.

Historical archaeology has produced some of the best examples of learning multiple meanings of artifacts. Studies in American historical archaeology have traced changes in the form and decoration of houses, cooking and serving pots, gravestones, and other items of everyday life over the last 200 years. These changes reflect trends away from an emphasis on communal social behavior toward the more individualistic and anonymous way of life typical of America today. Whereas two centuries ago people ate stews from a common pot, they now use individual plates and bowls. Where houses had been asymmetrical in layout and built to encourage entry into the living quarters (Fig. 3.6), they have changed to today's more symmetrical layout with entry halls to buffer or prevent the entry of visitors into the family's living space.

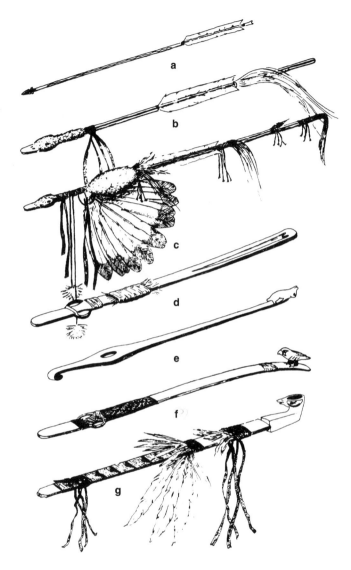

FIGURE 3.5

Historic (b–d, g) and prehistoric (e, f) materials illustrate similarities in form between spear-throwers (d, e) and *calumet* and other Native American pipes (b, c, g), as well as their co-occurrence sometimes in the same item (f). The arrow (a) is shown for scale. (After Hall, reproduced by permission of Robert L. Hall and the Society for American Archaeology from *American Antiquity* 42:4, 1977.)

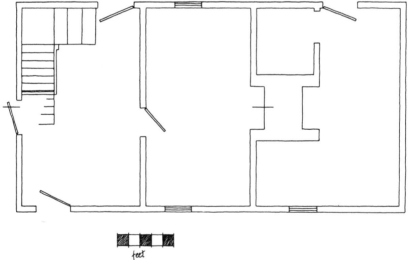

feet

FIGURE 3.6

(top) The Lesser Dabney House, an 18th-century Virginia dwelling. (bottom) Plan of the same house, showing direct access into living areas from outside, without the entry hall found in most American homes today. (After Glassie 1975.)

As these examples show, contextual archaeology has to be tied to specific cultural traditions to be able to reach levels of meaning not even attempted by other archaeological approaches. But this could make it less useful for the more general view of the past, beyond the confines of a particular cultural tradition. Because it is such a recent development, the ultimate contributions of the contextual approach have yet to be realized. It is already clear, however, that the impact of contextual archaeology will be in realizing how the archaeological record represents many levels of meaning, and how the diversity and patterns in that record represent how past peoples actively used and interpreted their world—a world that was often very different from our own.

SUMMARY

Archaeology today has a variety of means to reconstruct the past by applying a series of useful cultural models and interpretive frameworks. Following the general tenets of the scientific method, the cultural history approach gathers data and tests propositions, primarily to order the past into ever-larger temporal and spatial frameworks. Its descriptions are usually broad and general, founded in a normative concept of culture. The results of cultural history archaeology usually provide the essential foundations for the other two approaches.

The second major approach emphasizes identification and explanation of cultural processes—how cultures operate at any one point in time and why they change through time, sometimes relatively rapidly, or in other cases, almost imperceptibly. Multiple hypothesis-testing research is used to reveal the causal factors operating in specific cases. The approach is based on two complementary cultural models. The ecological model stresses synchronic study of human culture as a means of adaptation with the physical, biological, and cultural environment. This model contributes to a cultural systems framework, which views past societies as dynamic interactions between component parts. The materialist model emphasizes the role of the technological core of culture as it responds to changing human needs and environmental conditions by optimizing benefits relative to costs for society. Both models contribute to a multilinear cultural evolution framework to establish general cross-cultural trends of human prehistory, with technology usually seen playing the leading role.

The contextual approach focuses on understanding the past by using a more active or dynamic model of culture, studying a more human time scale, and focusing on individual, family, or ethnic group behavior. In contrast to other cultural models, the cognitive cultural model places individual humans in active control by portraying culture as the set of meanings people construct for making sense of their lives. These meanings define a culture constantly in flux. Where the cultural history and processual approaches use the archaeological record in the context of objective science, the contextual approach attempts subjective insight, seeking to reconstruct the point of view of the people who produced that record. Historical accounts may help discern this perspective, but it is far more difficult for an extinct prehistoric society. Contextual archaeology points to the need for multiple interpretations of the archaeological record and for a greater understanding of the meaning of that record, both for ancient societies and for our own.

Although archaeologists have debated the relative merits of these approaches, it seems clear that all contribute importantly to the most complete understanding of the past.

FOR FURTHER READING

THE CULTURAL HISTORY APPROACH
Kelley and Hanen 1988; Kidder (1924) 1962; Rouse 1962; Taylor (1948) 1967; Trigger 1968, 1989; Willey and Phillips 1958; Willey and Sabloff 1980

THE CULTURAL PROCESS APPROACH
Binford 1972; Gibbon 1989; Johnson and Earle 1987; Steward 1955; Trigger 1989; Watson, LeBlanc, and Redman 1984; Willey and Sabloff 1980

THE CONTEXTUAL APPROACH
Gero and Conkey 1991; Glassie 1975; Hodder 1989, 1991; Paddayya 1990; Pinsky and Wylie 1989; Preucel 1991; Shanks and Tilley 1987; Trigger 1989

ADDITIONAL SOURCES
Binford 1962, 1983a, 1983b; Conrad and Demarest 1984; Deetz 1977; Flannery 1967, 1976, 1986; R. A. Gould 1980; S. J. Gould 1985; Hall 1977; Haviland 1985; Hodder 1982; Meltzer, Fowler, and Sabloff 1986; Netting 1977; Schortman et al. 1986

How Archaeology Works

In this chapter we examine the information archaeologists work with and the ways it is acquired. You may have read about archaeologists piecing together the past by studying ancient pottery, arrowheads, or other artifacts found by excavation. These artifacts represent only one of several categories of evidence that archaeologists work with, and excavation is only one of several means of collecting information about the past.

ARCHAEOLOGICAL DATA

The material remains of past human activity, from the microscopic debris produced by chipping stone tools to the most massive architectural construction, become data when the archaeologist recognizes their significance as evidence and collects and records them. The collection and recording of these material remains constitutes the acquisition of archaeological data. Here we are concerned with the three basic classes of archaeological data: artifacts, features, and ecofacts, and how they cluster into larger units. These categories are not inflexible, as there is some overlap among them, but together they illustrate the variety and range of information available.

FIGURE 4.1

Artifacts are portable objects whose form is modified or wholly created by human activity, while ecofacts are nonartifactual remains that nonetheless have cultural relevance. Here a projectile point (an artifact) lies embedded among the bones (ecofacts) of an extinct form of bison at Folsom, New Mexico. (All rights reserved. Photo Archives, Denver Museum of Natural History.)

Artifacts

Artifacts are portable objects whose form is modified or wholly created by human activity (Fig. 4.1). Stone hammers or pottery vessels are artifacts because they are either natural objects modified for or by human use, such as a hammerstone, or new objects formed completely by human action, such as a clay pot. The shape and other traits of artifacts are not altered by removal from their place of discovery; both the hammerstone and the vessel retain their form and appearance after the archaeologist takes them from the ground.

Features

Features are nonportable human-made remains that cannot be removed from their place of discovery without altering or destroying their original form (Fig. 4.2). Some common examples of features are hearths, burials, storage pits, and roads. It is useful to distinguish between simple features such as these and

FIGURE 4.2

Features are artifacts that are not portable, in this case a partially excavated cremation burial pit.

composite features such as buildings and other remains with multiple parts. It is also useful to differentiate features that have been deliberately constructed—such as the examples just given—from others, such as trash heaps, that have grown by simple accumulation. Features usually define an area where one or more activities once took place.

Ecofacts

Ecofacts are nonartifactual natural remains that nonetheless have cultural relevance (Fig. 4.1). Although they are neither directly created nor significantly modified by human activity, ecofacts provide information about past human behavior. Examples include remnants of wild and domesticated animals and plants (bones, seeds, pollen, and so forth). These and other ecofacts such as soils contribute to our understanding of the past since they reflect ancient environmental conditions, diet, and resource exploitation.

Sometimes the line between ecofacts and artifacts is blurred. For example, bones with cut marks from butchering might be considered artifacts (reflecting human technology) as well as ecofacts (yielding clues to the ancient environment).

Sites

Sites are spatial clusters of artifacts, features, and ecofacts (Fig. 4.3). Some sites may consist solely of one form of data—a surface scatter of artifacts, for example. Others consist of combinations of the three different forms of archaeological data. Site boundaries are sometimes well defined, especially if features such as walls or moats are present. Usually, however, a decline in density or

FIGURE 4.3

Sites are spatial clusterings of archaeological remains. Stonehenge is an example of a site with well-defined boundaries. (English Heritage Photo Library.)

frequency of the material remains is all that marks the limits of a site. However boundaries are defined, the site is usually a basic working unit of investigation.

Sites can be described and categorized in a variety of ways, depending on the characteristics one wants to note. For instance, location—in open valleys or in caves, on the coast or on mountaintops—may reflect past environmental conditions, concern for defense, or the relative value placed on natural resources found in different areas. Sites may be distinguished by one or more functions that they served in the past. For example, one can speak of habitation sites, trading centers, hunting (or kill) sites, ceremonial centers, burial areas, and so on. Sites may also be described in terms of their age or cultural affiliation. For example, a southwest Asian site may be described as belonging to the Bronze Age or a Mexican site may be described as Aztec.

The nature and depth of cultural deposits at a site can reveal the time span of activities, indicating whether occupation was brief or extended. At some sites, occupation and deposition of artifacts is continuous. Other sites have had multiple occupations, with periods of abandonment marked by naturally deposited layers called nonartifactual or sterile. Depth of accumulation is not an automatic indicator of length of occupation, however; a great deal of mate-

FIGURE 4.4

Underwater excavation of the Roman shipwreck at Yassi Ada, off the coast of Turkey. (© National Geographic Society.)

rial can be deposited very rapidly at one spot while elsewhere a relatively thin deposit of trash might represent layers laid down intermittently over hundreds or thousands of years. Whether thick or thin, the remains of sites may be visible on the ground surface or completely buried and invisible to the naked eye.

Some sites that are not visible lie not underground but underwater, the most common being sunken ships (Fig. 4.4). However, sites that were once on dry land may also become submerged because of changes in water level (sometimes resulting from human activity such as dam building) or land subsidence. A famous example of the latter is Port Royal, Jamaica, a coastal city that sank beneath the sea after an earthquake in 1692.

Regions

Regions are the largest and most flexible spatial clusters of archaeological data. The region is basically a geographic concept: a definable area bounded by topographic features such as mountains and bodies of water (Fig. 4.5). But the definition of an archaeological region is also often based on ecological and cultural factors. For instance, a region may be defined as the area used by a prehistoric population to provide its food and water. By considering whole regions, the archaeologist can reconstruct aspects of a past society that may not be well represented by a single site.

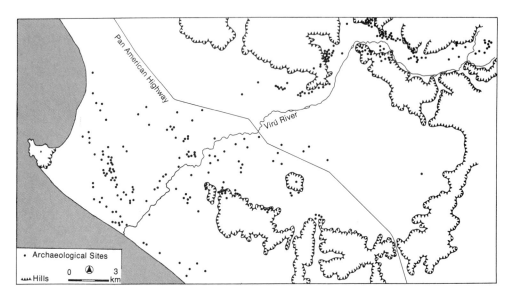

FIGURE 4.5

An archaeological region is often defined by topographic features. In this
case, hilly areas and seacoast define the limits of the Virú Valley, Peru.
(After Willey 1953.)

The definition and scope of an archaeological region vary according to the
degree of complexity of the society and its means of subsistence. Part of the
archaeologist's task is to identify the factors that define a particular region
under study, as well as to show how these factors changed through time. The
archaeologist usually works with a convenient natural region defined before-
hand by geographical boundaries and then seeks to determine that region's
ancient ecological and cultural boundaries as well.

DEPOSITION AND TRANSFORMATION

Archaeological data are the result of two factors: behavioral processes and
transformational processes. We will describe them in the order of their
involvement with archaeological data.

All archaeological sites are the products of human activity. While some
human behavior, such as storytelling, leaves no tangible trace, many activities
produce material remains. The activities responsible for these remains are
behavioral processes, comprising four consecutive stages: **acquisition, manufacture, use,** and **deposition** (Fig. 4.6). Artifacts such as tools are made from

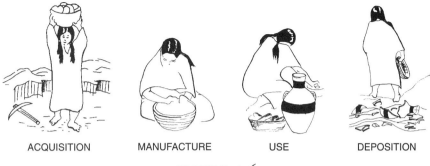

ACQUISITION　　MANUFACTURE　　USE　　DEPOSITION

FIGURE 4.6

Archaeological data represent at least one behavioral cycle of acquisition, manufacture, use, and deposition.

acquired raw materials, used for one or more specific purposes, and then discarded when broken or worn. Features such as houses are built from gathered materials, then occupied, abandoned, and destroyed or left to ruin. Ecofacts such as meat animals are hunted, butchered, cooked, eaten, and passed as waste products. The complex aggregate of these activities delineates the same stages in the life span of entire sites as well.

Some remains may pass through all four stages; others enter the archaeological record at intermediate points, as in a tool broken and discarded during manufacture. Other items may pass through more than one behavioral cycle, as in an old tool that is modified for new uses.

All forms of archaeological data, individually and together, are used to reconstruct the acquisition, manufacture, use, and deposition stages of ancient behavior. Clues to all four kinds of ancient behavior may be found in characteristics of the data themselves and in the circumstances of their deposition (Fig. 4.7).

These behavioral processes represent the first stage in the formation of archaeological data. The second stage, **transformational processes,** begins after material remains have been deposited. These processes include all conditions and events that affect those material remains from the time of deposition to the time the archaeologist recognizes and acquires them as data. Transformational processes include changes by natural agents—such as organic decay, disturbances by animal activity, or burial by volcanic deposits—as well as changes caused by humans, such as disturbances by plowing or looting. When the remains are plants or animals, the archaeologist draws on the field of **taphonomy**—the study of what happens to plants and animals after they die. An important book on taphonomy is appropriately titled *Fossils in the Making*.

The tangible products of ancient human behavior are never completely indestructible, but some survive better than others. As a result, the archaeo-

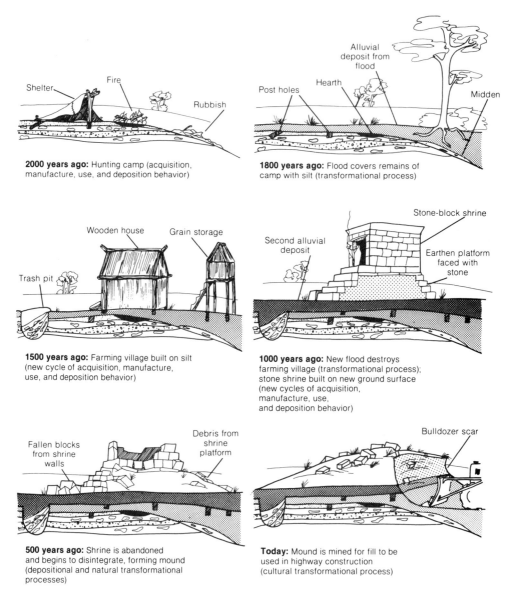

Shelter　　Fire

Rubbish

2000 years ago: Hunting camp (acquisition, manufacture, use, and deposition behavior)

Alluvial deposit from flood

Post holes　　Hearth

Midden

1800 years ago: Flood covers remains of camp with silt (transformational process)

Wooden house　　Grain storage

Trash pit

1500 years ago: Farming village built on silt (new cycle of acquisition, manufacture, use, and deposition behavior)

Stone-block shrine

Second alluvial deposit

Earthen platform faced with stone

1000 years ago: New flood destroys farming village (transformational process); stone shrine built on new ground surface (new cycles of acquisition, manufacture, use, and deposition behavior)

Fallen blocks from shrine walls

Debris from shrine platform

500 years ago: Shrine is abandoned and begins to disintegrate, forming mound (depositional and natural transformational processes)

Bulldozer scar

Today: Mound is mined for fill to be used in highway construction (cultural transformational process)

FIGURE 4.7

The characteristics of archaeological data and their deposition reflect both behavioral and transformational processes.

FIGURE 4.8

Tollund man, a corpse preserved for some 2000 years in a Danish bog. (Reprinted by permission of Faber & Faber Ltd. from *The Bog People: Iron-Age Man Preserved*, by P. V. Glob.)

logical record is never a perfect reflection of behavioral processes, but is always biased to some degree by the effects of transformational processes (see Fig. 4.7). To gauge these effects, it is crucial to determine the processes that have been at work in each archaeological situation. Natural and human events can either accelerate or retard destruction.

Natural agents are usually the most basic influences acting on the archaeological record. Temperature and humidity are generally the most critical: extremely dry, wet, or cold conditions preserve fragile organic materials, such as textiles and wooden tools, as well as bulkier perishable items such as human corpses (Fig. 4.8). Organic remains have been preserved under these circumstances along the dry coast of Peru, in the wet bogs of Scandinavia, and in the frozen steppes of Siberia.

Natural destructive processes such as oxidation and decay and catastrophic events such as earthquakes and volcanic eruptions also have profound effects on the remains of the past. Underwater remains may be broken up and scattered by tidal action, currents, or waves. Catastrophes such as volcanic eruptions may either preserve or destroy archaeological sites; often the same event may have a multitude of effects. For example, around 1500 B.C. both an earthquake and a volcanic eruption struck the island of Thera in the Aegean Sea near Greece

Excavations on Thera, where a blanket of volcanic ash sealed and preserved the remains of a large Bronze Age settlement. Here we see two views inside excavated buildings with pottery vessels and other artifacts in primary context. (Otis Imboden, © 1972 National Geographic Society.)

(Fig. 4.9). Part of the island disappeared in the explosion while the rest was immediately buried under a blanket of ash. The local population abandoned the island, but some settlement remains were sealed beneath the ash. Recent excavations have disclosed well-preserved buildings, some intact to the third story—a rarity in more exposed sites—as well as beautiful wall paintings and traces of fragile baskets.

One of the most decisive factors in transformation is subsequent human activity. People who later reoccupy an archaeological site may destroy all traces of previous occupation. Earlier buildings are often leveled to make way for new construction or to provide construction materials. In other cases, however, later activity may actually preserve older sites by building over and thus sealing the earlier remains (see Fig. 4.7). Of course, large-scale human events such as war usually have destructive consequences for archaeological preservation. Today one of the worst agents of destruction is the looting of archaeological sites, encouraged by a flourishing market in antiquities.

Obviously, archaeologists must determine what conditions and events have transformed the archaeological record before it is possible to reconstruct past human behavior. The specific behavioral and transformational processes differ from site to site, so each site must be evaluated individually. The archaeologist begins to reconstruct these processes from the circumstances under which the data are recovered, including their matrix, provenience, and association.

Matrix refers to the physical medium that surrounds, holds, and supports other archaeological data (Fig. 4.10). Most frequently it consists of combinations of soil, sand, gravel, or rock. The matrix provides important clues to understanding the artifacts, features, or ecofacts it contains. For instance, artifacts recovered from an alluvial matrix (deposited by running water) may have been deposited by natural action of a river. A matrix may also be produced by human activity such as the deposition of immense amounts of soil in order to construct an earthen platform. In this case, the soil is not only a matrix for any artifacts or ecofacts it contains, but also a constructed feature.

Provenience simply refers to a three-dimensional location of any kind of archaeological data within the matrix. Horizontal provenience is usually recorded relative to a geographical grid system using known reference points. Vertical provenience is usually recorded as elevation above or below sea level. Provenience information allows the archaeologist to record (and later to reconstruct) association and context.

Association refers to two or more artifacts (or any other kind of data) occurring together in the same matrix (Fig. 4.11). The associations of various kinds of data are crucial to the interpretation of past events (see Fig. 4.1). For instance, the artifacts found in association with a human burial, such as hunting weapons, may be clues to the individual's gender, status, and livelihood.

Context is an evaluation of archaeological data based on both behavioral and transformational processes. By considering the significance of provenience, association, and matrix for artifacts and ecofacts, the archaeologist identifies the transformational processes that have acted on these items and

FIGURE 4.10

In this photograph, a human burial has been excavated from most of its matrix, but the relationship of the remains to the matrix is readily apparent. (Courtesy of the Ban Chiang Project, University of Pennsylvania Museum.)

then reconstructs the original human behavior they represent. There are two basic kinds of archaeological contexts: primary and secondary, each of which may be divided into two further categories. We will define each and clarify their relationships with examples.

Primary context refers to conditions in which both provenience and matrix have remained undisturbed since the original deposition. Intact archaeological features are always in primary context, although later disturbance can remove portions of such features from primary context.

There are two kinds of primary contexts. **Use-related primary context** results from deposition in the place where the artifact was acquired, made, or used. The occurrence of two or more associated artifacts in use-related primary context ideally means that they were used and deposited at the same time. Such an occurrence then allows the reconstruction of the ancient activity of which the artifacts were a part. Undisturbed archaeological contexts are rare, for the archaeological record is always altered to some degree by natural transformational processes. But the behavioral significance will be preserved if the original associations and matrix have not been disturbed.

Use-related primary contexts are dependent both on the circumstances of the original behavior and on the occurrence of transformational processes that tend to preserve rather than destroy. Discoveries of chipped-stone projectile points in clear association with the bones of animals of prey have been important keys to the reconstruction of early human activities. In the mid-1920s,

FIGURE 4.11

A group of pottery vessels found in association as a result of intentional ritual deposition (primary context). This indicates they were used together as part of an ancient ceremony (ca. first century A.D., El Porton, Guatemala).

discoveries at Folsom, New Mexico, revealed such points in undisturbed use-related contexts associated with bones of a species of bison that has been extinct for at least 10,000 years (Fig. 4.1). The dates have been supplied by paleontological study, but archaeological association and context were critical in establishing the cultural meaning of these finds.

In some cases the preservation of use-related primary contexts is intentional. One of the best examples of this is the preparation of burials (Fig. 4.10) and caches (Fig. 4.11). In many areas of the world, elaborate funerary customs included the placement of offerings and other grave goods with the deceased. The resultant tombs, when found undisturbed, provide opportunities to reconstruct ancient ritual activity and belief systems. Other examples of use-related primary context have been preserved by natural events. The deposition of soil by wind and water has buried countless sites under deep layers of earth; a famous example of a dramatically buried site is the ancient Roman city of Pompeii, which was covered by volcanic ash from the eruption of Mount Vesuvius in A.D. 79 (see Fig. 2.1).

Transposed primary context refers to the deposition of artifacts and ecofacts after being moved from where they were acquired, manufactured, or used. This often happens when items are lost or discarded, as when a tool is thrown away after being damaged or worn out. Some discard activity produces **middens,** specialized areas for rubbish disposal apart from other activity areas. If used over long periods of time, middens may become stratified or layered,

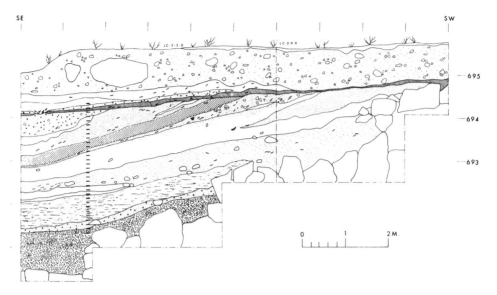

FIGURE 4.12

Cross-section drawing of a stratified midden representing nearly 2000 years
of accumulation at Chalchuapa, El Salvador. One of the characteristics of
transposed primary context, such as this midden, is that the artifacts from a
given layer are contemporaneous but cannot be assumed to represent the
same set of ancient activities.

with each layer corresponding to a period of rubbish deposition. Middens are
thus in primary context, but because of the way they were deposited, the only
past behavior directly reflected by this context is the practice of rubbish accumulation and disposal. If a midden is used over a long period of time, then relative position within the deposit (or within a particular layer of the midden) can
be used to assess relative chronological position (Fig. 4.12).

Secondary context refers to situations in which provenience, association,
and matrix have been altered by transformational processes. Use-related secondary context results from disturbances caused by human activity, ancient or
modern. Of course, if the later human disturbance is not recognized as such,
chaotic and misleading interpretation can result. For example, the contents of
a heavily disturbed tomb might include not only some portion of the original
furnishings, but also tools and containers brought in and left behind by the
looters. During the excavation of the tomb of the Egyptian pharaoh Tut-ankh-
amun, ancient looting was recognized by evidence of two openings and reclos-
ings of the entry; the final sealings of the disturbed areas were marked by
different motifs from those on the undisturbed portions. If the disturbance had
not been recognized, the associations and arrangements of recovered artifacts
might be wrongly interpreted as reflecting original burial customs.

Natural secondary context refers to disturbance caused by a variety of nonhuman agents, such as animal activity, tree roots, erosion, decay, volcanism, or earthquakes. For example, burrowing animals may place later artifacts in apparent association with earlier features and thereby make interpretation difficult. At Ban Chiang in northern Thailand, ancient burials are juxtaposed in a very complex fashion, with later pits intruding into and overlapping earlier ones. The job of segregating aboriginally distinct units was made even more difficult by the numerous animal burrows, including those of worms, crisscrossing the units, so that tracing pit lines and other surfaces was exacting and intricate work.

The archaeologist uses archaeological data to reconstruct both behavior and the cultural systems by which they were produced. As the first step in linking the data to a past cultural system, the archaeologist must assess how the processes we have discussed have affected the data: the kinds of ancient behavior that produced the evidence (behavioral processes) and the natural or human events that have affected the evidence from the time of deposition to the moment of archaeological recovery (transformational processes).

The types of archaeological context and the importance of accurately determining context can be illustrated by an example. As we have seen, any artifact may be modified to be reused for different purposes over its use span. Thus a single pottery vessel may be manufactured for the transport of water, but later modified for use to store food or other substances, and then (when inverted) as a mold for the shaping of new pottery vessels. If this vessel were abandoned during, or immediately after, any of these activities—say during its use as a pottery mold—and if it remained within an undisturbed matrix together with its associated artifacts, ecofacts, and features, then its archaeological context upon discovery would be primary (undisturbed) and use-related (part of pottery making). Knowing the provenience, associations, and context, in this case reflected in the finding of an inverted vessel surrounded by other vessels in various stages of manufacture along with clay-working tools and so forth, the archaeologist would be able to reconstruct both the type of activity and many specific techniques used in this instance of pottery making. But note that any prior uses, such as food storage, would not be directly detected.

On the other hand, if our vessel had been broken during use and its fragments swept with other debris into a rubbish pit, its context upon discovery would be primary (undisturbed) and transposed (the result of trash disposal). Because it was transposed, we could not assume the vessel was used for cooking or other culinary activity even if the pottery fragments were found associated with animal bones and food residues. We could only conclude that all these materials were deposited at the same time as a result of trash disposal activity.

Let us return to the original example of the vessel deposited during its use as a pottery mold together with its associated artifacts, ecofacts, and features. Suppose that after several centuries river erosion tore away this deposit and the vessel was redeposited on a sandbar downstream next to the remains of a drowned animal. Many years later archaeologists excavated the vessel from this spot, far removed from its original associations that reflected its use. It is now in natural secondary context: the vessel's provenience and association reflect only the natural forces of river deposition.

Finally, we have to recognize that any kind of excavation, by archaeologists or anyone else, *destroys* matrix, association, context and, therefore, information. The only way to preserve the information these factors convey is in drawings, photographs, and written records made at the time of excavations. Without them, even the most painstakingly controlled excavation is no more justifiable or useful than a looter's pit.

ACQUIRING DATA

Archaeologists gather evidence of past human activity as a first step toward understanding ancient behavior and toward meeting both the specific objectives of their research and the general goals of archaeology (see Chapter 1). Realization of these objectives requires discovering as much as possible about the archaeological record. Archaeologists seek to recover the full range of variation in the data relevant to their research questions. What was the range of activities carried on at a site? What was the range of places chosen for location and settlement? What was the range of forms and styles of artifacts? To the extent that such variation is not known, the picture of ancient life is incomplete and any inferences drawn may be wrong. In a sense, archaeological data are always unrepresentative; not all behavior produces tangible evidence, and even for that which does, not all the remains will survive. So the ideal goal of recovering the full range of variation is seldom realized. But understanding the processes that affected the production and preservation of the evidence can compensate to some extent for the unevenness in data availability. At this point, we need to consider how the archaeologist chooses data acquisition strategies in order to maximize the usefulness of the evidence that *is* available.

The first step in data acquisition is defining the limits of the region under investigation in terms of both time and space. This will impose a practical limit on the amount of evidence to be collected. A bounded research area may be referred to as a **data universe.** Thus an investigator may define a data universe as a single site, or even a portion of site. In research into a region, the research area corresponds to a much larger universe, such as an entire valley or coastal area containing many sites. The archaeologist may also draw temporal boundaries. One investigator may seek data corresponding to a relatively short era, such as the Pueblo II period of the American Southwest (ca. A.D. 900–1100), while another might be interested in a much longer span, such as a period of several thousand years corresponding to an entire interglacial period of the Pleistocene (Ice Age).

Once defined, the data universe is subdivided into **sample units.** A sample unit is the unit of investigation, which may be defined by either arbitrary or

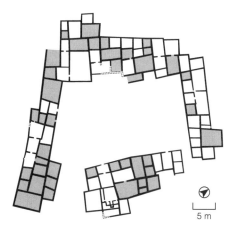

FIGURE 4.13

A universe with nonarbitrary units: in this case, rooms in a prehistoric Southwestern pueblo. The shaded rooms were the ones excavated. (By permission from *Broken K Pueblo, Prehistoric Social Organization in the American Southwest*, by James N. Hill, University of Arizona Anthropological Paper no. 18, Tucson: University of Arizona Press, copyright 1970.)

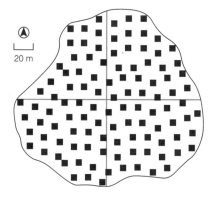

FIGURE 4.14

A universe with arbitrary units at Girik-i-Haciyan, Turkey; the black areas were the units investigated. (After Redman and Watson, reproduced by permission of The Society for American Archaeology, adapted from *American Antiquity* 35: 281–282, 1970.)

nonarbitrary criteria. **Nonarbitrary sample units** correspond either to natural areas, such as microenvironments, or to cultural entities, such as rooms, houses, or sites (Fig. 4.13). **Arbitrary sample units** are spatial divisions with no inherent natural or cultural relevance (Fig. 4.14). Examples of the latter include sample units defined by a grid system (equal-sized squares). *Sample units should not be confused with data:* If an archaeologist is looking for sites, the sample units will be geographical areas where sites might be located. If the data universe is a site, sample units are defined areas within that site; the data are the artifacts, ecofacts, and features within each sample unit.

The choice between arbitrary and nonarbitrary sample units is made by the investigator based on the specific objectives of the study and the characteristics of the data and sites. But in any case all sample units are (or are assumed to be) comparable. Arbitrarily defined units are comparable because they are always regular in size or shape or both. Even nonarbitrarily defined units of different sizes are assumed to yield similar or complementary information about ancient behavior. For example, if sites are the sample units, it is assumed that one cemetery site will give information similar to that from another cemetery site and complementary to that from habitation sites and other sample units within the data universe.

The aggregate of all sample units is the **population.** Note that when the universe is a region and the sample units correspond to all the known sites, the population will not include unknown sites or locations in the region without sites, even though these areas are part of the universe. Nevertheless, conclusions drawn about the population are often inferred to be true of the research universe as well.

Total data acquisition involves investigation of all the units in the population. Of course the archaeologist never succeeds in gathering every shred of evidence from a given data universe; new techniques of recovery and analysis are constantly being developed that broaden the very definition of archaeological data. A change in the research problem also alters the definition of what materials and relationships are considered appropriate data. It is nonetheless important to distinguish between attempts to collect all available evidence (by investigation of all sample units) and those that set out to collect only a portion of the available data. Something approaching total data acquisition, in this sense, is often attempted in salvage situations, as when a site or region is threatened with immediate destruction by construction of a new highway or dam.

Sample data acquisition refers to situations when only a portion or sample of the data can be collected from a given data universe. The limits to the sample recovered are often influenced by economic constraints—the archaeologist seldom has the funds to study all potential units. Nor is research time unlimited: seasonal weather conditions, scheduling commitments, and other factors often limit the time available to gather evidence. Access to archaeological data may be restricted, as when travel is hampered by natural barriers or lack of roads or areas are closed due to lack of permission from property owners. Even when there are no restrictions to access, however, it is still desirable to collect only a sample of the available archaeological data. Except in situations of threatened site destruction, most archaeologists recommend that a portion of every site be left untouched to remain available for future scientists, using techniques more sophisticated than today's. In this way future research can check and refine the results obtained using present methods.

RESEARCH DESIGN

Whether total or sample coverage is used, research must be planned carefully to ensure that its goals will be addressed and met. Traditionally, most archaeological research was site-oriented. The major goal was to excavate a particular site, often with the aim of collecting spectacular remains. With the emergence of archaeology as a scientific discipline, more systematic approaches to research have become the rule. Today, regional and problem-oriented investi-

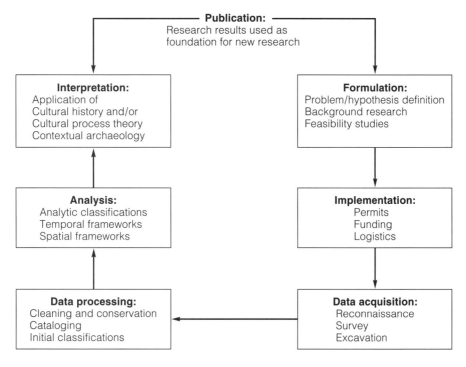

FIGURE 4.15

Diagram of stages of archaeological research.

gations are increasingly the norm. This kind of research aims at solving specific problems or testing one or more hypotheses by using controlled and representative samples of data.

In archaeology, **research design** refers to a sequence of stages that guide the conduct of an investigation (Fig. 4.15) to ensure the validity of results and to make efficient use of time, money, and effort. Each stage has one or more specific purposes. Although the stages may be ideally portrayed as a series of steps, the process is flexible in practice. Aspects of two or more stages may be carried out simultaneously, or accomplished in a different order, depending on particular circumstances. Furthermore, since each research situation is unique, this generalized research design must be capable of adapting to a wide variety of specific applications.

Formulation involves defining the research problem, performing background investigations, and conducting feasibility studies. Decisions regarding the problem to be investigated and the geographical area of study both limit and guide further work. Once these choices are made, the archaeologist conducts background research to locate and study any previous work that may be relevant to the investigation. Useful information at this point may include geographical, geological, climatological, ecological, and anthropological studies, if they are available. Such data may be found in publications, archives, or laboratories, and through consultation with individual experts. Because archaeological research generally requires fieldwork, a feasibility study involving a trip to the region or sites to be investigated is usually necessary in the formulation stage. The objective of such a trip is the evaluation of the archaeological situation and local conditions such as accessibility, availability of supplies, and so forth.

Thorough background investigations facilitate research by refining the problem under investigation and defining research goals. The goals of most archaeological research include testing one or more specific hypotheses. In some cases, these derive from previously proposed models; other times they arise during the formulation of the basic research problem. As the research progresses, of course, new hypotheses may be generated and tested. It is important to remember, however, that the initial formulation of research problems leads the archaeologist to look for particular kinds of data, and thus sets the course for the entire study.

Implementation involves completing all the arrangements necessary for the success of the planned fieldwork. These arrangements may be complex, especially if the research is to be done in a foreign country. The first step in implementing a study may be securing the necessary permits for conducting the research, usually from government agencies responsible for overseeing archaeological work. The owners of the land on which the work will take place must also grant permission before investigations can proceed. The laws governing archaeological work vary from country to country, and from state to state within the United States, so the archaeologist must be aware of the relevant regulations and customs within the area being investigated.

The archaeologist must also find funds to finance the research. In some cases this involves submitting a research proposal to either private or government agencies that support archaeological investigations. In many CRM situations (see Chapter 1), the agency issuing the contract provides the funding for the research.

When funding and permits have been secured, the archaeologist can turn to logistical arrangements. Research equipment and supplies must be acquired. In most cases, field facilities must be rented or built for the safekeeping of equipment and for laboratory processing and storage of artifacts and field records. Many projects require a staff that must be recruited, transported, housed, and fed, and these arrangements must be completed before work can begin.

Data acquisition involves three basic procedures: reconnaissance, survey, and excavation. We will treat these only briefly here since they will be considered in detail in Chapter 5. Reconnaissance is the means for identifying and locating archaeological sites, accomplished by on-the-scene visual search and by remote sensors. Survey is undertaken to record as much as possible about archaeological sites without excavation, using photography, mapping, remote sensors, and collecting samples of surface artifacts. Excavation is undertaken to expose the buried characteristics of archaeological sites, using a variety of techniques to both retrieve and record data revealed as a result.

Data processing refers to the manipulation of raw data (artifacts and ecofacts) and the creation and manipulation of records. Portable remains are usually processed in a field laboratory to ensure that they are recorded, preserved, and stored so as to be available for further analysis. Records referring to these data (descriptions, photographs, and scaled drawings) are also completed and filed to be accessible for later use.

Analysis provides the information about each data category used in archaeological interpretations. For example, analysis of artifacts includes classification, determination of age, and conduct of various technical studies designed to identify sources of raw materials, methods of manufacture, and uses. Some of these procedures can be done in the field laboratory, but the more technical or complex analyses are usually undertaken at specially equipped permanent scientific facilities.

Interpretation involves the synthesis of all the results of data collection, processing, and analysis to meet the original goals of the investigation. The use of the scientific method in these procedures is an important characteristic of modern professional archaeology. A variety of models are used and tested in the interpretive process, including both specific and general historical and anthropological frameworks.

Publication completes the research cycle by making the findings fully accessible so that the results can be used and retested by fellow archaeologists, other scholars, and all other interested individuals. This ensures that any research contributes to the broadest objectives of archaeology and of science in general.

ARCHAEOLOGICAL RESEARCH PROJECTS

Scientific archaeology demands a broad range of expertise. Today's archaeologist must be a teacher, a theoretical scientist, a methodologist, a technician, and an administrator. Since it is nearly impossible for one individual to do everything necessary for a particular research project, archaeologists usually bring together specialists from a wide variety of disciplines. This requires the coordination of many scientists, each of whom focuses upon a particular aspect of the research. By depending on scientific teams of botanists, ecologists, geologists, and other specialists, archaeologists can ensure that data are collected and utilized to the maximum degree possible. In some cases archaeologists may find most of the required support housed under one roof, as in the larger museums and research institutions in many parts of the world (Fig. 4.16). In the United States, the Smithsonian Institution provides one of the most complete support facilities for archaeology.

FIGURE 4.16

Conservation specialists are seen here restoring pottery artifacts excavated from the site of Copán, Honduras, in the field laboratory adjacent to the site. Copán has been the subject, since 1976, of a research project sponsored by many universities from many nations. (Courtesy of the Instituto Hondureño de Antropología e Historia and the Proyecto Arqueológico Acrópolis de Copán.)

The size and duration of archaeological research projects depend on the scale of the problems being investigated. A few months of a single individual's work may sometimes be all that is required to plan and conduct data acquisition, but that individual will also need some form of assistance from outside specialists in processing and analyzing the results. On the other hand, archaeological research concerned with complex civilizations, such as research at large urban sites in southwest Asia and Mexico, usually calls for a large archaeological staff and a huge labor force. In these and similar areas research projects employ large teams of on-site specialists and extend over many years.

Like most activities, archaeological research is limited by the availability of time and money. A far greater problem, one that threatens the very existence of archaeological research, is the increasing pace of destruction wrought by looting and the many modifications of our rapidly expanding world. The destruction of archaeological remains has reached such proportions that we may well ask, "Does the past have a future?" We will consider the problem of the destruction of our archaeological heritage in the final chapter of this book.

SUMMARY

Material remains from the past become archaeological data once they are recognized, collected, and recorded. The direct products of past human activity are either artifacts (portable remains) or features (nonportable remains). Indirect products of past human activity are called ecofacts. Archaeologists usually examine distributions of these data within sites (clusters of data) or within regions (clusters of sites). Further information is gleaned from recording the specific locations (proveniences), associations, and matrix that surrounds these classes of data. The context of these data—their depositional significance—is inferred by evaluating all of these factors. Understanding this context—and discriminating among the various kinds of context—is the crucial link that allows the archaeologist to reconstruct the kinds of ancient behavior the recovered data represent.

Ideally, the material record reflects four major categories of human activity—acquisition, manufacture, use, and deposition, which together constitute behavioral processes. But archaeologists can never recover data representing all kinds of past behavior. Some activity leaves no tangible trace. The evidence of other behaviors may be altered through time by transformational processes, both human and natural in origin. These processes act selectively either to preserve or to destroy archaeological evidence. Thus the data available to the archaeologist constitute a sample determined first by ancient human activity (behavioral processes) and then by human or natural forces acting after the remains are deposited (transformational processes).

The resulting data form the base that the archaeologist attempts to recover, either totally (by collection of all available evidence) or by sampling methods. Whatever collection method is used, the archaeologist seeks data that represent, insofar as possible, the full range of ancient human activity. With very few exceptions (such as cases where a site is about to be destroyed), it is generally practical and desirable to collect only a sample of the data. Specific research goals and field conditions usually require a flexible mix of sampling schemes to enable the archaeologist to learn as much as possible about the past.

Archaeological research is usually aimed at solving specific problems or testing specific hypotheses. To guide such investigations, archaeologists follow a research design that begins with formulation of the problem, based on background and feasibility studies; followed by implementation, involving fundraising, securing of permits, and making logistical arrangements. The next stage is data acquisition, often including reconnaissance (locating unknown sites), survey (mapping and collecting surface data), and excavation (removal of matrix to reveal buried data). This is followed by data processing and analysis, leading to interpretation (reconstruction of the past to address the specific research goals) and publication of the research.

To be successful researchers, archaeologists must command a broad range of expertise. They must master field methods, theory, administration, and a range of technical skills. Seldom can one individual perform all the tasks demanded by the complexity of archaeological investigation, so in most cases

archaeologists call on teams of specialists for assistance. The scale of archaeological research varies from that conducted by a single person in a few weeks
to that performed by large research teams over several years or decades. The
practical limits to such research are usually determined by time and money, but
the most severe threat to furthering our understanding of the past is posed by
the destruction of archaeological data caused by looting and the growth of our
modern world.

FOR FURTHER READING

ARCHAEOLOGICAL DATA
Binford 1964; Deetz 1967; Fish and Kowalewski 1990; Flannery 1976; Willey 1953

DEPOSITION AND TRANSFORMATION
Behrensmeyer and Hill 1980; Binford 1982; Butzer 1982; Glob 1969; Hoving 1978;
Schiffer 1976, 1987; Woolley 1934

ACQUIRING DATA
Hill 1970; Mueller 1975; Orton 1980; Pulak and Frey 1985; Redman and Watson
1970

RESEARCH DESIGN
Binford 1964; Clarke 1972a; Cronyn 1990; Gero and Conkey 1991; Taylor (1948)
1967

ARCHAEOLOGICAL RESEARCH PROJECTS
Agurcia 1986; Alexander 1970; Joukowsky 1980; Wheeler 1954; Willey 1974

ADDITIONAL SOURCES
Bass 1966; Binford 1972, 1981; Brain 1981; Champion 1980; Chang 1972; Fagan
1985; Frink 1984; Gladfelter 1981; Hamilton and Woodward 1984; Hester, Heizer,
and Graham 1975; Stein and Farrand 1985; Villa 1982; Wilson 1982

Fieldwork

WITH A WELL DESIGNED research plan in hand, the next consideration is the collection of archaeological data. Archaeologists use three means of collecting evidence about the past: reconnaissance, surface survey, and excavation. Although excavation dominates the popular image of what archaeologists do, both reconnaissance and surface survey are crucial to archaeological research, as are subsequent data processing and classification.

RECONNAISSANCE

Time transforms the sites of past human activity in a variety of ways. Some sites, such as Stonehenge (Fig. 4.3), may remain obvious to any observer. Others may be nearly destroyed or completely buried; in such cases, the task of identification may be extremely difficult. The systematic attempt to identify archaeological sites is called archaeological **reconnaissance.** Identification includes both the discovery of sites and the precise determination of their geographical location. Reconnaissance data can be used to formulate or refine hypotheses to be tested in later research stages. This is especially true when the work is taking place in geographical areas with no prior archaeological information or as part of a feasibility study for a larger overall project.

Archaeological reconnaissance yields data about the form (size and internal arrangement) of sites as well as their total number and spatial distribution within a region. This distribution may reveal patterns in the placement of sites

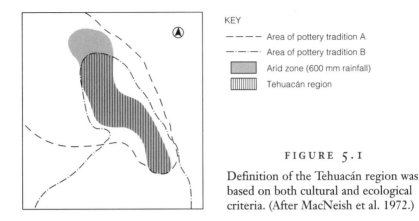

KEY

- - - - - Area of pottery tradition A
- · - · - · Area of pottery tradition B
▨ Arid zone (600 mm rainfall)
▥ Tehuacán region

FIGURE 5.1

Definition of the Tehuacán region was based on both cultural and ecological criteria. (After MacNeish et al. 1972.)

in relation to each other and to the natural environment, such as topography; plant, animal, and mineral resources; and water. Sometimes these findings may be used to define the region for later, more intensive study. For the Tehuacán Project (discussed further below), one phase of reconnaissance helped to define the study region by indicating the correlation between the limits of the arid Tehuacán Valley (Fig. 5.1) and the distribution limits of two pottery styles.

This example emphasizes the need for studies of a region's environmental resources, either prior to actual reconnaissance (as part of background research) or in conjunction with the site identification process. Defining ecological zones within a study area can guide the archaeologist in searching for sites if site location can be correlated with the distribution of different environmental variables. The archaeologist may thereby gain an initial understanding of possible ecological relationships between past peoples and their environment.

Discovering Archaeological Sites

Not all sites are found by reconnaissance. Some archaeological remains are never lost to history. In areas with long literate traditions, such as the Mediterranean basin, the locations and identities of many ancient cities have never been forgotten; Athens or Rome are obvious examples. Most sites, however—even many documented by history—have not fared so well. Many once-recorded sites have been lost, either razed by later conquerors or ravaged by natural processes of collapse and decay. Ancient Carthage, for example, was systematically destroyed by its Roman conquerors in 146 B.C. Only with archaeological research was it rediscovered near Tunis.

Sometimes histories and legends provide the clues that lead to the discovery of lost cities. The most famous quest of this sort was Heinrich Schliemann's successful search for the legendary city of Troy. As a child, Schliemann became fascinated with the story of Troy and decided that someday he would find that lost city. By age 30, he had become a successful international merchant and had amassed the fortune needed for his archaeological quest. He learned more than half a dozen languages, quickening his appetite for Troy by reading Homer's tales of the Trojan War in the original Greek. Textual descriptions of the location of the ancient city convinced him that it was to be found at Hissarlik in western Turkey. Accordingly, in 1870, he began excavations that ultimately identified Priam's legendary city. Later it was found that the burned remains Schliemann had called Troy were really an earlier settlement, and that in his determined digging he had cut right through the Trojan layers! Nonetheless, Schliemann is credited with the discovery of Troy, and his successful persistence gave great impetus to the search for the origins of Greek civilization.

Perhaps more archaeological sites come to light by accident than by any other means. The forces of nature—wind and water erosion, natural catastrophes, and so forth—have uncovered many long-buried traces of past human activity. The deposits of Tanzania's Olduvai Gorge, from which Mary and Louis Leakey recovered remains of early human ancestors, were exposed by thousands of years of riverine bed-cutting action. The famous Neolithic lake dwellings of Switzerland were discovered when extremely low water levels during the dry winter of 1853–54 exposed the preserved remains of the wooden pilings that once supported houses.

Chance discoveries of ancient sites occur all the time. For example, it was French schoolboys who in 1940 first happened on the Paleolithic paintings of Lascaux cave: the boys' dog fell through an opening into the cave, and when they went after their pet, they discovered the cavern walls covered with ancient paintings. As the world's population increases and the pace of new construction accelerates, more and more ancient remains are uncovered. More often than not, new sites are first found by farmers, ranchers, outdoor enthusiasts, and explorers rather than archaeologists. Unfortunately, and often despite the best intentions, many are destroyed before any archaeologist has a chance to observe and record them.

When archaeologists set out to discover and identify sites, reconnaissance is conducted in a variety of ways. The actual techniques and procedures used often depend on the kinds of sites being sought. The methods used to locate surface sites differ greatly from those intended to discover deeply buried sites. In most cases, limitations of time and money prevent the archaeologist from covering every square meter of the research area in attempting to identify sites. Accordingly, carefully selected sampling procedures should be used in order to maximize the chance that the number and location of sites in the areas actually searched are representative of the universe under study.

Some environments are more conducive to reconnaissance than others. Dry climates and sparse vegetation offer near ideal conditions for both visual detection of archaeological sites and ease of movement across reconnoitered terrain (Fig. 5.2). Such environments have greatly aided archaeologists in discovering sites in Southwest Asia, coastal Peru, highland Mexico, the southwestern United States, and similar areas.

(a) (b)

FIGURE 5.2

Present environmental conditions have a great influence on reconnaissance: (a) Tropical rain forest greatly reduces visibility, while (b) arid landscapes are often conducive to detection of surface sites. (Courtesy of the Tikal and Gordion Projects, University of Pennsylvania Museum.)

Good quality maps are essential for reconnaissance. Maps are often supplemented by aerial photos. Maps are used first to plot the grid squares or other boundaries for sample units and then to plot the location of new sites discovered. Plotting of sample unit boundaries enables the archaeologist to indicate which areas have been covered and which have not. Sampling adequacy can then be assessed and, depending on the pattern found in sites, the possible distribution of sites in nonreconnoitered areas can be posited. Plotting of new sites is necessary for distributional studies within the sampled area and, of course, for returning to the sites.

Methods of Reconnaissance

Three basic methods are used for archaeological reconnaissance: ground reconnaissance, aerial reconnaissance, and subsurface reconnaissance. Each requires specialized techniques, and each is effective in identifying sites under different conditions.

Ground reconnaissance is the oldest and most common method. It has been used since the days of antiquarian interest, when exploration by such men as William Camden in England or Stephens and Catherwood in Central America led to the discovery of countless sites. This approach is illustrated in recent years by numerous large-scale surveys in the United States and elsewhere. An example is the work in the Great Basin discussed in Chapter 1.

FIGURE 5.3

Traces of a building visible on the surface of Shahr-i-Sokhta. (Courtesy of Centro Studie Scavi Archeologici in Asia of IsMEO, Rome.)

Most ground reconnaissance is still conducted by walking—the slowest method, but the most thorough. The efficiency of reconnaissance on foot is increased by using teams to cover extensive areas. Attention to changing ground conditions is also useful; for example, in farming areas, plowing may bring shallowly buried items to the surface. Many archaeologists increase the speed of large-scale ground reconnaissance by use of horses, mules, or even motorized transport (four-wheel-drive vehicles are frequently necessary).

How does the archaeologist recognize archaeological sites on the ground? Some sites, of course, are identified by their prominence. Many ancient settlements in Southwest Asia are called *tell* or *tepe*—both meaning "hill"—because they stand out as large mounds against a relatively flat plain. In other cases, a slight rise or fall in the landscape may indicate a buried ancient wall or other feature. Many sites are identified by concentrations of surface artifacts such as pottery sherds and stone tools. Shahr-i Sokhta in eastern Iran was found because of its densely littered surface. Another sign of this site was differential absorption of salt, which made the tops of the buried mud-brick walls stand out as white against the rest of the surface (Fig. 5.3). Many sites, however, lack obvious surface traces and require more than surface observation for their discovery.

There are several methods for discovering sites in which the observer is not in direct contact with the archaeological remains. These remote sensing techniques may be divided into two major categories: aerial reconnaissance and subsurface reconnaissance.

Aerial reconnaissance includes a variety of established and experimental techniques, the most common being aerial photography. Although the most

FIGURE 5.4

Aerial photograph, shot by remote control, from a balloon moored over the site of Sarepta, Lebanon. (Photo by Julian Whittlesey.)

common platform for aerial photography is the airplane, less expensive options include balloons and kites equipped with remote-controlled cameras (Fig. 5.4).

Aerial photography is useful in several ways. It provides data for preliminary analysis of the local environment and its resources, and it yields information on site location. Aerial photography can reveal sites from their surface characteristics or prominence, and often it can even detect buried sites. Low-growing vegetation, such as grass, grain, and other ground covers, grows better where ancient human activity, such as the construction of canals, deposition of middens, or burials, has improved soil moisture and fertility. In contrast, solid construction features such as walls or roads immediately below the surface will often impede vegetation growth (Fig. 5.5). Either way, buried remains are revealed by patterns visible on aerial photos.

Archaeologists often use equipment more sophisticated than regular cameras and film. Infrared film can detect patterns invisible to normal light-sensitive film. Nonphotographic aerial images are also used, such as radar and thermography. Radar is effective in penetrating cloud cover, and it will see through dense vegetation to a certain extent. Thermography records differences in the absorption and reflection of heat and can detect archaeological features such as buried ditches and prehistoric fields.

Several nonmilitary satellites provide arrays of data useful for archaeology. Landsat has multispectral scanners that record the intensity of reflected light and infrared radiation. The satellite data are converted electronically to photographlike images which can be built up, in a mosaic, to form a very accurate

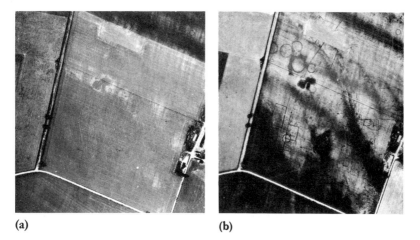

(a)   (b)

FIGURE 5.5

A pair of aerial photographs of the same area at different times. Detection
of buried archaeological features has been greatly enhanced with the mat-
uration of the barley growing in the field: (a) taken June 4, 1970; (b) taken
June 19, 1970. (Courtesy of the Museum Applied Science Center for
Archaeology, University of Pennsylvania Museum.)

map that reveals extensive features such as ancient road networks and is especially useful for regional studies (Fig. 5.6).

Geographic Information Systems (GIS) combine computerized data from
multiple sources, such as satellite imagery, historical maps, or ground survey.
The result is a data base on landforms, vegetation, water systems, and cultural
features for a specified region. Using a computer screen or a summary, the
archaeologist can view selected aspects of the landscape, highlighting individual elements, such as terrain or geological composition. At the same time, the
digitized data can be subjected to statistical analysis, such as looking for the co-
occurrence of cultural and natural features to analyze potential resources available to ancient settlements. GIS data allow archaeologists to locate and study
areas in which new sites are likely to occur. Searches of such signature areas can
then test hypotheses about site distribution.

As with data from all remote sensing techniques, aerial reconnaissance
results require knowledge of the corresponding **ground truth** for reliable
interpretation. This involves checking at ground level to determine what the
various contrasting patterns and features visible on photographs represent.

Subsurface reconnaissance includes a variety of methods used to identify
buried remains. These range from the rather simple to those requiring exotic
and expensive equipment. Most of these techniques provide limited coverage
and are time-consuming and costly. For these reasons they are usually used
only for subsurface identification of specific features within archaeological

FIGURE 5.6

Satellite image of a portion of the Nile Valley in Egypt, with the Great Pyramids visible on the desert margin at lower left. (Landsat imagery courtesy of EOSAT.)

sites. Sometimes, however, they may be the only means available for locating buried sites.

The most direct and simple methods are **augering, coring,** and **shovel testing.** An auger is a large drill run by human or machine power. It is used to find the depth of deposits such as topsoil or middens. Corers are hollow tubes that are driven into the ground. When removed, they yield a narrow column or core of matrix, providing a quick and relatively inexpensive cross-section of subsurface layers or construction. Simple shallow probes with shovels or post-hole diggers constitute the most common kind of reconnaissance technique in eastern North America and similar regions, where many sites lie invisible, just below ground level.

The **magnetometer** is an instrument that discerns minor variations in the magnetism present in many materials. Unlike the compass, which measures the direction of the earth's magnetic field, magnetometers measure that field's intensity. These instruments have been applied successfully to archaeological reconnaissance because some remains create anomalies in the magnetic field. For example, iron tools and ceramic kilns are especially easy to find with this instrument. Such buried features as walls made of volcanic stone, ditches filled with humus, and even burned surfaces may all be detected by the magnetometer (Fig. 5.7). Its primary use, then, is to locate features within a site.

A notable early use of the magnetometer, however, was in site reconnaissance during the search for the Greek colonial city of Sybaris. Founded in

(a)   (b)

FIGURE 5.7

Magnetometers are important aids in subsurface detection: (a) The person
in the foreground carries the detector, while the two in the background (b)
read and record the magnetic values. (© Nicholas Hartmann, MASCA,
University of Pennsylvania Museum.)

710 B.C., Sybaris had a history and a reputation but no tangible existence.
Notorious for the self-indulgence of its inhabitants, it was destroyed in 520 B.C.
It was known to be located somewhere on the plain of the River Crati in the
instep of Italy's boot, but all attempts at locating the ancient city had been
unsuccessful. In the 1960s, however, a joint Italian-American expedition succeeded in locating Sybaris (Fig. 5.8). The investigators used a variety of
approaches, including coring, but the magnetometer proved to be the instrument that located this elusive site.

The **resistivity detector** (Fig. 5.9) measures differences in the ability of
subsurface features to conduct electrical current. Moisture content gives most
soils a low resistance to an electrical current; solid features such as walls or
floors can raise resistance considerably. Another instrument, ground-penetrat-
ing radar (or pulse radar), sends electromagnetic waves into the earth to be
reflected back as echoes by subsurface discontinuities, such as soil strata and
constructed features.

Locating Archaeological Sites

Discovery is only half the task of reconnaissance. The other half is determining and recording the location of the sites or features as they are discovered.
The central purpose of recording is to relate the newly found sites to their spatial setting in order to place the previously unknown into the realm of the

FIGURE 5.8

Excavations at Sybaris, following reconnaissance by magnetometer, expose Roman construction superimposed on the remains of the earlier Greek colony. (Courtesy of the Museum Applied Science Center for Archaeology, University of Pennsylvania Museum.)

FIGURE 5.9

Subsurface detection by resistivity at a historical site in Pennsylvania. (Courtesy of the Museum Applied Science Center for Archaeology, University of Pennsylvania Museum.)

known. Usually this involves plotting the site location on a map or aerial photograph. Sometimes base maps have to be specially drawn to record the results of reconnaissance. In other cases, archaeological sites may already be indicated in some way on a map or visible on an aerial photo. Although this may lessen the job of the archaeologist conducting the reconnaissance, it does not remove the need for checking ground truth to ensure that a site actually exists at the indicated location.

The global positioning system (GPS) has been of tremendous help in accurately and quickly locating archaeological sites. Hand-held GPS receivers weigh only a few pounds. They can calculate the user's location very accurately by triangulation from a series of satellites in orbit 11,000 miles above the earth.

Along with plotting location, archaeologists give each new site a designation for identification. Numbers are often the easiest labels. The system commonly used in the United States combines a number designation for the state, a letter code for the county, and a number for each site. Thus, site 28 MO 35 refers to the 35th site designated in Monmouth County, New Jersey. Names are also used, for they can be easier to remember, although they can be more cumbersome. The crucial point is that each site must have a unique designation so that all relevant information—descriptions, surface collections, maps, photographs, and so on—can be linked to it. Although this information may come from reconnaissance, its collection actually falls under survey and excavation, which are discussed next.

SURFACE SURVEY

Surface survey refers to methods archaeologists use to acquire data from sites without excavation. The overall objective of surface surveys is to determine as much as possible about a given site or region based on both observing surface remains and detecting subsurface features through remote means.

The choice of surface survey methods depends on the characteristics of the site or region being studied and the kind of data being sought. In conducting surveys, archaeologists attempt to detect and record all surface features. Traces of many ancient remains, such as ruined buildings, walls, roads, and canals, exist on the ground, where they can be still be seen and recorded by mapping. On the other hand, buried features may not be directly detectable from the surface. In some cases, these buried remains can be located and mapped by one or more of the remote sensing methods already described.

Surface surveys also include detection and recording of artifacts and ecofacts. When these are found on the surface, their provenience is recorded. Because they are portable, they may be collected and taken to the field laboratory for further study. The detection of buried artifacts and ecofacts by remote sensors is usually difficult. In some cases, as noted earlier, augers, corers, and shovels can be used to determine the presence or absence of artifacts below ground, but recovery of buried artifacts and ecofacts must usually await excavation.

The objectives of reconnaissance and survey can sometimes be met most efficiently by combining them into a single operation. This is especially true if the same sample units can be used for site identification and for gathering surface data. In other situations, however, these operations are best pursued separately. For instance, an investigation may undertake total coverage of its data universe to identify and locate sites, but have the resources to record and collect surface remains for only a sample of the universe.

Whether or not it is combined with reconnaissance, surface survey is usually an essential complement to later excavation. It is even possible to conduct archaeological research by gathering data solely by surface survey. This may be the best and most obvious solution in cases of well-preserved surface sites with little or no depth. In other situations, lack of time, money, or necessary permits may preclude excavation so that surface survey becomes the only means available for acquiring data.

Survey Methods

As already mentioned, surface survey involves two basic methods: ground survey and remote sensing. Each of these will be considered in a little more detail before we turn to the results of surface survey.

Ground survey refers to walking over the site or sites under investigation to gather or record surface artifacts, ecofacts, or features. Surface features are recorded by making topographic or planimetric maps. The former depicts elevation differences by contour lines, while the latter uses symbolic representations of features (Fig. 5.10). Surface artifacts and ecofacts may be mapped as well, especially if their spatial distribution may reflect ancient activity areas or patterns. In many cases, however, the remains are too disturbed and numerous for mapping to be practical. In such situations, after keying provenience to mapped sample areas, surface artifacts and ecofacts are simply collected for field laboratory analysis.

Remote sensing is often used to detect and record buried features and sometimes to find artifacts. The techniques used are the same as described in the discussion of reconnaissance: aerial sensors such as cameras and radar; ground-based sensors, including magnetometers and pulse radar; and mechanical devices such as corers and shovels. Although the techniques are the same, in surface survey they involve different objectives. Instead of being used to discover unrecorded archaeological sites, they are used to detect and record internal components of sites as part of data acquisition. For example, aerial photography can reveal the form and extent of features such as building foundations and road networks whether they are present on the surface or detectable underground as crop marks.

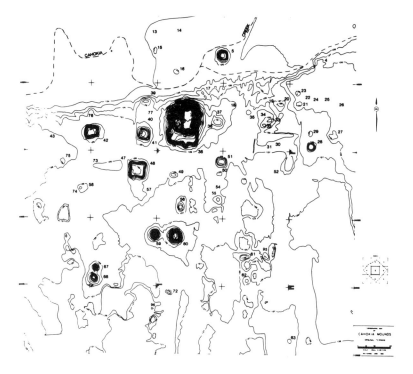

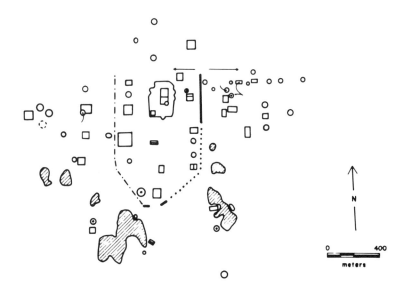

FIGURE 5.10

Comparison of information conveyed by (top) topographic and (bottom) planimetric archaeological maps of the same site, Cahokia, Illinois. (After Fowler 1989, courtesy of Melvin Fowler and the Illinois Historic Preservation Agency.)

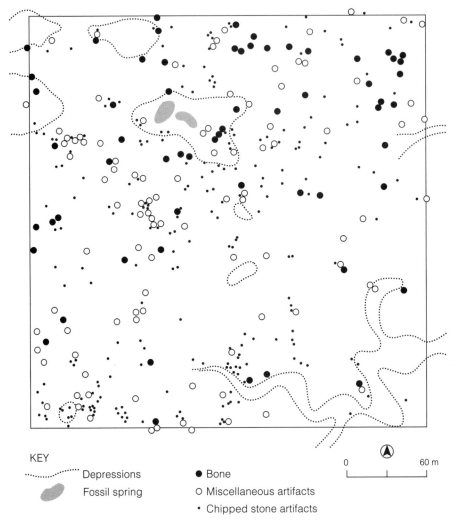

KEY

········· Depressions   ● Bone

🔲 Fossil spring   ○ Miscellaneous artifacts

· Chipped stone artifacts

0   60 m

FIGURE 5.11

Detailed plot of surface finds at China Lake, California. (After Davis 1975, reproduced by permission of The Society for American Archaeology, adapted from *American Antiquity* 40: 51, 1975.)

Preliminary Site Definition

A well-executed surface survey using one or more of these methods provides the archaeologist with a preliminary definition of the study universe, whether it consists of a single site or a region containing many sites. The preliminary definition should also include data bearing upon the form, density, and structure of archaeological remains within the universe. The range in the forms of features may be assessed by both ground survey and remote sensing; the ranges

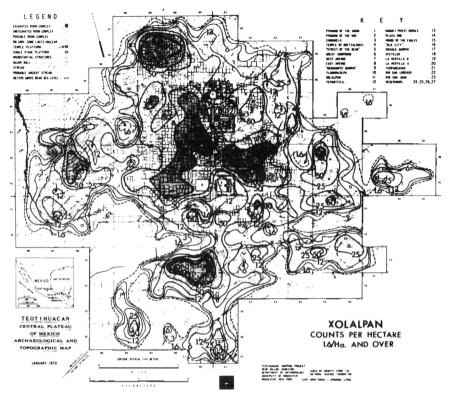

FIGURE 5.12

Surface densities of recovered pottery at Teotihuacán, Mexico, ca. A.D. 450–650. (After Cowgill 1974.)

in forms of artifacts and ecofacts are assessed from surface collections. Surface survey information may then be used to determine the relative density of each form, together with their interrelationships (their structure). By plotting the spatial distribution of one artifact class—say, grinding stones—the investigator may find areas in which these artifacts cluster. Furthermore, it may be possible to relate these relative densities to the distribution of other classes of artifacts, ecofacts, and features. Surface survey data of this kind are often presented as maps to show the distribution and density of artifacts, ecofacts, and features within a site. From these maps, the archaeologist may be able to formulate working hypotheses to account for the distributional patterns. For example, in the China Lake Valley of California, artifact and ecofact distributions were used to infer that two different stone tool types represented different parts of one tool kit rather than occupation by distinct human groups (Fig. 5.11). At Teotihuacán, in central Mexico, surface potsherd density was plotted for different time periods to study the growth and decline of population (Fig. 5.12). In surface-oriented research, these findings are an end product of the investigation. In most cases, however, such survey results are preliminary, for they guide the archaeologist in choosing where to excavate to explore promising areas and test specific hypotheses.

EXCAVATION

The principal means by which the archaeologist gathers data about the past is **excavation,** used both to discover and to retrieve data from beneath the ground surface. As we have seen, surface survey is often an essential prelude to excavation. Collections of artifacts and ecofacts from the surface often provide clues about what lies beneath the ground and help the archaeologist plan excavations. Remote sensors such as magnetometers or pulse radar equipment may also detect the existence of buried features. But the only way to verify the presence and characteristics of subsurface data is through excavation.

Data retrieved through excavation are especially important for the archaeologist since subsurface remains are usually the best preserved and the least disturbed. Surface artifacts and ecofacts are seldom in primary context and are usually poorly preserved. Surface features such as ancient walls or roads, though they may still be in primary context, are often less well preserved than similar features buried, and therefore protected, below the surface. In addition, excavation often reveals associations of artifacts, ecofacts, and features in primary contexts. As we have seen, this kind of data is the most useful to the archaeologist for inferring ancient function and behavior.

The two basic goals of excavation are to reveal the three-dimensional patterning or structure in the deposition of artifacts, ecofacts, and features; and to assess the functional and temporal significance of this patterning. For example, stone tools, pottery vessels, and animal bones may be found together adjacent to house remains or other areas in which they were used. Determination of this three-dimensional patterning depends on documenting provenience and associations of the individual artifacts, ecofacts, and features with respect both to each other and to their surrounding matrix. At the same time, evaluation of provenience and association allows the archaeologist to assess context. Attention to these relationships clearly differentiates the archaeologist from the looter.

By knowing which elements were found together (from their provenience and association) and by inferring how they got there (from association and context), the archaeologist can reconstruct ancient behavior. As a result, proper excavation records are as crucial to interpretation as proper methods of excavation. Of course, reconstructing behavior also depends on the ability to determine the functions of the individual artifacts, ecofacts, and features; this analysis, as we shall discuss in Chapter 6, is based not only on their provenience and association, but also on their form and other attributes.

The three-dimensional structure of an archaeological deposit is especially important. There is a fundamental distinction between the single vertical

FIGURE 5.13

Recovery of evidence representing a single moment in time at Ceren in El Salvador. Excavations have exposed the remains of an adobe house and adjacent cornfield buried by a local volcanic eruption that collapsed and carbonized the roof beams and thatch. Later eruptions are represented by the upper deposits of ash. (Courtesy of Payson D. Sheets.)

dimension that shows depth and the two horizontal ones that determine lateral extent. Ideally, the horizontal dimensions represent the associated remains of a single point in time. The case of Pompeii, where a whole community was buried and preserved as if in suspended animation, provides an extreme illustration. The point is that artifacts and features on the same horizontal surface often represent use or discard that is approximately contemporaneous (Fig. 5.13). Over time, new surfaces cover the old, and repetition of this process creates a vertical dimension (Fig. 5.14). Thus the vertical dimension in an archaeological deposit represents accumulation through time.

Stratigraphy

Archaeological **stratification** refers to the observed layering of matrices and features. These layers or **strata** may be sloping or roughly horizontal, thick or thin. In some cases, they are well-defined by contrasts in color, texture, composition, or other characteristics. Just as often, however, boundaries may be difficult or even impossible to see; one stratum may simply grade into another. But in all cases stratified deposits reflect the geological **law of superposition:** the sequence of observable strata from bottom to top reflects the order of deposition from earliest to latest. The individual strata of an archaeological

Two contemporary houses at same ground level

One house is abandoned, collapses, and is used as a rubbish dump.

Resulting mound is leveled and a new house is built on its summit, which is now contemporary (although at a higher level) with still-occupied house at right.

FIGURE 5.14

An example of one means by which accumulation of occupational debris results in vertical buildup.

deposit may represent the superimposed remains of different occupations at the site; they may result from the sequential disposal of material, such as accumulated layers of trash in a midden; or they may reflect deposits made naturally, as when floods cover an area with layers of alluvium. Whatever the source of deposition, the lowest levels were those *deposited* the earliest.

Note, however, that the law of superposition refers to the sequence of deposition, not to the age of the materials in the strata. Although in most cases the age of materials does follow their depositional sequence, there are exceptions. For example, strata may be formed of redeposited material, as when water erosion removes soil from a location upstream and redeposits it in a new location downstream. If this soil contains cultural material, chronologically late artifacts could be removed and redeposited, then covered by chronologically earlier artifacts (Fig. 5.15). Thus the redeposited matrix contains later artifacts in its lower strata and earlier artifacts in its upper strata. Note, however, that

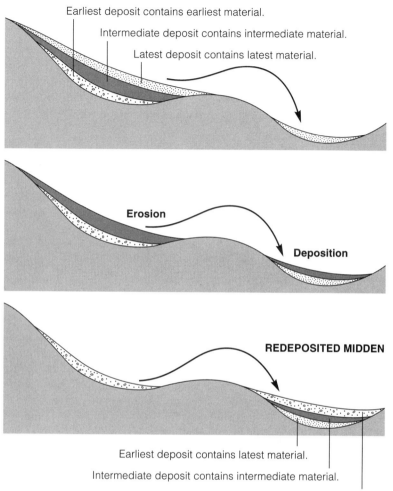

FIGURE 5.15

Schematic depiction of inverted layering. The uppermost (latest) material in the original deposit erodes first and is redeposited as the lowermost layer downstream.

even in this case of reversed stratification, the law of superposition holds: the lower layers were *deposited* first, followed by the upper layers. The same reversal effect can result from human activity, as when stratified deposits are mined and reused for construction fill. Another reason superposition of artifacts or ecofacts may not directly reflect age is because of intrusive strata. Pits or burrows dug by humans or by animals may insert later materials into lower levels.

The interpretation of stratification is called **stratigraphy.** That is, stratigraphy refers to the archaeological evaluation of the temporal and functional meaning of the observed strata. In stratigraphic analysis, the archaeologist combines use of the law of superposition with a consideration of context. Since intact archaeological features are invariably in primary context, problems of temporal determination usually arise with portable data—artifacts and ecofacts. In essence, the archaeologist must judge whether the artifacts and ecofacts found in each stratum are the undisturbed result of human activity (primary context) or have been rearranged or redeposited by human agents or natural events (secondary context).

In some cases this judgment is aided by **conjoining studies,** in which fragments of broken bone, stone, or other material can be fitted back together. For example, at Site FxJj50 in the Koobi Fora area on the east shore of Lake Turkana, Kenya, conjoining studies linked enough scattered stone flakes to suggest that they represented remains of tool manufacture and use within a 170-square-meter site area. Bone pieces were also conjoined with the same interpretation, and the weathering on the bone suggested it had lain exposed to the elements for little more than a year at most, before burial by flood-laid soils. Together, these inferences established the 1.5 million-year-old site as a single complex feature, and strengthened the behavioral interpretations for the distribution of these materials.

If, through means such as conjoining studies, archaeologists can demonstrate primary context with reasonable assurance—that is, if there is no evidence of redeposition or disturbance—then the temporal sequence of the archaeological materials within a deposit may be assumed to follow that of the strata. In this way, a stratigraphic sequence is established.

Let us consider an example of stratigraphy. In northern Colorado, bison hunters some 11,000 years ago camped in the area now called the Lindenmeier site. The hunting groups left stone tools, toolmaking debris, hearths, and the bones of prey animals. Although each individual group probably spent only a brief time camped at Lindenmeier, repeated use of the campsite over time led to a gradual accumulation of occupation debris. During this time span, the level of the ground surface was being raised by natural processes: small depressions flooded with water from a nearby stream, and plants grew in the wet areas, died, and decayed to form soil filling the old depressions. The new, raised surfaces created by such filling-in were used as hunting camps, and older cultural debris was buried and sealed in place when it was flooded. In this way, the combined effects of geological buildup and repeated reoccupation produced a stratified deposit in which the natural matrix accumulation included (and preserved) evidence of human occupation. At Lindenmeier the law of superposition is relatively unaffected by disturbing factors: the basic stratigraphy is simply vertical accumulation through time, and the relative age of the artifacts correlates well with stratigraphic position.

The functional dimension of stratigraphy involves distinguishing natural activity from cultural activity. In essence, the archaeologist attempts to determine which layers in the stratified deposit result from human activity and which are naturally laid soils. For some deposits, evidence of past human activity is obvious, as in burials, house foundations, and middens. In the absence of clear indicators, however, determining if a given stratum was produced by human agents may be more difficult. Clues to past human occupation include the presence in the soil of unusually high concentrations of diagnostic residues, such as phosphates, or of pollen from domesticated plants. Archaeologists make other functional distinctions as well, such as between architectural and nonarchitectural features. Nonarchitectural features include middens, burials, hearths, and quarries. Architectural features include walls, floors, platforms, staircases, and roadways.

Stratigraphic evaluation, then, incorporates both temporal and functional aspects. Combining the law of superposition with assessments of context, the archaeologist interprets the depositional history of the excavated matrix. Functional interpretation begins with a distinction between those parts of the sequence that are natural strata and those that are cultural features. On the basis of these evaluations, the archaeologist establishes first a stratigraphic sequence for each excavation and then, by comparing stratigraphy between excavations, a composite stratigraphic sequence for the entire site. This stratigraphic sequence forms the underlying temporal framework for all further interpretation.

Stratigraphy thus emphasizes sequence and accumulation over time and follows from the vertical dimension of archaeological deposits. Distribution in the two lateral dimensions—that is, the spread of features and artifacts through a given horizontal layer—associates these data with one another within a single period or time span. Because horizontally associated materials within a stratum are ideally the remains of behavior from a single period of time, these lateral distributions provide data to reconstruct the range of activities carried on simultaneously. Taken together, stratigraphy and association—the vertical and the horizontal—define the three-dimensional physical structure that excavation attempts to reveal.

Excavation Methods

An archaeological excavation is usually a complicated, time-consuming process. The aim of an excavation program is the acquisition of as much three-dimensional data relevant to its research objectives as possible, given available resources. The success of any particular program depends upon a variety of factors, the most important of which is the overall organization or strategy of the excavations. This strategy guides the archaeologist in choosing the location, extent, timing, and kinds of excavation to meet the research goals with maximum efficiency.

Obviously each situation is unique, but the range of choices among which the archaeologist must decide is limited. To make the best decisions for a given project, the researcher must be thoroughly familiar with all the alternatives and the ends each is best suited to accomplish.

FIGURE 5.16

View of an earthen structure at Las Tunas, Guatemala, revealed by a
trench; a second, smaller trench has now penetrated this structure and
its supporting platform. (Verapaz Project, University of Pennsylvania
Museum.)

The two basic kinds of excavations mirror the three-dimensional physical
structure of most sites.

1. **Penetrating excavations** are primarily deep probes of subsurface deposits.
   Their main thrust is vertical, and their principal objective is to reveal, in
   cross-section, the depth, sequencing, and composition of archaeological
   remains. They cut through sequential or adjacent deposits. This category
   includes test pits, trenches, and tunnels (Fig. 5.16).

2. **Clearing excavations** aim primarily at the horizontal investigation of
   deposits. Their main thrust is outward or across, and their principal objective is to reveal the horizontal extent of an archaeological deposit and the
   arrangement of objects within the deposit. Clearing excavations emphasize
   tracing continuities of single surfaces or deposits of varying extent (Fig.
   5.17).

Archaeologists frequently use a combination of these types of excavation to
meet the diverse goals of their research.

Many strategies are possible for excavating an archaeological site. More
than one archaeologist has compared excavation to solving a three-dimensional
jigsaw puzzle. Of course, excavation does not attempt to put the pieces togeth-

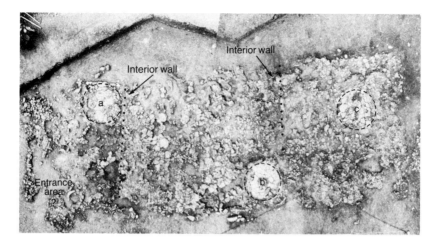

FIGURE 5.17

A labeled photograph of House 14 at Divostin, Yugoslavia. This was the largest dwelling (18 m long) found and cleared at that Neolithic site. Three hearths (a, b, c) and nearly 100 pottery vessels were found on the fired mud-and-chaff floor. (Courtesy of Alan McPherron.)

er, but takes them apart. The archaeologist reassembles the pieces later, on paper or by computer. This need to reassemble the pieces explains the importance of using care in taking them apart (excavating) and in observing and recording precisely how they originally fit together. We will briefly consider the techniques for conducting and recording excavations—techniques that, when properly executed, enable the archaeologist later to reconstruct and interpret the original three-dimensional site.

Provenience Control

Archaeologists have developed a variety of methods to ensure accurate control of vertical and horizontal provenience during excavation. Horizontal location is determined with reference to a site grid. Within each excavation or other data-collection operation, then, the location of artifacts and features discovered can be related to the grid system by direct reference to specific grid coordinates or to edges of the excavation (Fig. 5.18). Vertical location is determined with respect to a known elevation; this may be done with surveyors' instruments or by direct measurement. A leveling instrument or transit may be used to measure relative elevation from a known elevation datum. Alternatively, elevation above or below a point nearby may be measured with a line level, steel tape, and plumb bob (Fig. 5.19). Elevation is given in relation to sea level.

Provenience control for artifacts and ecofacts is often complicated by their small size and abundance. When artifacts are relatively sparse, or when they are

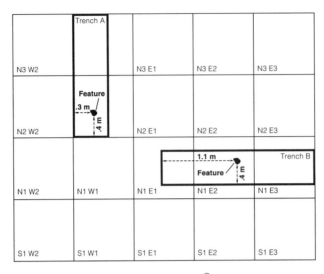

FIGURE 5.18

A site grid may be used to designate the horizontal provenience of excavated features in two ways. In Trench A, measurements are made north and east of the N2 W1 stake, to record the provenience as "(N2).4m/(W1).3m." In Trench B, horizontal provenience is measured from the limits of the trench, as "1.1 m east of the trench's west wall, .4 m north of the trench's south wall." The latter is convertible to a site grid designation as long as the location of the trench walls in relation to the grid is known.

encountered in primary contexts, the location of each item is precisely plotted. Otherwise, provenience can be recorded by reference to a specified area within an excavation, such as a single stratum. The most common means of recovering artifacts and ecofacts under such circumstances is by screening, or trapping small finds by passing matrix through a wire mesh (see Fig. 5.20); and flotation, or catching small organic materials by immersing matrix in water. After recovery, artifacts are often bagged and ecofacts are put in suitable containers. Then both are taken to the field laboratory for processing. From this point on, of course, they must carry a label relating them to their provenience.

Recording Archaeological Data

Apart from artifacts, ecofacts, and other samples physically removed from their provenience, all data retrieved by archaeologists are in the form of records. Because the portion of a site that is excavated is thereby destroyed, the way archaeological research is recorded is of crucial importance. The only record of the original matrices, proveniences, associations, and contexts of the data are preserved in the field notes, scaled drawings, photographs, and standardized forms produced by the investigator.

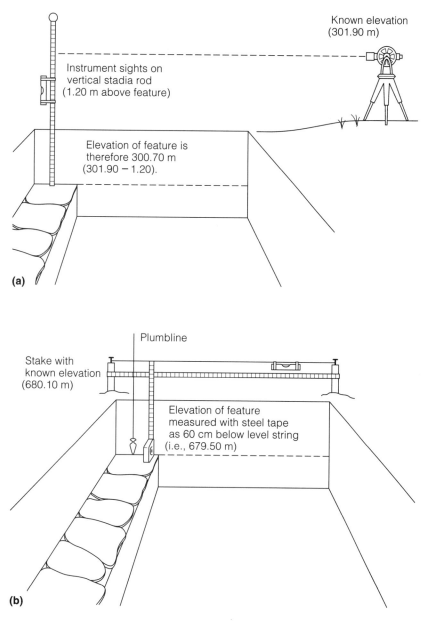

(a)

Known elevation
(301.90 m)

Instrument sights on
vertical stadia rod
(1.20 m above feature)

Elevation of feature is
therefore 300.70 m
(301.90 − 1.20).

Plumbline

Stake with
known elevation
(680.10 m)

Elevation of feature
measured with steel tape
as 60 cm below level string
(i.e., 679.50 m)

(b)

FIGURE 5.19

Two ways of determining vertical provenience: (a) an instrument of known
elevation is used in conjunction with a stadia rod; (b) an elevation is measured along a plumb line intersecting a level string of known elevation.

FIGURE 5.20

Screening at Copán, Honduras. This technique is a means of recovering small artifacts and ecofacts that might otherwise be missed during excavation. (Courtesy of the Peabody Museum of Harvard University and Gordon R. Willey.)

These four kinds of data records are used for all types of data collection, but they are generally more detailed when used to record archaeological excavations. In such cases, the most common and important are photos and scaled drawings (which are either rendered by hand on paper or electronically by computer drafting programs). Scaled drawings include sections, which depict the vertical or stratified relationships as exposed by excavation, and plans, which depict the horizontal relationships of features and other material remains. Sites and features are thoroughly photographed before, during, and after excavation. Initial photos document the appearance of sites and features before excavation disturbs them. Once excavation is under way, a continuous series of photographs is taken to chronicle everything as it is revealed (Fig. 5.21).

DATA PROCESSING

Once archaeological data are collected and recorded in the field, the recovered materials and records must be organized. The processing of these raw forms of data ensures their preservation, security, and availability for study. Although this step seems self-evident, it is an essential prerequisite to any further work. Imagine trying to do research in a library in which books and other publications are simply piled on the floor as they arrive without cataloging. This suggests the importance of orderly processing of all forms of archaeological data for continued use.

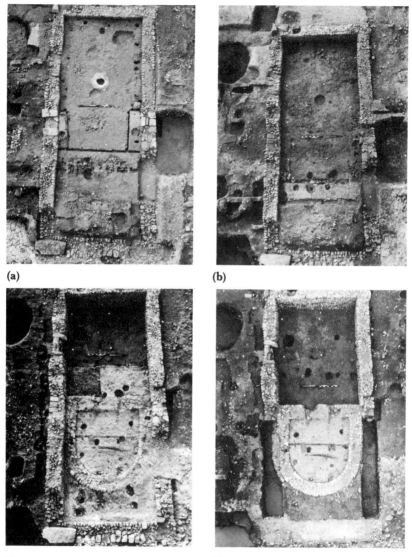

(a)　(b)

(c)　(d)

FIGURE 5.21

Views of successive stages, (a) through (d), in the excavation of the Church of St. Mary, Winchester, England. Foundations visible in (a) date from ca. A.D. 1150; those exposed in (d) represent an earlier building dated at ca. A.D. 1000. (Courtesy of Martin Biddle, © Winchester Excavations Committee.)

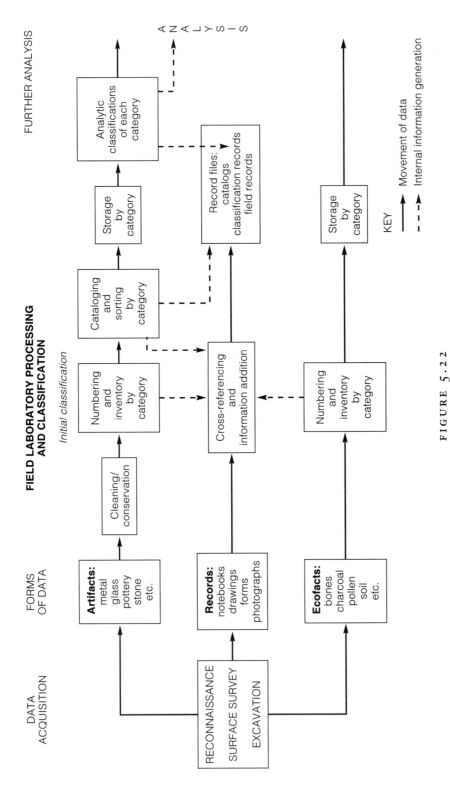

FIELD LABORATORY PROCESSING AND CLASSIFICATION

Initial classification

FURTHER ANALYSIS

DATA ACQUISITION

FORMS OF DATA

Artifacts: metal glass pottery stone etc.

Records: notebooks drawings forms photographs

Ecofacts: bones charcoal pollen soil etc.

RECONNAISSANCE SURFACE SURVEY EXCAVATION

Cleaning/ conservation

Numbering and inventory by category

Cataloging and sorting by category

Storage by category

Analytic classifications of each category

ANALYSIS

Cross-referencing and information addition

Record files: catalogs classification records field records

Numbering and inventory by category

Storage by category

KEY
Movement of data
Internal information generation

FIGURE 5.22

Flow chart to illustrate the data-processing and analysis stages normally undertaken in a field laboratory.

For artifacts and ecofacts, processing consists of cleaning them, conserving them, labeling them by provenience, and sorting them into basic categories to prepare them for later analysis. Such processing is usually done during the course of fieldwork. In this way, the archaeologist can evaluate the data as they are recovered and can continue to formulate and modify working hypotheses for testing while the research progresses. For example, if the archaeologist recognizes that evidence being recovered indicates occupation that is not consistent with a current hypothesis, further excavation can be carried out to test this finding. Should this expanded work validate the initial indications, the original hypothesis may be altered or replaced by a new proposition.

Artifacts usually undergo the most steps in processing and are often classified in some way in the field as well. Ecofacts are generally more delicate and are usually turned over to a specialist for identification. Features, of course, are not processed beyond being recorded as they are revealed. Of course, constituents of some features, such as the bones and mortuary offerings in a burial, are portable and can be taken to a laboratory to be processed as artifacts and ecofacts. Recorded data such as notebooks and drawings also pass through the processing stage in the field laboratory (Fig. 5.22).

CLASSIFICATION

In all branches of science, classification provides the working basis for further study. As mentioned in Chapter 2, much of the work of early archaeologists was devoted to the description and classification of their collections. Although classification is no longer the archaeologist's major concern, it remains as a first step toward reconstructing the past.

Before investigators can analyze and interpret collected data, they must place the data in some kind of order. Classification refers to the process of arranging or ordering objects into groups on the basis of the sharing of particular characteristics called **attributes.** An attribute is any observable trait that can be defined and isolated. Three basic categories of attributes apply to archaeological data (Fig. 5.23).

1. **Stylistic attributes** usually involve the most obvious descriptive characteristics of an artifact believed to reflect choices of its maker: its color, texture, decoration, alterations, and other traits.
2. **Form attributes** include the overall three-dimensional shape of the artifact and aspects of that shape. These include measurable dimensions (or *metric attributes*) such as length, width, thickness, and weight.
3. **Technological attributes** include the characteristics of the raw materials used to make artifacts (called *constituent attributes*) and any other traits that reflect the manufacturing process.

STYLISTIC ATTRIBUTES

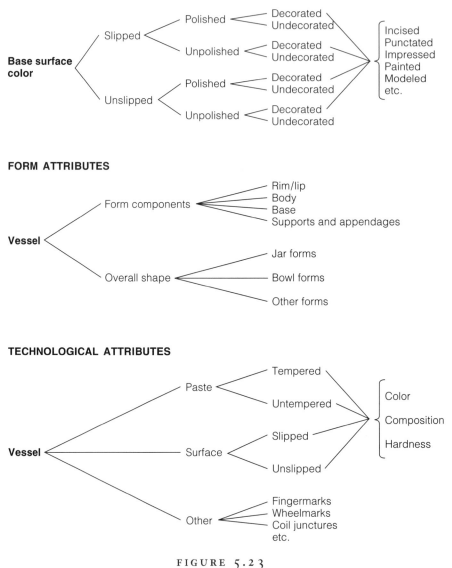

FORM ATTRIBUTES

TECHNOLOGICAL ATTRIBUTES

FIGURE 5.23

Classification of pottery: examples of kinds of attributes used to define stylistic, form, and technological types.

The kind of attribute selected will, of course, determine the kind of archaeological classification that results. These define **technological types, form types,** or **stylistic types.** Examples of technological types include Southwest Asian metal artifacts where different copper alloys can be distinguished by their constituents, such as brass (copper and zinc) or bronze (copper and tin or copper and arsenic). In defining form types, component shape attributes—for example, the inward or outward curve of a vessel's walls—are especially important in classifying fragmentary artifacts such as pottery sherds; metric attributes such as vessel height are usually more applicable to intact specimens. An example of form types is the common classification of hand-held grinding stones by their cross-sectional shape (round, ovoid, rectangular, and so on). Stylistic types are generally based on color, surface finish, and decorative attributes. Pottery classifications usually derive from such attributes, including types based on the presence or absence of painted decoration and, if decorated, the number of colors and style of painting.

These kinds of classifications are based on directly observable traits. Artifacts can also be classified using inferred characteristics, which are attributes measurable only by tests such as spectrographic or chemical analysis. Classifications based on these kinds of criteria are seldom carried out in the field, however, since they usually require specialized laboratory facilities and technicians.

All classifications serve a variety of purposes. First and most fundamentally, classifications create order from apparent chaos by dividing a mass of undifferentiated data into groups (classes). Classification thus allows the scientist to organize vast arrays of data into manageable units. We have already done this by distinguishing artifacts from ecofacts and features for their respective collection and processing requirements. Artifacts are often further subdivided into gross categories such as chipped stone, pottery, or metalwork. These classes may then be subjected to more detailed classification, breaking them down into kinds of chipped stone artifacts, kinds of pottery, and kinds of metalwork.

The second purpose of classification is to allow the researcher to summarize the characteristics of many individual objects by listing only their shared attributes. Most archaeological classifications result in definition of **types.** Types represent clusters of attributes that occur together repeatedly in the same artifacts. For example, the potsherds and whole vessels in a given pottery type will share attributes such as color and hardness of the fired clay; other attributes, such as evidence of ancient vessel repair or of ritual vessel breakage, may not be defining traits of the type class. Thus, reference to types enables the archaeologist to describe large numbers of artifacts more economically, ignoring for the moment other attributes that may be used to differentiate among members of a single type.

Third, classifications define variability. The explanation of such variability often leads to further understanding of the past. For example, recognition of different pottery styles can suggest distinctions in social status within an ancient society.

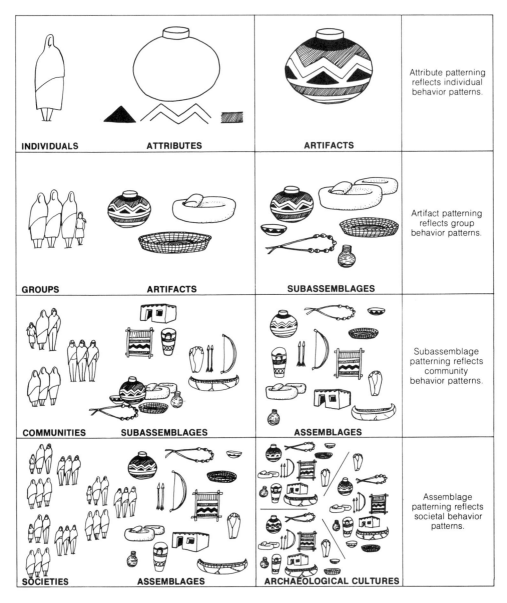

INDIVIDUALS ATTRIBUTES ARTIFACTS — Attribute patterning reflects individual behavior patterns.

GROUPS ARTIFACTS SUBASSEMBLAGES — Artifact patterning reflects group behavior patterns.

COMMUNITIES SUBASSEMBLAGES ASSEMBLAGES — Subassemblage patterning reflects community behavior patterns.

SOCIETIES ASSEMBLAGES ARCHAEOLOGICAL CULTURES — Assemblage patterning reflects societal behavior patterns.

FIGURE 5.24

Behavioral reconstruction based on hierarchical classification, independent of archaeological context. (After *Invitation to Archaeology*, by James Deetz, illustrated by Eric Engstrom, copyright © 1967 by James Deetz. Reprinted by permission of DOUBLEDAY, a division of Bantam, Doubleday, Dell Publishing Group, Inc.)

Finally, by ordering and describing types, the scientist suggests a series of relationships among classes. These relationships generate hypotheses that stimulate further questions and research. For instance, the most obvious kind of question that emerges from a classification concerns its source: how did the order originate and what is its significance? In classifications of artifacts, the described order and relationships among categories or types represent aspects of the artifacts' raw materials, techniques of manufacture, use (function), and decorative style.

The point to remember is that classification is a convenient working tool, organizing artifacts or other archaeological data into manageable and meaningful groups, and facilitating further analysis. There is no single right classification. The attributes the investigator chooses to look at depend on the research issues he or she wants to explore. For example, a researcher interested in food storage patterns in different parts of a community or in different time periods would look at shapes and sizes of storage vessels rather than designs used to decorate them.

One approach attempts to reconstruct the past by correlating hierarchical classifications with various levels of behavior. The most widely cited example of such behavioral reconstruction is that outlined by James Deetz (Fig. 5.24). According to this scheme, the individuals who created artifact types adhered to culturally defined standards. Patterned sets of artifacts used by occupational groups (defined by form and functional attributes), such as the various tools used by farmers or hunters, are called **subassemblages.** Patterned sets of subassemblages, representing the sum of social activities, define the **assemblage** of an ancient community. At the highest level, patterned sets of asssemblages are used to define **archaeological cultures** (the sum total of material remains assumed to represent the culture of a past society).

The usefulness of this kind of behavioral reconstruction, often based on style and form types, relies on the validity of the assumption that archaeological classifications reflect the structure of ancient cultural patterns. The best test of the utility of this kind of hierarchical classification rests with the context and associations of the data upon which it is based.

SUMMARY

Archaeological fieldwork involves the collection and processing of data. Fieldwork may begin with reconnaissance to discover and locate sites. Ground reconnaissance is the oldest and most thorough way to identify sites, but it is often slow and unable to detect deeply buried sites. Aerial reconnaissance provides rapid coverage of wide areas and is efficient for identifying sites that have at least some surface indications. Subsurface detection methods, using mechanical probes or electronic instruments, are slow, but may be the only way to find buried sites.

Once sites are identified and located, surface survey is used to gain representative data without resorting to excavation. Sometimes this may be the only way data are acquired; more often, however, surface survey is a prelude to excavation, aiding in selecting areas to excavate and producing hypotheses to be tested by excavation. Ground survey is the most common method, acquiring data by mapping sites and by collecting surface artifacts and ecofacts. Subsurface sensors, like those used to discover sites, may be used as part of surface survey as well. Together, ground survey and subsurface detection methods are used to produce maps showing the distributions and densities of features, artifacts, and ecofacts at sites and within regions.

Excavation is used to investigate the three-dimensional structure of buried archaeological data and to determine the functional and temporal significance of these data. These three dimensions reflect the processes of site formation: activities that took place at any one point in time are represented by the horizontal dimensions, while sequential activities are represented by the vertical dimension. Archaeologists, therefore, investigate stratigraphy—the interpretation of the sequence of deposition—to determine which data reflect simultaneous (and functionally related) activities and which reflect the sequence of activities through time. There are two basic kinds of excavations: penetrating excavations cut through deposits to reveal the depth, sequence, and composition of sites; clearing excavations expose the horizontal extent and arrangement of remains within a single stratum.

Provenience control is crucial to the collection of archaeological data: to reconstruct later how a site was formed, the location of all recovered materials must be accurately recorded. All data from excavations or surface collections are given distinctive labels and plotted with reference to horizontal location and vertical elevation. Data acquisition is a destructive process, so records—field notes, standardized forms, scaled drawings, and photographs (the first three are often rendered in paper and computerized formats)—are essential to all later analysis and interpretation.

Both data and records are usually processed in a field laboratory, to ensure that they are preserved, secured, and available for further study and analysis. After this, portable data, such as artifacts and some ecofacts, are classified by attributes (stylistic, form, and technological) that the archaeologist selects to address particular research questions. Classification is a convenient means of ordering, summarizing, relating, and understanding a mass of data, and each classification is only one of many possible organizing schemes. All, however, are useful to the archaeologist in providing a starting point for further analysis and interpretation.

FOR FURTHER READING

RECONNAISSANCE AND SURFACE SURVEY
Allen, Green, and Zubrow 1990; Ammerman 1981; Cowgill 1974; Davis 1975; Ebert 1984; Fish and Kowalewski 1990; Hester, Heizer, and Graham 1975; Joukowsky

1980; King 1978; MacNeish et al. 1972; Plog, Plog, and Wait 1978; Schliemann (1881) 1968

EXCAVATION
Bunn et al. 1980; Dillon 1989; Harris 1989; Hester, Heizer, and Graham 1975; Joukowsky 1980; Rapp and Gifford 1985; Stein and Farrand 1985; Wheeler 1954

DATA PROCESSING
Cronyn 1990; Dillon 1985, 1989; Hester, Heizer, and Graham 1975; Joukowsky 1980; Kenworthy et al. 1985

CLASSIFICATION
Deetz 1967; Ford 1954; Hill and Evans 1972; Spaulding 1953; Whallon and Brown 1982

ADDITIONAL SOURCES
Bass 1966; Bunn 1981; Butzer 1982; Champion 1980; Coles 1984; Cowgill 1974; Davis 1975; Dorrell 1989; Elachi 1982; Estes, Jensen, and Tinney 1977; Flannery 1976; Hamilton and Woodward 1984; Levin 1986; Limp 1974; MacNeish et al. 1972; Parrington 1983; Pulak and Frey 1985; Villa 1982; Willey 1953

6

Analyzing the Past

Archaeologists use various studies to analyze artifacts, ecofacts, and features. Since each of these broad categories covers a wide variety of archaeological remains, we will consider here only those most commonly encountered by archaeologists. This study includes consideration of the characteristics that differentiate one kind of data from others to show the ways each can contribute to an understanding of past behavior. Bear in mind that the information gleaned from these remains is influenced by their physical characteristics, their state of preservation, and the specific questions being asked.

ARTIFACTS

Artifacts are classified into **industries,** which are defined according to both materials used and manufacturing techniques. Our discussion will highlight lithic and ceramic industries because stone and fired clay are the most commonly encountered archaeological materials.

Lithic Artifacts

Stone tools were undoubtedly among the earliest implements used by human societies; in fact, their use predates the emergence of modern *Homo sapiens* by more than a million years. The first stone tools used by the ancestors of modern humans were probably unmodified rocks or cobbles used only once for tasks such as hammering or pounding. But **lithic technology** has its roots in the first attempts to modify and shape stone to make tools.

There are two basic kinds of lithic technology: one involves fracturing or flaking stone (the chipped stone industry); the other is based on pecking and grinding or polishing stone (the ground stone industry). Because chipped stone is the oldest preserved form of culture and technology, archaeologists have used it to name the earliest period of cultural development, the Paleolithic (Old Stone) period. In this traditional scheme, the later development of a stone technology involving grinding signals the advent of the second developmental age, the Neolithic or New Stone Age. Ground stone tools did not, of course, replace chipped stone; rather, the two technologies coexisted for thousands of years in both the Old and New Worlds. Of the two, chipped stone is more commonly encountered.

Chipped stone technology takes advantage of the characteristics of several hard, nonresilient, and homogeneous minerals, including flint or chert, obsidian (a natural volcanic glass), basalt, and quartz. When struck, these materials fracture in a uniform manner, not following any natural cleavage planes in the rock. Instead, shock waves from the blow spread through the struck stone or **core** in a cone-shaped pattern, detaching a fragment called a **flake** (Fig. 6.1). Chipped stone tools are produced either by removing flakes to give a sharp edge to the core (core tools), or by utilizing one or more of the detached flakes (flake or blade tools).

Chipped stone tools can be made by a variety of techniques; we will briefly summarize the more important of these. Some techniques have been inferred from traces left on the tools themselves, others from ethnographic observations of peoples still manufacturing stone tools, and still others through archaeologists' experiments in duplicating the ancient forms. Some of these techniques are as old as the origins of stone tools; others represent later refinements during the long development of lithic technology.

The shape and size of the flake detached from a core depend on the physical characteristics of the stone itself, on the angle and force of the blow being struck, and on the physical characteristics of the tool being used to detach the flake. Short, rather thick flakes are produced by **direct percussion,** which is achieved by either striking the core with a hammerstone or striking the core against a fixed stone called an anvil (see Fig. 6.2a). The earliest recognizable stone tools, manufactured during the earliest part of the Paleolithic period more than 2 million years ago, were produced by these methods.

A basic refinement of the percussion technique used in forming both core and flake tools is the **indirect percussion** technique, in which a punch made of bone or wood is placed between the core and the hammerstone to direct and soften the resultant blow, producing longer and thinner flakes. Another refinement called **pressure flaking** uses steady pressure on the punch to detach flakes (Fig. 6.2b). The usual result of either indirect percussion or pressure flaking is a series of long, thin, parallel-sided flakes called **blades.** True blades produced from prepared cylindrical cores are typical of the later Paleolithic

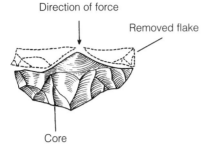

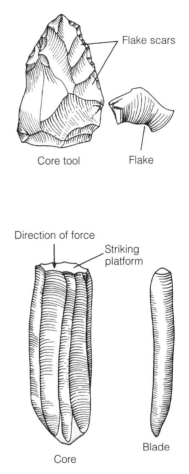

FIGURE 6.1

Terminology used in describing lithic core, flake, and blade tools, reflecting manufacturing technology. (After Oakley 1956, by courtesy of the British Museum [Natural History].)

in the Old World and of much of the pre-Columbian era in the New World.

Once a flake or blade tool has been detached, it may be ready for use as a cutting or scraping tool, or it can be further modified. Edges that required strength and durability rather than sharpness, such as those on scrapers, were **retouched** by finely controlled pressure flaking to remove small, steep flakes. Skillful pressure flaking can sometimes completely alter the shape of a flake, as in production of barbed or notched projectile points and miniature forms (microliths).

Archaeologists have traced the development of chipped stone technology through a span of more than 2 million years. During that time, new techniques and forms gradually emerged that increased both the efficiency of tool production and the available inventory of tool forms. By the end of the Paleolithic period, however, a new lithic technology was also being developed—the shaping of harder, more durable stone by pecking and grinding against abrasives such as sandstone. These tools, which took the form of axes and adzes, had much longer-lasting edges than their chipped counterparts and were thus more

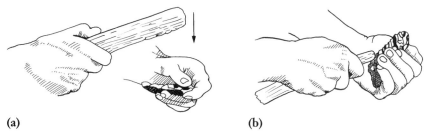

(a)   **(b)**

FIGURE 6.2

Some manufacturing techniques for chipped stone tools: (a) direct percussion using an antler; (b) pressure flaking using an antler.

efficient for such tasks as cutting trees and splitting lumber. Ground stone techniques were also used to shape large basins (**querns** or **metates**) used for grinding grain and other tasks.

Lithic analysis has traditionally involved classification based on form, often using direct or implied functional labels such as *scrapers* and *handaxes*. Although still used, form classifications have been refined to specify more precisely the sets of criteria that distinguish form types.

To a large extent, lithic typologies based on overall form have given way to more sophisticated attribute analyses based on either manufacturing technology (technological types) or actual use (functional types). Stone tools are particularly well suited to such analysis and classifications because stone working and use are subtractive actions: each step in shaping and use permanently removes more of the stone. Clues to most steps in ancient manufacturing and use are preserved and can be detected in flake scars, striking platforms, and other identifiable attributes (see Fig. 6.1). By analyzing the full range of lithic material, both artifacts and workshop debris (**debitage**), the archaeologist can often reconstruct most or all of the steps in tool manufacture (Fig. 6.3).

In order to test and refine reconstructions of ancient tool manufacture, lithic specialists such as François Bordes and Don Crabtree have attempted experimentally to duplicate ancient chipped stone technology. Through these experiments, and through their training of other archaeologists in the techniques used to manufacture stone tools, lithic specialists have increased the precision with which ancient manufacturing practices can be analyzed, as well as proposing alternative methods that may have been used in the past. Several studies have shown that what were once considered waste flakes were in fact cutting tools.

Microscopic or chemical examinations of stone are sometimes useful for establishing the source of the raw material. By comparing quarry samples with artifact samples microscopically, analysts can sometimes identify distinctive quarry signatures—particular patterns of constituent minerals that come from one source alone. For example, Herbert Thomas demonstrated in 1923 that the bluestones of Stonehenge had been brought from the Prescelly Mountains

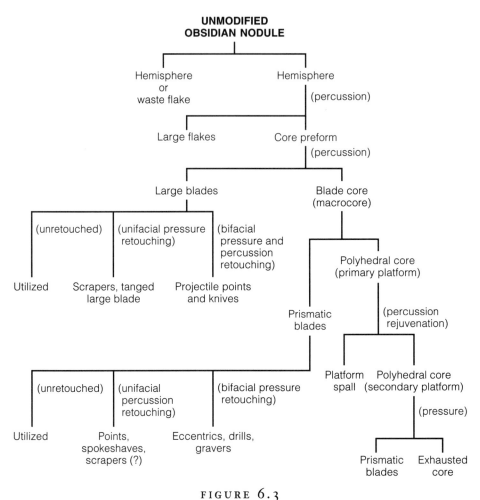

FIGURE 6.3

A technological classification representing manufacturing steps used in production of chipped stone artifacts at Chalchuapa, El Salvador. (Courtesy of Payson D. Sheets.)

of Wales, some 240 miles away, by a feasible transport route. Diagnostic trace elements within lithic materials such as obsidian can be identified and measured by neutron activation (measuring the material's response to brief and harmless bombardment by neutrons) or similar analyses. The use of these techniques for detection of raw-material sources has allowed reconstruction of ancient exchange networks in many parts of the world.

Determining how stone tools were used requires other approaches. At one time inferred function was often a primary criterion for lithic classifications. One common distinction was between supposedly utilitarian objects (those with domestic or household uses) and ceremonial objects (having ritual or non-domestic uses). This categorization might work for artifacts from secure contexts, such as tools from household living floors versus those from burials. But the distinction was often misused by automatically associating elaborate forms with ceremonial use and those of simpler shapes with utilitarian use. Artifacts from secure ceremonial contexts may once have served multiple functions, including utilitarian ones, prior to their final deposition in a burial or cache. Today, lithic analysts usually identify stone tool function through detailed attribute study. They examine specific aspects of form, such as angle of the cutting edge, and attributes of wear resulting from use—microscopic fractures, pitting, or erosion of the edge—to establish the range of tasks an artifact once performed.

These analyses of form and wear use analogy—comparing the attributes of archaeological materials with those of modern examples whose function is known—to determine probable ancient function. For example, ancient spear points are identified by the similarity of archaeological forms to modern versions. In other cases, analogs are provided by imitative experiments in which archaeologists make stone tools and use them to chop, scrape, slice, whittle, or saw various materials such as meat, bone, or wood. After an experimental tool is used, its edges are examined microscopically to detect the pattern of wear resulting from each kind of use. Wear signatures can be identified and used to infer the functions of archaeological specimens that have similar wear patterns.

Residues left on working edges may provide direct clues to ancient function. Thomas Loy has found that edges of stone tools may preserve traces of blood that allow identification of the kinds of animals killed by these weapons, even after thousands of years. Another well-known example of residue detection is the identification of silica, which provides evidence of the harvesting of grains or other grassy plants in sites occupied during the early stages of agricultural development.

Ground stone tools can also preserve clues to manufacture and use. Examination of residues may reveal what was ground on the implement in question. For example, a quern or mortar could have been used to grind food or pigments; only analysis to detect possible residues or wear will tell.

Ceramic Artifacts

The term **ceramics** covers all industries in which artifacts are modeled or molded from clay and then made durable by firing. In addition to pottery, this category includes ceramic figurines, musical instruments, and spindle whorls (used for spinning thread or yarn). Although clay figurines—such as the Venus figurines from Dolni Vestonice in the Czech Republic, which date from the European Upper Paleolithic—appear to be the earliest known form of ceramic technology, pottery is undoubtedly the most abundant and widespread kind of ceramics.

Pottery is a distinct ceramic industry because of its unique manufacturing techniques and specialized functional attributes. Archaeological evidence throughout the world indicates that pottery originated with humanity's first

(a)

(b)

(c)

(d)

attempts at settled life. In Southwest Asia, East Asia, and South America, pottery developed as part of a more complex, expanding technology that was fostered by the relative stability of settled village life. Pottery was and still is used to transport, cook, and store a wide range of foods, liquids, and other supplies. But as societies became increasingly complex, pottery also assumed other, specialized functions, including such ritual uses as burial urns and incense burners.

Compared with the age of the chipped stone industry, pottery's 12,000-year history seems short. But the widespread occurrence of pottery vessels, combined with their extreme durability and capacity for great variety in form and decoration, make pottery one of the most frequently analyzed and useful kinds of artifacts available to archaeologists. The importance of the common potsherd in archaeological research can hardly be overstressed; one unabridged dictionary even defines *potsherd* as "a broken pottery fragment, esp. one of archaeological value."

Pottery technology ranges from simple household hand-production to specialized mass-production methods. First, however, the potter must acquire and prepare the proper clay. The moist clay must be thoroughly kneaded (or wedged) to drive out air bubbles and create a uniform, plastic mass. (*Plasticity* refers to the capacity to be molded and shaped.) As part of the clay processing, nonplastic substances such as sand or ground shell that retain their shape and size may be added—as *temper*—to reduce shrinkage and thus lessen the chance that the completed vessel will break during drying or firing.

Hand-forming pottery involves modeling a vessel either from a clay core or by adding coils or segments and welding the junctures with a thin solution of clay and water (Fig. 6.4). It is the oldest kind of pottery technology and is usually associated with small-scale production. Mold-forming is commonly used to mass-produce pottery and small clay artifacts such as figurines and spindle whorls. Wheel-forming, a relatively recent invention that appeared in Southwest Asia sometime before 3000 B.C., is the most common means of mass-producing pottery vessels throughout the world. The potter's wheel is used to form the vessel by manipulating a rapidly rotating clay core centered on a vertically mounted wheel, powered by the potter's hands or feet or by other power sources.

FIGURE 6.4

Selected steps in pottery manufacture: (a) hand-forming vessels (Chinautla, Guatemala); (b) applying a slip (Senegal); (c) decorating the vessel shoulder by incising with a shell (Senegal); (d) firing pottery in an open kiln (Chinautla). (Photos b and c courtesy of Olga F. Linares; photos a and d by author.)

Once the vessel is formed, it is usually smoothed to create a uniform surface, often using a coating of a thin clay solution or **slip.** Slips or paints may be used to decorate the vessel in a variety of patterns and colors. Specialized slips that vitrify during high-temperature firing are called **glazes.** A vessel may be further modified or decorated by modeling, either adding clay (welding appliqués) or subtracting clay (incising, carving, cutting, and so on). When dry, the vessel may be polished by rubbing with a smooth hard object such as a beach pebble to compact the surface and give it a shine.

Firing transforms clay from its natural plastic state to a permanent non-plastic one. During the firing process, clay may pass through as many as three stages:

1. Dehydration or loss of water, occurring at temperatures up to about 600° C.

2. Oxidation of carbon and iron compounds in the clay, occurring at temperatures up to about 900° C.

3. **Vitrification**—a complex process in which glass and other new minerals are formed in the clay, occurring at temperatures above about 1000° C. Vitrification fuses the clay so that the vessel walls become waterproof. The earliest glazed pottery appears to have been produced in China by 1500 B.C.

Pottery analysis uses a variety of approaches, depending on the objectives of the research. Any of the three broad approaches discussed earlier—studies based upon stylistic attributes, form attributes, and technological attributes—are frequently used with pottery.

Stylistic analyses of pottery have usually received greatest emphasis. Pottery lends itself to a variety of stylistic and decorative treatments—painting, appliqué, incising, and so on—that have no effect on the vessel's usefulness as a container. Because of this underlying freedom of choice in pottery decorations, it is often assumed that stylistic patterns represent culturally guided choices rather than technological or functional limitations. Stylistic classification remains one of the most important methods of analyzing ancient pottery, using decorative attributes to trace ancient social and cultural links in time and space.

The analysis of vessel form may be combined with stylistic classifications to assist in the definition of types. Because they can take a wide variety of shapes, differences in form among pottery vessels may represent the potter's choices rather than technological limits (Fig. 6.5). Of course vessel form is also a clue to function. The use of general shape-function analogs is common in archaeological studies. For instance, ancient jars with necks were often used for storing and dispensing liquids, as they are today in most areas of the world without running water; the restrictive neck helps to control spills and thus to reduce waste.

Vessel function may also be determined by detecting residues from use, whether those remnants are visible or discovered through microscopic analysis.

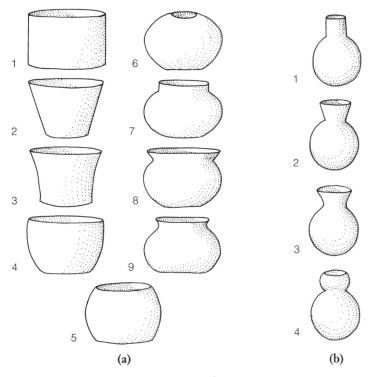

FIGURE 6.5

An example of pottery form classification: (a) nine defined bowl categories;
(b) four defined jar categories. (After Sabloff 1975.)

For example, cooking vessels may have identifiable interior residues. In such cases, the archaeologist can not only infer vessel function but also reconstruct ancient cooking practices and food preferences. Other residues, such as incense resins, cereal pollen, or unfired clay can also help in identifying the function of incense burners, grain storage jars, or potter's equipment.

The provenience of pottery may also allow the investigator to determine past uses. Vessels associated with burials are usually regarded as ritual paraphernalia used in funerary rites. Funerary vessels, however, often show traces of prior use, indicating that they served different purposes before being assigned their final, ritual function. Identifying all the multiple uses of recycled pottery vessels is often not possible, but these complicating factors should be kept in mind in interpreting vessel function.

Analysis of ancient pottery remains may reveal clues about manufacturing behavior, but in contrast to a subtractive technology such as the manufacture of stone tools pottery involves a plastic, additive technology. Manipulation of the clay in the later stages of manufacture often obliterates the diagnostic markings and features left by earlier stages. The only way to overcome this difficulty is to use analogy with documented instances of pottery production today. Clues may be recognized by observing actual production and matching these with similar features on ancient pottery.

Metal Artifacts

Metallurgy is the complex technology used to extract metal from ores and produce metal artifacts. The earliest examples of this technology are found in Southwest Asia, where between 8000 and 9500 years ago people began to shape copper into simple tools and ornaments. An independent tradition of metal working appeared in the New World, beginning with making copper ornaments in the upper Great Lakes region by 3000 B.C. Somewhat later a more sophisticated metallurgy developed in the Andes of South America and in Mesoamerica. Since that time, metallurgy has developed and spread throughout the world, almost completely replacing lithic technology. Today, of course, sophisticated metal technology has become an essential part of our own civilization.

Metal technology originated in the prehistoric exploitation of three hard metals—copper, tin, and iron—and, to a lesser degree, of two rare or precious metals, silver and gold. Because the development of metallurgical technology followed a fairly regular sequence, gradually replacing the two established lithic industries in the Old World, 19th-century archaeologists classified the apparent progress of Old World civilization with labels referring to successive ages of metal. Thus, the first metal to be used gave its name to the Copper Age, or Chalcolithic. The combination of copper and tin that was produced in later times gave its name to the Bronze Age, which was followed in turn by the Iron Age.

Since the 19th century, archaeologists have learned a great deal more about the origin and development of prehistoric metallurgy. As a result, the course of technological innovation can now be traced not only in Southwest Asia but also in Southeast Asia, China, Africa, and the New World. The picture is by no means complete; for instance, discoveries at Non Nok Tha and Ban Chiang in Thailand have generated new support for the hypothesis that tin-bronze metallurgy developed independently in Southeast Asia.

The sequence of metallurgical development is still best known for Southwest Asia, however. The first uses of metal in that area, some time before 7000 B.C., involved **cold hammering** of copper. Copper is malleable enough to be shaped by hammering, but the progressive pounding cracks and weakens the metal. **Annealing**—heating and slow cooling—heals the cracks and stresses produced by hammering, thus providing renewed strength to the metal tool. Before 4000 B.C., copper technology had changed. The metal was now being melted and cast in molds into a growing variety of shapes, from axe heads to spearpoints, swords, and ornaments. At the same time, intense heat was used to **smelt** copper from ores, thereby greatly expanding the range of sources for the raw material.

FIGURE 6.6

A grouping of bronze vessels from the first millennium B.C. found in a
tomb chamber at Gordion, Turkey. (Courtesy of the Gordion Project,
University of Pennsylvania Museum.)

Another significant advance involved deliberate production of metal
alloys. Most scholars believe that experimental attempts to remove impurities
from copper led to the realization that some of these apparent impurities were
beneficial. Most notably, inclusion of small quantities of tin or arsenic in copper forms a new metal combination, or alloy, called *bronze.* Bronze has several
advantages over copper. Its melting point is lower, and it also cools into a harder
metal capable of retaining a sharper, stronger edge. Further hammering, after
cooling, hardens it further. Bronze was being produced in Southwest Asia by
about 3000 B.C. (Fig. 6.6); as noted above, Southeast Asia has yielded some
bronze artifacts that date to about the same era. Bronze metallurgy spread
swiftly. Some of the most sophisticated products of bronze casting were created in China during the Shang Dynasty, which extended from about 1500 to
1027 B.C.

Ironworking was the next major development in metallurgical technology.
Meteoritic iron was known and used during the Bronze Age, but in the later
part of the second millennium B.C. ironworking displaced bronze casting as the
principal means of metal tool production. Since iron melts at a higher temperature than bronze, ironworking is also more complicated than bronze casting.
The principal iron output of early Southwest Asian furnaces was a spongy mass
called a *bloom,* which was then reheated in a forge and hammered by a black-
smith to shape the tool, increase the metal's strength, and drive out impurities.
Even so, forged iron is relatively soft. Use of a charcoal fire for the forge,

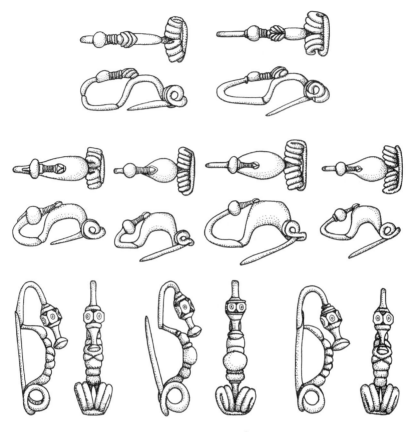

FIGURE 6.7

Three hypothesized stylistic types of bronze fibulae from an Iron Age grave at Münsingen, Switzerland. (After Hodson 1968.)

however, introduces carbon and strengthens the iron, producing carburized iron—or steel—a much harder and more durable metal. By the end of the second millennium B.C., Southwest Asian blacksmiths were making steeled iron tools, and the age of iron metallurgy was under way.

The analysis of metal artifacts has varied with the geographical area and reflects differing research priorities. Because metal—especially molten metal—is a malleable material, like pottery, it is well suited to stylistic analyses and classifications. One example is the classification of bronze fibulae, or safety-pin brooches, from La Tène sites of Iron Age Europe (Fig. 6.7). Other studies have focused on the form of metal artifacts and on functional attributions based on form variation, similar to studies done for stone and ceramic artifacts.

The general focus in metal artifact analysis, however, is reconstruction of ancient technology. Classifications divide the metal industry into subindustries according to the metal being worked. More technical analyses are then performed, including constituent analysis and microscopic examination of the metal structure. These studies help the archaeologist understand the range of technology involved in production, the procurement of raw materials, and refinement of the final product. Constituent analysis not only can identify the metals and nonmetallic materials present but also may allow specification of the metal sources. Examination of the microstructure of an artifact may yield clues about the precise techniques used in its production—hammering, annealing, quenching, and so on.

A complicating factor in these analyses is that metallurgy, like pottery, is an additive and correcting process in which mistakes can to some extent be covered and smoothed away by subsequent treatment. Unlike pottery, however, in which firing permanently alters the raw material, metal artifacts can also be melted down and the raw material reclaimed and reused. Such recycling may, for example, account for a relative lack of bronze artifacts early in the Iron Age: to save valuable alloying materials, many whole implements may have been refashioned into a succession of new tools, with only the final version left to the archaeological record.

Organic Artifacts

The class **organic artifacts** includes a variety of objects made from organic materials such as wood, plant fibers, bone, antler, ivory, and shell. Although such items are known to be important—and even dominant in the material culture of some modern societies, such as the Inuit (Eskimo)—they are especially susceptible to decay processes and thus are encountered by archaeologists only under special conditions. Many kinds of organic materials have been used to produce artifacts, each of which involves a specialized technology. We shall restrict discussion here to the most frequently encountered artifact categories: bone and related materials (such as antler and ivory), wood, and shell.

Despite some controversy over the precise origins of bone technology, there is no doubt that by the Upper Paleolithic, people were making artifacts from a variety of animal parts. In both the Old and New Worlds, bone was split and carved with stone tools to form spear points, fishhooks, and other tools. Antler, usually from deer, was split or carved to make projectile points, especially barbed points for spears or harpoons. In the Arctic, the prehistoric tradition of carving ivory with stone to make harpoons and other artifacts has survived to this day (Fig. 6.8).

The technology involved in the production of bone, antler, and ivory tools is subtractive, like stoneworking. The simplest such tools were those that involved no form modification, as when an animal bone could be used as a club. The same bone could also be broken to produce a sharp or jagged edge. The earliest finds suggest that such working was first confined to chipping and cracking, but by the Upper Paleolithic, the production of bone, antler, and ivory tools shows great variety, skill, and sophistication; some forms even have engraved decoration.

FIGURE 6.8

Bone harpoon heads from Alaska, with flint inserts, illustrate one kind of artifact fashioned from organic materials. (Courtesy of the University of Pennsylvania Museum.)

FIGURE 6.9

An example of a Hohokam decorated shell from Arizona (ca. A.D. 800–1200). The design was etched with acid from a saguaro cactus. (Arizona State Museum Collections, University of Arizona.)

Because wood is even more perishable than bone, antler, and ivory, the origins of woodworking remain obscure. Isolated finds, particularly from waterlogged sites, attest to woodworking by the Lower Paleolithic in Africa and the Middle Paleolithic in Europe. Being a subtractive industry, this technology is preserved in the finished implements themselves, but due to the rarity of their discovery, methods of manufacturing (cutting, sawing, or carving) are more often inferred indirectly, from stone or metal woodworking tools.

Shell artifacts have been found the world over, even substituting for stone tools where stone is scarce. Other shell artifact forms include cups, spoons, fishhooks, and a variety of ornaments. Shellworking is another subtractive industry; one of the most remarkable ancient means of modifying shell surfaces was a delicate etching by application of a cactus-derived acid, used among the Hohokam in the American Southwest (Fig. 6.9).

Analysis of organic artifacts yields information on the range of biotic resources exploited by an ancient society and may give clues to communication links with other areas, as when shell artifacts at an inland site are found to be marine (saltwater) species. We will consider the ecofactual aspects of organic artifacts in more detail later on.

Most classifications of organic artifacts are based on criteria of form. Sometimes these form taxonomies have stylistic overtones, but more often they involve functional inferences, and the types may be labeled with direct or implied functional names. For example, the well-known artifact assemblages of the European Upper Paleolithic include a great variety of barbed bone projectile points, almost always referred to as *harpoons*. Such designations provide convenient easy-to-remember names, but they do not establish the actual function of these artifacts.

ECOFACTS

Because they are natural objects, ecofacts yield more indirect information about technology, but they are no less important than artifacts as clues to understanding past human societies. For example, at the Olsen-Chubbuck site in southeastern Colorado, a series of bison skeletons was found associated with some stone tools, all strewn along the base of a ravine (Fig. 6.10). The site represents the remains of human hunting behavior some 8500 years ago. The location and arrangement of both ecofacts and artifacts have been used to infer a good deal about hunting strategy (how and from what direction the animals were driven over the ravine edge, including which way the wind may have been blowing), butchering techniques (how the carcasses were dismembered, which bones were stripped of meat on the spot, and which were carried off to the presumed campsite), and yield (how much meat and byproducts would have been available from the kill).

Ecofacts can also tell us about noneconomic activities such as ritual. Analysis of the heavy concentration of pollen found scattered over Burial IV in Shanidar cave, northern Iraq, implies that when this Neanderthal man was buried some 60,000 years ago, his survivors covered him with flowers, including daisies, cornflowers, and hollyhocks. Because such flowers now bloom locally in May and June, it has been inferred that the burial took place at that time of year.

Most frequently, however, ecofacts are used to reconstruct the environment in which past societies lived and the range of resources they exploited. Grahame Clark and his coworkers analyzed pollen samples from Star Carr, a 10,000-year-old site in northern England, and inferred that the surrounding area was largely covered by forest of birch and pine; the presence of pollen from plants that thrive in open areas points to localized clearings, one of which became the site of Star Carr. By examining both the plant remains and the abundantly recovered antlers of red deer, roe deer, and elk, the investigators

FIGURE 6.10

Remains of bison killed and butchered by hunters some 8500 years ago, excavated at the Olsen-Chubbuck site, Colorado. (Reproduced by permission of the Colorado State Museum and the Society for American Archaeology, from *Memoirs of the Society for American Archaeology* 26: ix, 1972.)

could establish the times of year the site had been occupied. This was done by comparing the distribution of antlers broken from the animals' skulls with those that had simply been collected after being shed naturally, and correlating the results with the known seasonal cycles of deer antler growth and shedding. The work at Star Carr was a landmark, showing the wealth of interpretation that could be gained from ecofactual data.

As with artifacts, the first step in analysis of ecofacts is classification. Clearly, however, the classification of ecofacts must use different criteria than used for artifacts, borrowing schemes from botany, zoology, and geology. Once these preliminary steps are completed, ecofacts may be classified in many specific ways, according to properties that might relate them to past human soci-

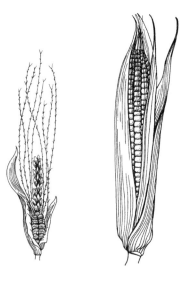

FIGURE 6.11

Comparison between a reconstructed view of wild maize (now extinct) on the left, and domesticated maize on the right. Over time, selection favored more and longer rows of kernels.

eties. For example, some plants and animals are available for harvesting only at limited times of the year; these, as the Shanidar and Star Carr cases indicate, may be used to determine seasonality of exploitation. Animals can also be studied in terms of the amounts of meat they would yield and therefore the size of the human population they could support. Soils can be classified as to their relative potential fertility under given kinds of agricultural exploitation.

Floral Ecofacts

Floral remains in archaeological contexts fall into two basic categories: microspecimens and macrospecimens. Microspecimens include pollen as well as the more durable silica bodies formed in plants called **phytoliths.** Macrospecimens include seeds, leaves, casts or impressions, and so forth. Both categories require technical identification. As part of this process, many plants (and animals) are identified as wild or domesticated. The domestication of plants and animals in the Old and New Worlds was a significant cultural development, giving people more direct control over the quantity and quality of their food supply. Accordingly, a good deal of study has been done concerning when, where, and how this process was carried out. Critical to such study, of course, is the ability to identify wild and domesticated forms. Since domestication is a gradual result of repeated selection for desired traits—as when larger or quicker-growing strains are deliberately replanted and nurtured—there is no single "original" domesticated maize cob or wheat kernel. Rather, one can discern trends in form from fully wild to fully domesticated (Fig. 6.11).

Another dimension in the study of floral ecofacts is the context in which they are found. The Shanidar IV context is one of ideological or symbolic use of plants. On the other hand, the only sure indication that a plant was a food resource is contextual—from its occurrence in the digestive tracts of mummies or bog corpses, or in human **coprolites** (preserved feces). Food remains and residues may also be found adhering to the interiors of food storage vessels or to preparation surfaces such as grinding stones.

Faunal Ecofacts

Animal remains in archaeological contexts take a number of forms, from intact specimens to partial ones, such as bones or coprolites. Bones and teeth, the most commonly recovered forms, have received the most attention.

A basic question of faunal studies involves the kinds of animals being exploited. Archaeologists attempt not only to identify the species distinctions, but to establish the proportions of adult versus juvenile and, for some adult animals, male versus female. Tallies of this kind have been used as evidence for the very beginning of animal domestication, before bone changes due to selective breeding can be detected. In this case, the presence of large numbers of young-animal remains may indicate direct access to and control of a herd or selective culling before breeding age to remove certain characteristics. In other cases, the presence of immature animals may point to use of the site in the season when the young animals would have been available. In contrast, changes in bone mass of sheep and goats of the third millennium B.C. in Israel suggest that older females were more numerous in later occupation levels: from this shift in herd composition, the same analysts inferred a rising emphasis on milk production.

Archaeologists can also examine the parts of animals present at a site. At Star Carr, the occurrence of stag frontlets as well as detached antlers gave evidence not only of the season during which the site was occupied but also of the range of antler raw materials that were used by the site's occupants. At Olsen-Chubbuck, study of the presence or absence of various skeletal elements led to inferences about butchering techniques by indicating which parts of the animals were taken back to the residence area for more leisurely consumption.

Special characteristics of particular animals may lead to specific interpretations. Some small animals, such as snails, are very sensitive to climate and thus can serve as indicators of local climatic change or stability. An increase in white-tailed deer could, for example, signal an increase in cleared areas or a decrease in local forest cover. Presence of large mammals as prey often suggests organized group hunting practices, and hunting herd animals requires different tactics from those for hunting solitary animals. Ideological interpretations may also be made from faunal evidence.

Contextual associations can be related to various kinds of human-animal relations. For example, the occurrence of mummified cats in ancient Egypt and jaguar remains in elite Maya burials reflect the high symbolic status enjoyed by those animals in the two societies. Bones found in middens, on the other hand, are usually interpreted as remains of food animals or scavengers.

As part of the consideration of context, the archaeologist must be careful to distinguish, as far as possible, which animals are related to human presence and exploitation and which are not. For example, burrowing animals such as gophers or opossums found in graves may have gotten there on their own, independent of the ancient burial. Other animals may simply take advantage of the shelter provided by occupation areas, such as bats roosting in abandoned Maya temples. As an example of how critical such a determination can be, consider the debate over Makapansgat, an early site in South Africa. Raymond Dart used the pattern of occurrence of the nonhuman bones—how they were broken, what elements were present, and how they were deposited—to argue that these bones include tools, as well as ecofacts, used by early human ancestors 2 million years ago. Other scholars, however, argue the bones are neither artifacts nor ecofacts, but are the result of animal activity and breakage like those found in the dens of modern carnivores.

Human Remains

Human remains are the domain of a branch of anthropology—biological or physical anthropology. More than anything else encountered and studied by archaeologists, human remains raise significant ethical issues. This is most apparent when living descendants of the dead express their concerns about the excavation and analysis of skeletal remains. We will consider the professional responsibilities of the archaeologist in the treatment of human remains in our final chapter. Here we shall simply review some of the ways in which human remains from an archaeological context may further the understanding of the ancient society being investigated. Studies of human remains can also reveal the health and nutritional status, genetic patterns, and other factors that affected individuals and groups in the past, which can be of use to people today.

Forms of human remains include intact or well-preserved examples, such as mummies; fragmentary bones and teeth; and coprolites. Bones and teeth are most often preserved, and they will receive most attention.

Analysis of human remains begins with identification of the particular elements (bones, teeth) present and of the number of individuals represented. Since people are often buried in individual graves, this may not be a difficult task, but mass graves or reused ones present special problems. Once the elements are identified, however, an assessment is made of each individual's sex and age at death. Some skeletal elements are more reliable or easier to interpret in these assessments. For example, sex can be most readily judged from the pelvis. Age can be assessed by a variety of means, including eruption sequence and degree of wear on teeth, fusion between bones of the skull, and fusion of the ends (epiphyses) to the shafts (diaphyses) of limb bones.

Once age and sex identifications are made, a number of other studies may be done. Paleodemographic analysis seeks to understand the structure of the ancient population under investigation, including determination of sex ratio and life expectancy (Fig. 6.12).

Aspects of ancient diets can be reconstructed from skeletal samples. One technique is stable carbon isotope analysis of human bone collagen. Because plants metabolize carbon dioxide according to different ratios of two carbon isotopes, ^{13}C and ^{12}C, measurement of the ratios can indicate which plant

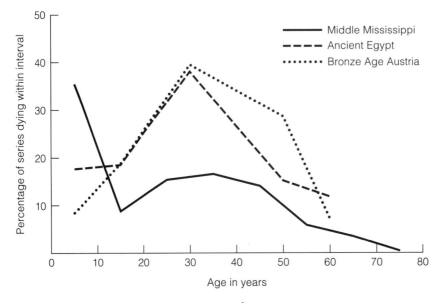

FIGURE 6.12

Comparative mortality profiles from selected ancient populations. Middle Mississippians of the southeastern United States after A.D. 1000 were two to three times as likely to die before 10 years of age than were ancient Egyptians or Austrians of the Bronze Age several thousand years earlier. Once past childhood, however, members of all three groups reached a peak death rate between ages 25 and 35. (From Blakely 1971; courtesy of Robert L. Blakeley and the *American Journal of Physical Anthropology*.)

groups were used in the ancient diet. Such important foods as maize, sorghum, sugar cane, and millet, for example, belong to one major group, called C_4 plants, while spinach, manioc, barley, sugar beets, and peas belong to another, the C_3 group. Among the results of these studies is independent corroboration of the conclusion that maize, a C_4 plant, was domesticated in Mexico and Peru and later became a staple crop in North America. Stable carbon isotope analysis of human skeletal material from Tehuacán, Mexico (discussed in Chapter 5) by Farnsworth and his colleagues revealed that C_4 plants (including maize) composed 90 percent of the diet by 4500 B.C. and remained at this level for the remainder of the pre-Columbian era. This contrasts with far lower estimates of plant use in the Tehuacán diet based on preserved macrospecimens (seeds and other plant remains). The discrepancy seems due to a sampling bias, since the pollen samples came from only one type of habitation site (dry caves). The stable isotopic analysis of the human skeletal sample more likely represents the complete dietary inventory of the Tehuacán population.

Other isotopes present in human skeletal remains also provide clues for dietary reconstructions. Stable nitrogen isotope analysis reveals distinctions between reliance on marine versus land-based food resources. Strontium isotope analysis can detect distinctions between meat and plant diets.

Human remains also yield information on the health and nutrition of the population. Not all diseases or injuries affect the skeleton, but many do. Obvious examples are bone fractures and tooth caries; other maladies, including arthritis, yaws, and periodontal disease, leave tangible marks. (Of course, if mummified bodies are available for study, analysis can be much more complete, akin to a regular autopsy.) These diagnostic traces make ancient human remains important to the study of the origins and development of diseases such as tuberculosis.

Human bones also offer clues on ancient social standing. William Haviland has attributed differences in male stature at the Maya site of Tikal, Guatemala, to social class and accompanying wealth differences. The taller males, found in richer tomb burials, were probably also richer in life and thus able to secure better food supplies than could their shorter counterparts, buried in less well-made and well-furnished interments.

Some cultural practices also leave their mark on skeletal remains. One example is cranial deformation, practiced in pre-Columbian times in North, Central, and South America. According to this custom, the head is tightly bound until it takes the desired form (Fig. 6.13); the past Chinese practice of binding girls' feet to make them smaller is comparable.

Inorganic Remains

Inorganic remains include one of the most important categories of ecofacts— the various soils uncovered by excavation. The soil in an archaeological deposit is more than just a matrix in which culturally relevant materials may be embedded. It is only in the last quarter century or so, however, that the full importance of archaeological soils has begun to be recognized. Two principal aspects of soil should be examined: how it was deposited and of what it is composed.

Deposition of soil layers can result from human activities or from natural geological processes. It is basic to stratigraphic evaluation to distinguish between natural and cultural origins for all deposits encountered. But in some cases the soils have a particularly dramatic story to tell. For example, Alan Kolata has found water-laid soils capping the occupation levels at 750-year-old sites on the south shore of Lake Titicaca, in Bolivia. He suggests the soils likely account for sudden decline in this part of the ancient Tiwanaku state: flooding and a rise in the lake level may have waterlogged and thereby ruined what had been a productive agricultural landscape.

Even more dramatic is the fate of the island of Thera (now called Santorini) in the Aegean, where an earthquake destroyed the town of Acrotiri in about 1500 B.C. In Chapter 4, we discussed the explosion of the volcano on that island and how this event completely disrupted local human occupation. However, excavations at Acrotiri have established that a considerable time elapsed between the earthquake and the volcanic explosion, since a thin humus layer (the result of natural, gradual soil formation processes) was found between the remains of the fallen abandoned buildings and the volcanic deposits. Indeed, two distinguishable eruptions apparently took place—a small

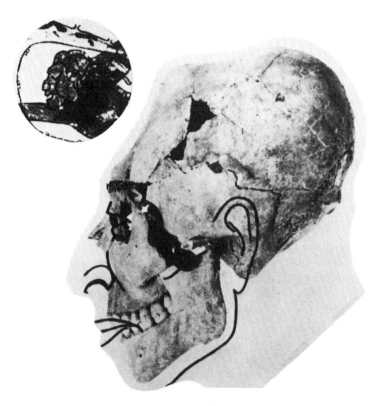

FIGURE 6.13

Photograph of an artificially deformed skull from the Classic Maya site of
Altar de Sacrificios, Guatemala, with a superimposed reconstruction of the
individual's profile in life. The inset shows an individual with a similarly
deformed skull painted on a pottery vessel from the same site. (Courtesy
of Dr. Frank P. Saul, Medical College of Ohio.)

one followed by the catastrophic destruction. The smaller eruption apparently
worked as a warning, allowing most of the residents of Thera to leave: the finds
at Thera are relatively lacking in human remains compared to Pompeii, where
many residents had no time to flee before the eruption of Vesuvius in A.D. 79.

Soil characteristics were observed by ancient inhabitants as well as modern
investigators. Soil surveys in many areas of the world have indicated that occupation by agriculturalists correlates well with the distribution of well-drained
and fertile areas. Fertility potentials must be tested, however, and not simply
assumed. For example, volcanic ash is generally a fertile parent material for
agricultural soils. But the ash fall from the eruption of Ilopango volcano in El
Salvador around A.D. 200, traced by Payson Sheets and his associates, blanketed
the area with an infertile layer that would have decreased local agricultural
production capacities for as long as several centuries.

FEATURES

Features, like artifacts, owe their form to human intervention, so it is not surprising that analysis of features is similar to that for artifacts. Formal, stylistic, and technological analyses are all appropriate approaches to the study of features. As when dealing with artifacts, the archaeologist attempting to understand the significance of a particular feature makes use of provenience, association, and context. Two characteristics of features are particularly important in analysis: location and arrangement. Intact features directly reflect the original makers' and users' intentional placement, while the locations of artifacts are used to infer (by determination of context) whether a use-related placement has been preserved. Features are most valuable in understanding the distribution and organization of human activities, for they represent the facilities—the space and often some stationary equipment—with which these activities were carried out. Sometimes, of course, features are not intact and, as with artifacts, some interpretations can only be inferred. For example, when a multistory house collapses, features from the upper floors, such as hearths or grain-grinding bins (Fig. 6.14), may still be inferred from their disarrayed component parts, but the original form, placement, and arrangement of the feature can only be estimated.

We shall discuss features in two categories that have behavioral implications: constructed features and cumulative features.

Constructed Features

Constructed features were built to provide space for some activity or set of activities. Examples range from simple windbreaks to elaborate houses (Fig. 6.15) and temples, from burials and tombs to roadways and fortification walls, and from artificial reservoirs and stone-lined hearths to agricultural terraces and irrigation canals. The important criterion is that there is some human construction that formally channels the ongoing use of space.

Classification and analysis of constructed features may examine attributes of form, style, technology, location, or some combination of these. Technological analysis includes consideration of the materials used in the construction and the ways these materials were put together. When complex architecture is involved, as with such imposing features as the Egyptian pyramids, intricate analysis is required. The technological analysis of such features usually yields data not only about the physical act of construction, such as the use of particular materials and the sequence of their incorporation in the growing structure, but also about related social aspects of the construction process. For instance, in the prehistoric Moche Valley in Peru, adobe bricks from large structures were marked with distinctive labels. Michael Moseley has concluded that each mark represents a separate group of brick producers (a little more than 100 of these marks were identified). Each work force responsible for supplying a certain number of bricks could thus have verified that its proper contribution had indeed been made.

FIGURE 6.14

Features may often be identified even after disturbance: (a) an intact mealing bin, where stones were set for grinding grain, in a prehistoric pueblo from the south western United States; (b) a feature presumed to be a collapsed mealing bin, the disturbance seemingly resulting from destruction of the building's roof or upper story. (Photo a by author; photo b by M. Thompson, Arizona State Museum, University of Arizona.)

(a)

(b)

FIGURE 6.15

House 1 at Skara Brae, in the Orkney Islands of Scotland, provides a good illustration of features. Not only is the house itself a complex feature, but its furnishings are features too, from the bed platforms at upper left to the stone hearth at center and cupboard at upper right.

Well-preserved structures can yield complex data about construction methods and materials. For example, among the oldest known roadways are wooden tracks built to cross wetlands, which have then helped preserve these features. The oldest known example, the Sweet Track in the Somerset Levels of southwest England, dates to about 4000 B.C. (Fig. 6.16). Its excavation has led to a wealth of information about technology, environment, and other aspects of life in the Neolithic, including a variety of preserved wooden implements dropped by people walking across the track and then preserved in the bog below.

Even seemingly simple constructed features can have great significance. For example, bedrock mortars of the western Sierra Nevada mountains of California are roughly circular depressions, of various sizes, ground into granite outcrops or huge boulders. They and associated cobbles are mortars and pestles, used together for pulverizing seeds and other plant materials. These features are known to have been used by women of the Mono and related Native American groups to prepare acorn flour and other food. Thomas L. Jackson's combined archaeological and ethnographic study shows that bedrock mortars are keys to understanding Mono society and economy. Archaeologists had previously argued the variation in mortar depths was due to differential wear: the longer a mortar was used, the deeper it got. Jackson questioned this

FIGURE 6.16

An artist's reconstruction (left) of the Sweet Track in use can be compared
with (right) a photograph of its archaeological traces as revealed by excavation. ([l] Painting by Patricia J. Wynne, from "The World's Oldest
Road," by John M. Coles. Copyright © 1989 by Scientific American, Inc.
All rights reserved. [r] By permission of John M. Coles.)

conclusion, citing accounts of Mono women who describe their mortars as
being of three deliberately distinct depths, each for a different phase in acorn
processing. The location, spacing, and associations of the mortars also reflect
deliberate decisions to accommodate annual movements across the landscape
to collect and process food. Because the mortars were made and owned by
Mono women, the site distribution leads to a new appreciation for the central
role of women's activities and decision-making in structuring Mono life.

Internal arrangement, elaboration, and orientation of features are often
important attributes. A good example of this is the range of features now being
studied as astronomical observatories. In the 1960s Gerald Hawkins analyzed
the astronomical alignments found in the component parts of Stonehenge,
interpreting the range of observations that could have been made from this
Bronze Age station. Although many of Hawkins's findings are now disputed,
his work led scholars to examine other monuments to see if their arrangements
suggest similar use. The kinds of features under investigation range from the
Big Horn Medicine Wheel in northern Wyoming to entire community plans
that may incorporate astronomical layouts.

Location of constructed features can also be informative for particular research questions. For example, location of burials in special mortuary structures or elite areas, such as the North Acropolis of Tikal, Guatemala, or the Great Pyramids of Egypt, may indicate special social status and privilege. Study of locations of these or other particular kinds of features may suggest factors involved in siting or placement decisions, such as preference for elevated ground or proximity to water sources in locations of houses. With the increased use of quantitative methods and with the adoption of analytical techniques from fields such as geography, archaeologists are beginning to study the attributes of different locations more thoroughly and to specify more rigorously whether the choices of location that we observe are due, in fact, to human preferences and decisions or to chance.

Cumulative Features

Cumulative features are those formed by accretion rather than by a pre-planned or designed construction of an activity area or facility. Examples include middens, quarries (the result of subtraction of the exploited resource, sometimes accompanied by an accumulation of extracting tools), and workshop areas. We have already seen, in Chapter 5, how conjoining studies helped define a cumulative workshop feature at Koobi Fora.

Conjoining studies also aided interpretation of the features defined by some 16,000 lithic artifacts at Meer II, a 9000-year-old campsite in northern Belgium, dispersed vertically through nearly 50 cm of deposit. Enough of the lithics could be refitted, however, to see that this site was a single complex feature—and still essentially intact. Evidence on manufacturing sequences among the conjoinable pieces was used to show spatial relations between making and using the stone tools. When data were added concerning general debris density, hearth location, and wear patterns on the tools, a detailed map of overall activities could be created, defining a domestic area in the southwest, where hide processing and bone and antler working took place around a hearth. From wear patterns, Daniel Cahan and Lawrence Keeley could even show that the bulk of the rough work was done by a right-handed person, with a left-hander working alongside for perhaps a shorter time.

Although stylistic analysis is rarely appropriate here, cumulative features can be analyzed according to attributes of form, location, and sometimes technology. Form attributes include size and content. Because we are dealing with accumulated entities, size can indicate either the duration or the intensity of use. For example, a midden will be larger if it is used for a long time or with great frequency in a short period of time. It is not always possible to distinguish the relative importance of these two factors in cumulative features. But, when available, long-term stratified middens are particularly valuable to the archaeologist because they yield evidence concerning the temporal span of occupation at a site.

Analysis of the location of cumulative features may give information on the distribution of ancient activities. For example, distribution of quarries relative to habitation sites might indicate how far people were willing to travel to obtain stone raw materials, and the location of workshop areas reveals the distribution of manufacturing activities within or among settlements.

Because they are unplanned accretions of artifacts and other materials, cumulative features have different technological attributes from constructed features. That is, even though cumulative features were not built, they may still yield technological information. For example, quarries may preserve extraction scars as well as abandoned mining tools; these may indicate various techniques used to mine raw materials. A study of the debris from stone-chipping stations may help in reconstructing the chipping technology, and artifacts from a midden—molds or bowl sherds containing unfired clay or pigments—may indicate the nearby presence of a pottery production area and aid in determining the technology involved in its use.

SUMMARY

In this chapter we have reviewed the analysis of the three categories of archaeological data—artifacts, ecofacts, and features. Analysis of these remains is influenced by their physical characteristics, their state of preservation, and the specific questions being asked of the data.

Artifacts are divided into industries based on shared raw materials and manufacturing techniques. The industries most commonly encountered by archaeologists are those of stone (lithic) and fired clay (ceramic). Lithic industries involve subtractive production processes that often preserve evidence of the steps taken during manufacture. This makes technological analysis, especially with chipped stone tools, a rewarding avenue of understanding. Functional analysis of lithic artifacts is also useful in reconstructing past activities when based on detectable wear and residues.

Ceramic industries, such as pottery, are made by additive processes that often destroy evidence of manufacturing steps, so that technological analysis is more difficult. But clay is a plastic and easily manipulated substance that can be shaped and decorated in a variety of ways, thus lending itself to stylistic classifications that define variations in both time and space. Pottery vessel shapes and the identification of residues are used to infer function as a means to reconstruct past activities.

Metal artifacts also possess characteristics that allow technological, stylistic, and functional analyses. Artifacts made from organic materials are usually classified by form as a basis for functional inferences. Constituent analyses of most kinds of artifacts can identify raw material sources and allow the reconstruction of past trade and distribution networks.

The various categories of ecofacts—plant, animal, human, and inorganic remains—can be analyzed to yield culturally meaningful information. Floral remains include both microspecimens (pollen and phytoliths) and macrospecimens (seeds, plant fragments, and impressions). Faunal remains include mummies, skeletal remains, and coprolites. Once identified as to species, both floral and faunal samples can yield information on ancient environments and subsistence activities, as well as medical and ritual behavior. Human remains provide direct evidence about ancient nutritional and health status, vital to understanding not only the past, but also the present (as in the origins and evolution of human disease). Inorganic remains, especially the analysis of soils, can yield clues to the presence or absence of past human activity and information about ancient land use and environments.

Features preserve in their form and location a record of the spatial distribution of past human activities. Some features are deliberately constructed to house activities; others represent cumulative activities (additive or subtractive) that modify the environment. Constructed features usually represent attempts to channel use of space. Their analysis allows reconstruction of past technologies, while their attributes of form and location yield inferences about ancient behavior and culture. In addition, variations in building or decorative style provide important markers of age or cultural identity. Cumulative features result from gradual accumulation of artifacts and ecofacts, as in workshops or middens, or progressive removal of materials, as in mines or quarries. Both provide important clues to ancient technology and other forms of behavior.

FOR FURTHER READING

ARTIFACTS
Arnold 1985; Benson 1979; Bordaz 1970; Clark (1954) 1971; Gero 1991; Keeley 1980; Lechtman 1984; Madden, Muhly, and Wheeler 1977; Oakley 1956; Rice 1987; Sabloff 1975; Torrence 1989

ECOFACTS
Bass 1986; Binford 1981; Brothwell 1981; Chapman, Kinnes, and Randsborg 1981; Dimbleby 1985; Gilbert and Mielke 1985; Hart 1983; Hassan 1981; Klein and Cruz-Uribe 1984; Olsen 1964; Ubelaker 1989; Wheat 1972; White 1990; Wing and Brown 1980

FEATURES
Coles 1984; Coles and Coles 1986; Hawkins 1965; Hyslop 1984; Jackson 1991; Stein and Farrand 1985; Van Noten, Cahan, and Keeley 1980

ADDITIONAL SOURCES
Andresen et al. 1981; Binford 1967; Binford and Binford 1969; Bordes and de Sonneville-Bordes 1970; Cahan, Keeley, and Van Noten 1979; Champion 1980; Crabtree 1972; DeNiro 1987; Farnsworth et al. 1985; Haviland 1967; Hester, Heizer, and Graham 1975; Joukowsky 1980; Jovanovic 1980; King 1978; Kolata 1987; Loy 1983; Moseley 1975; Potts and Shipman 1981; Rovner 1983; Toth 1987; van der Merwe 1982; van der Merwe and Avery 1982; Villa 1982; Wertime and Wertime 1982

7

Dating the Past

To RECONSTRUCT THE PAST, we must first control the time dimension. That is, we need to determine which remains are from the same period and which are from different periods. Only then can we examine behavior systems at single points in time and how these systems change through time.

Throughout much of its history, archaeology has emphasized methods for establishing the age and proper sequence for the evidence from the past. As a result, archaeologists now have a variety of ways to determine the age of this evidence. Recent advances in chemistry and nuclear physics have greatly expanded the inventory of available dating techniques, freeing archaeologists from much of the traditional work of determining the age of their evidence. Because of the radiocarbon revolution in the 1950s and a host of newer age-determination methods, the archaeologist today can focus research on behavior-oriented studies rather than chronological issues.

Before we discuss a few of the specific techniques, however, we should consider a few basic definitions. First, age determination may be direct or indirect. **Direct dating** uses analysis of the artifact, ecofact, or feature itself to arrive at its age. **Indirect dating** uses analysis of material associated with the artifact, ecofact, or feature being studied to evaluate its age. For example, an obsidian blade found in a tomb might be dated directly by the obsidian hydration method (explained later); other artifacts found in the same tomb and the tomb itself can then be dated indirectly by assigning them the same age as the obsidian blade with which they were associated. Of course, the reliability of indirect dating depends on the security of the context—in this case, the evidence that the obsidian and the other materials were deposited at the same time.

TABLE 7.1

Major Archaeological Dating Techniques

RELATIVE METHODS	ABSOLUTE METHODS
Seriation	Obsidian hydration
Sequence comparison	Dendrochronology
Stratigraphy	Radiometric (radiocarbon,
Geochronology	potassium-argon, etc.)
Bone chemistry	Archaeomagnetic

The second distinction is that between relative and absolute (also called *chronometric*) dating techniques (Table 7.1). **Relative dating** refers simply to evaluating the age of one item of data relative to other items; for example, determining that artifact A is older than artifact B. In relative dating, actual ages are not assigned to data. **Absolute dating** refers to placing the age of a sample on an absolute time scale, usually a calendrical system (for example, determining that artifact A was used from ca. 400 to 300 B.C.). Although absolute methods assign an age in years, they are seldom precise. Instead, as our example indicates, most absolute methods assign an age expressed as a range in years, and often include a statement of the degree of statistical probability that the true age of the sample falls within that range (expressed by a "±" symbol).

The most precise dating is possible with artifacts or features inscribed with calendrical notations, even if these refer to a calendar different from the one in use today. For instance, most coins minted during the Roman Empire carry at least one reference to a specific year in the reign of a particular emperor. And in the Americas, most monuments carved by the Maya of the Classic Period (ca. A.D. 250–900) are inscribed with one or more dates in their calendrical system. In both of these cases, the ancient calendrical system can be correlated to our own, so that the Roman and Maya notations can be assigned to a date in our system—in some cases, down to the month and day. This precise dating can, in turn, be used for indirect absolute dates for materials associated with such calendrical inscriptions.

A series of either relative or absolute dates arranged in order of their age defines chronological sequences. These sequences provide time frameworks used to organize all subsequent data. Establishing these sequences is crucial since they enable archaeologists to reconstruct the order in which ancient events took place. In many areas of the world, these sequences are well defined, and newly discovered data can simply be placed in the existing scheme. In other areas, however, basic chronologies have yet to be established.

In the following section, we shall briefly discuss a few of the most important methods used by archaeologists to determine age and chronological

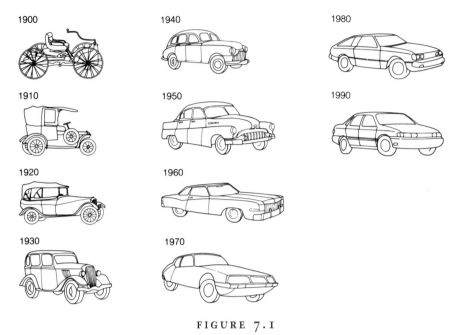

1900 1910 1920 1930 1940 1950 1960 1970 1980 1990

FIGURE 7.1

Gradual changes in design are clearly evidenced in familiar aspects of our own culture, such as automobiles.

sequence. It is important to note that each method has some limits or built-in inaccuracies. Thus, a chronology based on several different methods and many dated samples is more reliable than a sequence based on a single method or just a few dated samples.

SERIATION

Patterns of human behavior change continually, and as behavior changes, so do its material products. We have all observed how changes through time in design and style alter familiar objects in our own society. Many of us can identify the trends of change well enough to place any particular item in its approximate time period. For instance, when shown automobiles of varying ages, many of us can arrange them in rough chronological sequence (Fig. 7.1); similar sequential changes are noticeable in clothing styles, art, music, and so on.

The artifacts and features of past societies also exhibit changes through time, and by observing and studying their attributes, archaeologists can usually discover the trends. By identifying the attributes that are most sensitive to change—the traits that change most rapidly—the archaeologist can construct a sequence that will most accurately reflect the passage of time. Surface decorative or stylistic attributes usually shift most rapidly and freely and tend to be the best chronological indicators because they are least affected by functional or technological requirements. For example, a water storage jar must be deep enough to hold water and should have a restricted mouth to lessen evaporation and spills, but it can be any color or design. Artifacts made from such plastic materials as clay or metal are usually good sources for deriving temporal sequences because they can be decorated in a variety of ways.

Seriation is a relative dating method derived from these cultural regularities. It refers to a variety of techniques that seek to order artifacts in a series so that adjacent members in the series are more similar than members farther apart in the series. Seriation has two basic applications: stylistic seriation and frequency seriation.

Stylistic Seriation

Stylistic seriation is a technique for ordering artifacts and attributes according to similarity in style. The variation may reflect either temporal change or spatial distance; the archaeologist must determine which factor (or both) was involved in each situation. Generally, the more limited the source area of the artifacts in question, the more likely the seriation reflects the passage of time.

One of the first studies to use stylistic seriation was the Diospolis Parva sequence outlined by Sir Flinders Petrie at the close of the 19th century. Petrie was faced with a series of pottery jars from predynastic Egyptian tombs that were not linked stratigraphically. He ordered the pottery by shape and ranked their similarities by using a series of numbers (Fig. 7.2). The numbers, of course, did not refer to age in years, but indicated instead the relative age of each jar within the seriation. This technique allowed Petrie to organize the pottery chronologically and, by association, to order the sequence of tombs as well.

Petrie's study also provides evidence that the archaeologist cannot assume that the trend of change is always from simple to complex or that it implies progress as our own culture defines that term. In the Diospolis Parva sequence, the vessel handles began as functional attributes and ended as decorative lines mimicking handles. Thus, for a sequence to be valid, the archaeologist must ensure that it is free from presumptions of progress, increasing complexity, or other ethnocentric biases. Of course, one must also have some idea of which end of the resulting seriation is the beginning—that is, which is the earlier end and which is the later. In most cases, links with other dating methods (usually absolute) will provide this information.

Frequency Seriation

Frequency seriation orders the sequence of sites or deposits by studying the relative frequencies of their artifact types. This is based on the assumption that the frequency of each artifact type follows a predictable career, from the time of its origin to an expanding popularity and finally to total disuse. The length

ARBITRARY SEQUENCE DATES

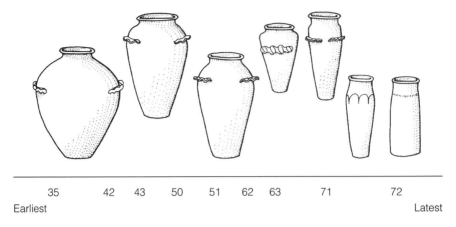

| 35 | 42 | 43 | 50 | 51 | 62 | 63 | 71 | 72 |

Earliest   Latest

FIGURE 7.2

One of the earliest applications of stylistic seriation was Petrie's chronological ordering of tombs at Diospolis Parva, Egypt, based on changes in
associated pottery vessels. (After Petrie 1901.)

of time and the degree of popularity (frequency) varies with each type, but
when presented diagrammatically most examples form one or more lenslike
patterns known as **battleship-shaped curves.** The validity of this pattern has
been verified by plotting the frequencies of artifact types from long-term stratified deposits and by testing historically documented examples. The best-known
historical test, by James Deetz and Edwin N. Dethlefsen, involved dated tombstones from 18th- and early 19th-century New England. This study demonstrated that the popularity of various decorative motifs on the headstones did
indeed show battleship-shaped distribution curves over time (Fig. 7.3).

SEQUENCE COMPARISON

If seriation cannot be used for the artifacts being studied, the archaeologist has
another recourse. If other well-documented artifact sequences exist in the geographical area being investigated, the artifact classes in question may be compared to those already defined from nearby sites and placed into a temporal
order corresponding to those already established. This is **sequence comparison,** and it presumes the existence of past cultural connections, such as trade,
so that the resemblances are not accidental. But even if such connections can
be documented, there is no guarantee that two similar types are exactly the
same age. The work of Deetz and Dethlefsen, for example, showed that even
among neighboring colonial communities, the time ranges for particular tomb-

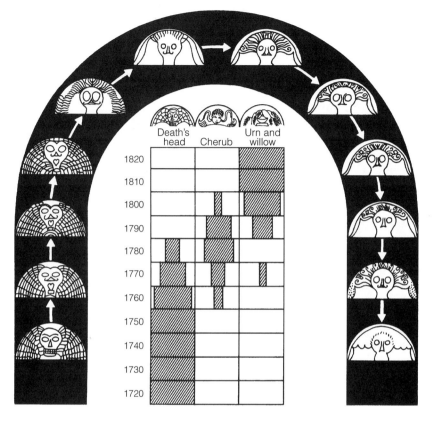

FIGURE 7.3

A study of dated New England tombstones shows that the changes in popularity of particular styles is aptly described by battleship-shaped curves,
and it supports assumptions used in both stylistic seriation and frequency
seriation. The outer ring shows the gradual change in one motif, the
death's head. (After *Invitation to Archaeology* by James Deetz, illustrated by
Eric Engstrom, copyright © 1967 by James Deetz. Reprinted by permission of Doubleday, a division of Bantam, Doubleday, Dell Publishing
Group, Inc.)

stone motifs were rather variable. Because of these difficulties, the comparative
method is usually the weakest means for inferring a local chronological
sequence; it is usually used only when other means are impossible.

Sequence comparison is very useful, however, for building broad
chronologies for a region. By matching sequences already established for individual sites or regions, archaeologists produce the time-space grids important
to the reconstruction of cultural history (see Chapter 3), allowing the identification of trends in cultural change and stability across broad expanses of space
and time.

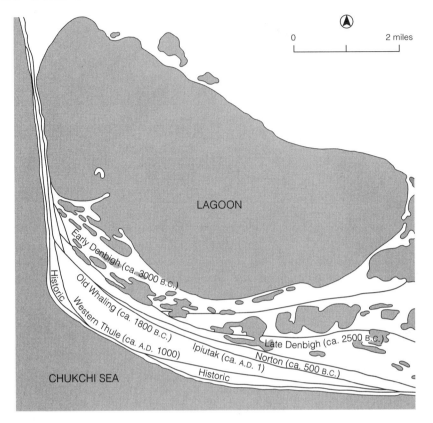

FIGURE 7.4

This map of Cape Krusenstern, Alaska, emphasizes some of the series of
ancient beach ridges that have been related to particular periods of occupation during the last 5000 years. (Redrawn from *Ancient Men of the Sea* by
J. Louis Giddings. © estate of J. Louis Giddings, New York: Alfred A.
Knopf, Inc., 1967.)

STRATIGRAPHY

The age of archaeological materials can sometimes be assessed by their association with geological deposits or formations. Often these assessments are
relative, as in cases based on superposition, where materials in lower strata
were deposited earlier than those in higher strata. As stated in Chapter 5,
stratigraphy refers to the archaeological interpretation of the significance of
stratification. We have also seen how archaeological stratigraphy may represent
a combination of both behavioral and natural transformation processes (as in a
midden composed of alternating strata of cultural materials in primary context
and redeposited alluvium). As long as the context—and, therefore, the tempo-

ral order—of a stratified deposit is clear, the archaeologist can use stratigraphy to determine the relative age of the deposition of artifacts and other materials in the deposit.

GEOCHRONOLOGY

Many methods have been developed for determining the age of geological formations. Since the earth existed for billions of years before humans appeared, however, only a few techniques of **geochronology** apply to the relatively recent span of archaeological deposits. Often these assessments are relative, based on stratigraphy. But when geologists have determined the absolute age of geological formations using radiometric or other techniques (discussed below), the archaeologist can, in turn, assign an indirect date to artifacts found in these matrices.

The effects of long-term geological processes, such as glacial advance and retreat or fluctuations in land and sea levels, can sometimes be quite useful in dating archaeological remains. Again, if the chronology of the geological events is known, associated archaeological materials can be fit into that scheme. For example, the successive formation of post-Pleistocene shorelines at Cape Krusenstern, Alaska, provided J. Louis Giddings with a means of ordering sites chronologically. As the beach expanded seaward through time, people continued to locate their camps near its high-water limit. In this progression, the younger beaches—and, by association, the more recent sites—are those located closer to the current beach front. More than 100 old beach lines are discernible at Cape Krusenstern, representing some 5000 years of accumulation (Fig. 7.4). Through this relative sequence—which some have called **horizontal stratigraphy**—Giddings arranged the sites in temporal order. By applying other dating techniques, he then converted the relative dating to an absolute scheme.

OBSIDIAN HYDRATION

In 1960, Irving Friedman and Robert L. Smith announced a new age determination technique based on the cumulative **hydration,** or adsorption of water, in **obsidian.** Over time, the adsorbed water forms a hydration layer on the exposed surfaces of obsidian (see Fig. 7.5). The thickness of this layer is measured in microns ($1\mu = 0.001$ mm) and is detectable microscopically. Since the hydration layer penetrates deeper into the surface over time, the thickness of this layer can be used to determine the amount of time that the surface has been exposed. In other words, the age of manufacture or use—either of which could fracture the obsidian, exposing a new surface for hydration—can be calculated if the rate of hydration is known. Once this rate is established, the

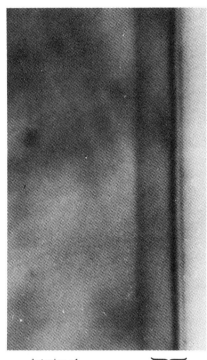

FIGURE 7.5

In this magnified view, a 3μ-wide hydration zone appears as a wide band at the edge of the obsidian. (From Michels 1973; by permission of the author and Seminar Press.)

Interior of obsidian specimen

Hydration zone

thickness of the hydration layer from any obsidian sample can be compared to a chronological conversion table to provide the sample's age.

Since the method was originally applied, problems have emerged that have had to be corrected to furnish reliable dates. First, the hydration rate varies with the composition of the obsidian, which differs from one source deposit to another. Second, the hydration rate also changes in response to temperature variations of the matrix in which the obsidian was deposited. As long as the correction factors for these variations are known and applied, obsidian hydration can still be an accurate, simple, and inexpensive means for directly dating obsidian artifacts.

FLORAL AND FAUNAL METHODS

There are several methods based on floral and faunal remains that can provide either direct or indirect dates for archaeologists. We will discuss two of the most familiar techniques.

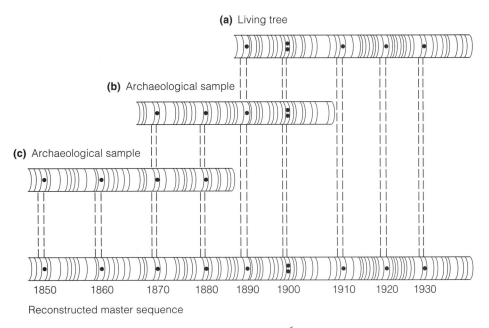

FIGURE 7.6

A master dendrochronological sequence is built by linking successively older specimens, often beginning with living trees (a) that overlap with archaeological samples (b, c), based on matching patterns of thick and thin rings. Provided the sequence is long enough, specimens of unknown age can be dated by comparison with the master sequence. The rings are marked with dots at 10-year intervals for ease of reading. (After Bannister 1970.)

Dendrochronology

Dendrochronology, or tree-ring dating, is the best-known method of directly determining absolute age for floral materials. This approach is based on counting the annual growth rings observable in the cross-sections of cut trees. As early as 1848 Squier and Davis (see Chapter 2) determined the minimum age of mounds in the Mississippi valley from the age of the oldest trees growing on them. Assuming that trees would not be allowed to grow on earthen constructions while they were in use, they reasoned that, if the oldest tree growing on these mounds were 300 years old, the site itself would have to be at least three centuries old.

The modern method of dendrochronology involves a refinement of such tree-ring counts. It uses the cross-linkage of ring-growth patterns among a series of trees to extend a sequence of growth cycles into the past, far beyond the lifetime of a single tree (Fig. 7.6). The compilation of a long-term sequence of tree-ring growth patterns was first established by astronomer, A. E. Douglass, working in the southwestern United States in the first decades of the 20th century. Douglass's original research was aimed at relating past climatic cycles—as reflected in patterns of wider and narrower tree-ring growth—to sunspot cycles. Although variations in tree-ring growth do provide valuable clues to past climatic cycles, the added benefit of this method in establishing an absolute chronological sequence for archaeology was soon realized. By counting back from a known starting point and matching patterns of rings from trees with overlapping lifetimes, the tree-ring sequence could be projected back for thousands of years. Then a given tree segment from an archaeological context could be dated by matching its ring pattern to the known sequence. The longest tree-ring sequences are those of oak trees in Germany (some 9500 years) and bristlecone pines in southeastern California (more than 8000 years and discussed further later on).

Although it would seem potentially useful anywhere in the world where trees were used by prehistoric peoples, dendrochronology has in fact been applied in only a few parts of the world, most notably in the southwestern United States, Alaska, northern Mexico, Germany, Norway, Great Britain, and Switzerland. The method is limited by its dependence on four conditions that cannot be met everywhere:

1. The proper kind of tree must be present: the species must produce well-defined annual rings and be sensitive to minute variations in climatic cycles. Many species of trees cannot be used because they produce roughly uniform rings regardless of climate changes.

2. The ring-growth variation must depend primarily upon one environmental factor, such as temperature or soil humidity.

3. The prehistoric population must have made extensive use of timbers, especially in construction.

4. Cultural and environmental conditions must allow for good preservation of timbers in archaeological contexts.

Dendrochronology determines the date a tree was cut down by placing its last or outermost growth ring within a local sequence. If the outermost ring is missing from the sample, the exact cutting date cannot be assessed. Even with a cutting date, the validity of an archaeological date based on dendrochronology also depends on correct evaluation of the archaeological context and association of the timber. Specimens that form parts of construction features—and thus are in primary context—are more reliable. Even so, Bryant Bannister has listed four types of errors in interpreting tree-ring dates:

1. The wood may have been reused and therefore its cutting date is older than the construction in which it was used.

2. The use of the feature—such as a house—may have extended well beyond its construction date, so that the timber's cutting date is much older than the final use or abandonment of the house.

3. The replacement of old, weakened timbers by newer, stronger ones may result in the wood being younger than the original construction.

4. Wooden artifacts or ecofacts found within a feature—such as furniture or charcoal in a house—may be either *younger or older* than the building's construction date.

To help offset these problems, the archaeologist tries to recover multiple samples for dendrochronological analysis. The dates from the various specimens can then be used to check each other. Good agreement among several samples from the same feature makes it far more likely that the results reflect an accurate date.

Bone Chemistry

Bone chemistry techniques enable the archaeologist to see if bones found in the same matrix were indeed deposited together. Bone buried at the same time in the same deposit will lose organic components, principally nitrogen, and gain inorganic components, such as fluorine and uranium, at the same rate. Since the rates of nitrogen loss and fluorine gain differ because of varying local environmental conditions (temperature and humidity), the rates vary from one deposit to another. Thus these rates can only be used to determine relative dates, that one bone is older than another from the same deposit. They cannot be used to establish absolute dates.

The classic applications of these relative dating techniques involved human skeletal remains of disputed antiquity, the most dramatic of which was the exposure of the great Piltdown hoax. The Piltdown finds, unearthed between 1911 and 1915, revealed an apelike mandible (jawbone) apparently paired with a modern-looking human cranium. The two were anatomically mismatched overall, but the apparent geological association, combined with the uniformly discolored appearance of age in all the bones and some humanlike traits in the otherwise apelike jaw, convinced all but a few disbelievers that Piltdown Man represented a significant new discovery that altered conceptions about the course of human evolution. The skeptics held out, however, and finally prevailed. In 1950, Kenneth Oakley tested the bones for fluorine content and later for nitrogen; he found that the mandible was much younger than the cranium (see Table 7.2). Uranium tests reinforced these findings. On further examination, the apparently human traits of the mandible and its discoloration were shown to be due to deliberate alteration of a modern ape jaw.

RADIOMETRIC METHODS

Several age-determination techniques exploit the principle of radioactive decay, the transformation of unstable radioactive isotopes into stable elements. These methods are all termed **radiometric** techniques. Although they can sometimes be used to date archaeological materials directly, they more frequently provide indirect age determinations. Because the radiometric technique most

TABLE 7.2

Fluorine, Nitrogen, and Uranium Content of Piltdown and Related Bones

REMAINS	PERCENTAGE OF FLUORINE	PERCENTAGE OF NITROGEN	URANIUM PARTS PER MILLION
Fresh bone	0.03	4.0	0
Piltdown fossil elephant molar	2.7	—	610
Piltdown cranium	0.1	1.4	1
Piltdown jaw	0.03	3.9	0

SOURCE: *After Oakley 1970, Table B, p. 41.*

commonly used by archaeologists is radiocarbon dating, the following discussion will emphasize this particular technique. Most other radiometric techniques are applicable to extremely long time spans (Table 7.3), beyond the time range of human existence. They are used mainly by geologists to determine the age of geological formations.

The physical properties of radioactive decay can only be used for dating purposes if three facts are known: the original amount of the radioactive isotope present at the onset of decay; the amount now present; and the rate of radioactive decay. In most cases the first factor must be computed indirectly. The amount of the radioactive isotope now present is counted directly, using different methods according to the isotope being measured. Since the decay of any unstable isotope is a random process, it does not produce a steady rate of decay; it is possible, however, to calculate the statistical probability that a certain proportion of the isotope will decay within a given time (Fig. 7.7). This rate is usually expressed as the **half-life** of the isotope—the period required for one half of the unstable atoms to decay and form the stable daughter isotope. It is important to remember that the half-life of any radioactive isotope represents not a fixed rate, but rather a statistical average with a specified range of error.

Radiocarbon

Radiocarbon dating is the most important radiometric technique for archaeologists. Carbon dioxide enters plants through photosynthesis, and the plants are in turn eaten by animals. Thus all living things constantly take in both ordinary carbon (^{12}C) and radioactive carbon (^{14}C) throughout their lifetimes. The proportion of ^{14}C to ^{12}C in an organism remains constant until its death. At that point, no further ^{14}C is taken in, and the amount of radioactive carbon present at that time begins to decrease through radioactive decay. Thus, measurement of the amount of ^{14}C still present (and emitting radiation) in plant and animal remains enables the determination of the amount of time elapsed since death.

TABLE 7.3

Half-Lives and Utility Ranges of Radioactive Isotopes

ISOTOPES	HALF-LIFE (IN YEARS)	LIMITS OF USEFULNESS FOR ARCHAEOLOGICAL DATING
$^{14}C \rightarrow {}^{14}N$ (radiocarbon) (Cambridge half-life)	5730 ± 40	Normally 100,000 years and younger
$^{40}K \rightarrow {}^{40}Ar$ (potassium–argon)	1.3 billion ± 40 million $(.04 \times 10^9)$	100,000 years and older
$^{235}U \rightarrow {}^{207}Pb$ (uranium-235–lead)	ca. 700 million	Too slow to be of archaeological value
$^{238}U \rightarrow {}^{206}Pb$ (uranium-238–lead)	ca. 4.5 billion	Too slow to be of archaeological value
$^{232}Th \rightarrow {}^{208}Pb$ (thorium–lead)	ca. 14 billion	Too slow to be of archaeological value
$^{87}Rb \rightarrow {}^{87}Sr$ (rubidium–strontium)	ca. 50 billion	Too slow to be of archaeological value

Any archaeological specimen of organic origin is potentially a candidate for direct radiocarbon dating. Charcoal from burned materials, such as is found in ancient hearths or fire pits, is most commonly used, but unburned organic materials such as bone collagen, wood, seeds, shells, leather, and so forth—even the carbon in worked iron—can also be dated. Most of these latter materials require larger sample amounts, however, because they contain a smaller proportion of carbon.

In the original method developed in the late 1940s by Willard F. Libby, the amount of ^{14}C is detected by Geiger counters, used to measure the rate of decay emissions from a sample, usually for a period of 24 hours. A more recently developed procedure using a tandem accelerator allows the physicist to measure directly the amount of ^{14}C in a sample. Although the new technique is more expensive, such direct measurement does offer a significant advantage since dates can be obtained from samples, such as seeds, too small for the traditional method.

Radiocarbon age determination has revolutionized archaeological dating. It provided the first means of relating dates and sequences on a worldwide basis, because, unlike other methods available at the time, it did not rely on local conditions. The great wave of enthusiasm led, however, to uncritical acceptance and overconfidence in the precision of radiocarbon dates. Although

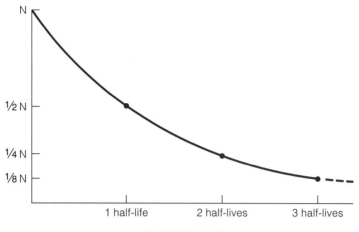

FIGURE 7.7

The decay rate of a radioactive isotope is expressed by its half-life, or the period after which half the radioactive isotopes will have decayed into more stable forms. After two half-lives, only one quarter of the original amount of radioactive isotopes will remain, and by the end of the third half-life, only one eighth ($1/2 \times 1/2 \times 1/2$) will remain radioactive.

it is still the most popular method and among the most useful of all dating techniques available to the archaeologist, it does have a number of limitations.

The limitations begin with the archaeologist. Any radiocarbon date is only as meaningful as the evaluation of the archaeological context from which it derives. Organic samples from disturbed deposits—that is, from secondary contexts—can furnish dates, but these often have no bearing on the ages of associated materials. To use radiocarbon to date associated materials indirectly, the archaeologist must establish that all were deposited together.

The second limitation derives from the small amount of ^{14}C available for detection. The third is the built-in statistical uncertainty inherent in all radiometric techniques, since both the decay rate *and* the half-life are averages. Thus, a radiocarbon age expressed as 3220 ± 50 years B.P. (before present) does *not* mean that the analyzed sample died 3220 years ago, but that there is a 67-percent probability that the original organism died some time in the 100-year span between 3170 and 3270 years before A.D. 1950 (the arbitrary zero date used in all radiocarbon analyses). The probability that a reported range includes the right date can be improved to 97 percent by doubling the range of error—in this case to 200 years or from 50 to 100 years on either side of the central date.

A fourth limitation to the radiocarbon technique is the documented fluctuation of past levels of ^{14}C on earth. Measurements of radiocarbon dates for wood samples with ages determined by dendrochronology demonstrate these fluctuations. The result is that earlier than 1500 B.C., radiocarbon age determinations furnish dates that are increasingly out of line (Fig. 7.8). At 1500 B.C.,

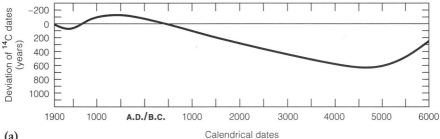

(a)

(b)

FIGURE 7.8

(a) A representation of the discrepancy between the ideal ^{14}C chronological scale (straight line) and a plotted series of samples, dated by radiocarbon analysis, whose age was independently determined by dendrochronology. The discrepancy is due to past fluctuations in the amount of ^{14}C on earth. (After Michael 1985.) (b) The bristlecone pine, found in the White Mountains of California, is the longest-living tree species known and is the key to increasing the accuracy of age determinations using the radiocarbon method. (Photo by Henry N. Michael, courtesy of the Museum Applied Science Center for Archaeology, University of Pennsylvania Museum.)

radiocarbon dates are about 150 years too recent; by 4000 B.C., they are about 700 years too young. The solution to this problem has emerged from the same source that exposed the error—dendrochronology. Extensive radiocarbon testing of known-age samples of wood has yielded a calibration formula, which allows a date calculated in radiocarbon years to be corrected to a more accurate time value. The correction tables are limited by our ability to secure known-age samples of wood; but use of the oldest living tree, the bristlecone pine found in southeastern California, has enabled scientists to extend the correction range back more than 8000 years.

Recent revisions and refinements in radiocarbon dating have provided what Colin Renfrew has called the "second radiocarbon revolution." The first revolution was the original development of this dating method, giving a uniform means to develop absolute chronologies applicable anywhere in the world; the second has been the realization of the archaeological implications, particularly in the Old World, of the dendrochronological calibrations that have revised many of the most ancient radiocarbon determinations, making them older still.

Before radiocarbon dating was available, archaeologists had used dating techniques based on stylistic and form comparisons to interrelate European and Southwest Asian sequences. Whenever a question arose as to the source of an Old World invention or innovation—such as copper metallurgy or the construction of megalithic (monumental stone) tombs—the usual assumption was that it had come from civilized Southwest Asia to barbaric Europe. The first sets of radiocarbon dates seemed to support these assumptions. Now, however, calibrated radiocarbon dates indicate that many archaeological remains, such as megalithic constructions, which had been thought to be the result of Southwest Asian influence, actually occurred earlier in Europe! The traditional belief in a Southwest Asian monopoly on innovation and cultural advance has been tossed aside, and archaeologists are now seriously reexamining interpretations of ancient long-distance communication in the Old World.

Potassium-Argon

Potassium-argon dating is based on the radioactive decay of a rare isotope of potassium (^{40}K) to form argon (^{40}Ar) gas. The half-life of ^{40}K is 1.31 billion years, but the method can be used to date materials as recent as 100,000 years old. The technique is used principally to determine ages for geological formations that contain potassium. The basic principles of radiometric age determination, already described for the radiocarbon method, are used with rock samples to measure the ratio of ^{40}K to ^{40}Ar. A refinement of the potassium-argon technique has recently been developed; it allows several age determinations to be made from each sample, thus increasing the reliability of the date.

The K-Ar technique has been particularly helpful in dating geological formations associated with the remains of fossil hominids (human ancestors) and Lower Paleolithic tools. When Mary and Louis Leakey found the remains of

Zinjanthropus, an early hominid (now included in the genus *Australopithecus*), they were able to assign the bones an age of about 1.75 million years on the basis of potassium-argon dating of the volcanic strata in which the remains were found. More recently, potassium-argon dates have been determined for formations associated with early hominid finds in the Lake Turkana/Omo Valley area on the border between Kenya and Ethiopia, extending the chronology of hominid existence there back more than 2 million years.

ARCHAEOMAGNETISM

Dating by **archaeomagnetism** relies upon the fact that the earth's magnetic field varies through time, shifting in the horizontal plane (expressed as *declination* angle) as well as vertically (expressed by the *dip* angle). The course of these shifts over the past few hundred years has been determined from compass readings preserved in historical records. This changing magnetic course can be extended back in time by the analysis of certain mineral compounds, such as clay, that contain iron particles that may align to magnetic north just as a compass does. This occurs when clay is heated above its *curie* point, the temperature at which the particles lose their magnetic orientation. When the minerals cool again, the new magnetic alignment of the iron particles is frozen in the clay body. Thus, if a sample of baked clay is not disturbed, it will preserve the angles of dip and declination from the time when it was heated. By using known-age samples of fired clay, such as hearths dated by radiocarbon associations, archaeologists have traced the location of the magnetic pole into the past. When enough cross-dated archaeomagnetic samples have been analyzed, the variations in dip and declination can be matched to a time scale, thus allowing newly discovered fired clay samples to be dated directly, using the archaeomagnetic data alone (Fig. 7.9).

OTHER METHODS

There are numerous dating methods beyond those we have discussed, and new techniques are being developed all the time. Most of these are less frequently used or more limited in their application than are the ones considered here. Nonetheless, some of these additional methods are well established and accurate, such as calendrical dating (using deciphered ancient calendars), varve analysis (using strata deposited annually in lakes by retreating glaciers), and other radiometric techniques (fission track and uranium series dating). Others remain more experimental, such as electron spin resonance (or ESR, used to date shell or bone), thermoluminescence (used to date ceramics), and aspartic acid racemization (used to date bone).

(a)

(b)

FIGURE 7.9

Age determinations based on archaeomagnetism: (a) Careful collection
and recording in the field are essential. One sample has been removed and
preserved in the small square container to the left (above the leveling
device); another is about to be removed (behind the compass). (b) The
specialist measures and analyzes magnetic alignments in the laboratory
later by replicating the original orientation of the sample. (Photo (a) Santa
Bárbara Project, Honduras; photo (b) M. Leon Lopez and Helga Teiwes,
© 1967 National Geographic Society.)

SUMMARY

Control over the dimension of time is crucial; reconstruction of the past
depends on the archaeologist's ability to distinguish contemporaneous and
sequential events. Various techniques are used to determine the age of recovered data, either directly (by dating the artifact, ecofact, or feature itself) or
indirectly (by association with other remains that can be dated). Absolute dating refers to age in calendrical years or years before present (B.P.). Relative dating refers to age in relation to another date (older, younger, or the same age).

Archaeologists have long used relative dating techniques based on provenience, such as stratigraphy, or based on the characteristics of recovered
remains, such as stylistic or frequency seriation. Geological associations may
also provide dates for archaeological evidence, as in use of geochronological
sequences. Obsidian hydration yields direct and absolute dates for obsidian
artifacts based on hydration rates. Floral and faunal remains can be dated by
several means, including absolute age from tree-ring sequences (dendrochronology) and relative age from the detection of chemical changes in

bones. Radiometric methods are based on the radioactive decay of unstable isotopes; the most useful, radiocarbon dating, relies on an isotope of carbon (^{14}C) present in all living tissue. Potassium-argon dating determines the age of some geological deposits and can provide indirect dates for associated archaeological remains. Traces of ancient magnetism, preserved in features such as hearths, can be dated by correlation to magnetic sequences (archaeomagnetism) of known age.

New and improved methods continue to be developed. But all archaeological dating techniques have some limiting factors. While the various methods of age determination can lead to accurate control of the time dimension for archaeological data, archaeologists must be aware of each method's limits and, whenever possible, compensate for inaccuracies by applying two or more methods as cross-checks to produce an internally consistent chronological sequence.

FOR FURTHER READING

SERIATION
  Deetz and Dethlefsen 1967; Petrie 1901

STRATIGRAPHY
  Harris 1989; Rapp and Gifford 1985

GEOCHRONOLOGY
  Giddings 1967; Rapp and Gifford 1985

OBSIDIAN HYDRATION
  Friedman and Trembour 1983; Michels 1973

FLORAL AND FAUNAL METHODS
  Baillie 1982; Oakley 1970

RADIOMETRIC METHODS
  Hedges and Gowlett 1986; Michael 1985; Renfrew 1971, 1973

ARCHAEOMAGNETISM
  Wolfman 1984

ADDITIONAL SOURCES
  Aiken 1985, 1990; Bannister 1970; Biscott and Rosenbauer 1981; Joukowsky 1980; Orme 1982; Sharer 1994; Taylor and Longworth 1975; Zeuner 1958

Reconstructing the Past

Now THAT WE HAVE described how archaeologists control the time dimension of their data, we can consider the ways data are used to reconstruct the past. Here we move from analysis, or gaining information by breaking down the data into its essential elements and their relationships, to interpretation, or putting these elements back together to form a meaningful reconstruction that addresses the research goals.

There is no definite line between analysis and interpretation. As we noted in discussing research design in Chapter 4, the collection and analysis of archaeological data often overlap in time, and the archaeologist is always looking for new ways to answer the questions formulated as the research progresses. Even in examining the tiniest bit of evidence—such as a decorative motif on a painted sherd—the archaeologist works with an eye to how this might bear on the larger questions the investigation is attempting to answer. This chapter will consider how archaeologists reconstruct activities that took place at any one point in time by using analogy and the spatial patterning of data.

ANALOGY

A basic paradox underlies archaeology: the archaeological record exists in the present, while the archaeologist is interested in the past—specifically in the past conditions and human activities that created that record. Since events in

FIGURE 8.1

Manufacture of chipped stone tools in Ethiopia. Lithic technology survives today in several parts of the world, providing analogs for understanding similar technologies in the past. (Photo by James P. Gallagher.)

the prehistoric past cannot be observed directly, the archaeologist reconstructs those events using **analogy**—a form of reasoning whereby the identity of unknown things or relations is inferred from those that are known. Everyone uses this kind of reasoning, but its application in archaeology merits a more detailed consideration at this point. Reasoning by analogy is founded on the premise that if two classes of phenomena are alike in one respect, they may be alike in other respects as well. In archaeology, analogy is used to infer the identity of and relationships among archaeological data by comparing them with similar phenomena documented in human societies that are living or recorded historically.

On the most basic level, it is analogy that allows the archaeologist to identify artifacts, features, ecofacts, and sites as the remains of past human behavior. After all, the archaeologist does not observe the ancient human activity that produced chipped stone implements. However, ethnographers and other observers have recorded hunters and gatherers in several remote parts of the world continuing to make and use similar tools into this century. Because of the similarity in form between the artifacts and the ethnographically observed examples, analogy has identified many of the ancient tools and, by extension, has allowed reconstruction of manufacturing techniques and use behaviors associated with them (Fig. 8.1).

Analogy underlies all prehistoric archaeological reconstruction, but historical archaeology can often rely on documentary sources to identify archaeological remains. In cases that can be directly linked to later records, this historical information is sometimes projected back in time to assist archaeological reconstructions. But in clear-cut prehistoric situations, with no direct links to historical information, the archaeologist must rely on inferences using analogy.

In many cases, the archaeologist's use of analogy to identify a familiar artifact or feature is not a conscious process. An automatic association takes place drawing on everyday experience; in this way, an archaeologist relates masonry foundations that support modern houses to a similar archaeological feature as the remains of a dwelling. Often the archaeologist will encounter a feature or an artifact that is not familiar to his or her experience; in such cases, identification by analogy becomes most clearly a conscious, rational process.

A good example of detailed analogical reasoning is Lewis Binford's study of a certain type of feature encountered in sites of the middle and lower Mississippi River Valley and adjacent areas after A.D. 1000. These features are fairly small pits dug into the ground, averaging about 30 cm or less in length and width and slightly more than that in depth. They contain charred and carbonized twigs, bark, and corncobs, and are found around houses and domestic storage areas, never near public buildings. It is clear that the charred contents had been burned in place, in an oxygen-starved atmosphere that must have produced a lot of smoke, so these features were called "smudge pits." But their specific function was unknown, although a variety of suggestions were made, ranging from offerings of corncobs to ovens to fires built to drive away mosquitoes.

In seeking a firmer way to interpret these smudge pits, Binford went through the ethnographic literature describing the Native American groups in the area. These accounts included descriptions of hide-smoking procedures in which untanned deerskins were tied over small pits. Smoldering, smoky fires were then set in the pits and allowed to burn until the hides were dried and toughened, ready to be sewn into clothing. Binford pointed out that the details in the ethnographic accounts on the form and contents of the hide-smoking pits corresponded well with equivalent attributes of the archaeological smudge pits. Because there was a high degree of correspondence in form between ethnographic and archaeological examples, because the geographical areas involved were the same, and because a good case could be argued for the continuity of practices in that area from the archaeological past (after A.D. 1000) to the time of ethnographic observations (1700–1950), Binford argued—by analogy—that the archaeological smudge pits represented facilities for smoking animal skins.

More precisely, Binford offered this interpretation based on analogy as a hypothesis to be tested. If this identification were correct, other aspects of hide smoking described in ethnographies should also be found associated with the archaeological smudge pits. For example, since the ethnographic accounts describe tanning activities as occurring between, rather than during, peak hunting seasons, the smudge pits should be found in sites used in the spring and summer rather than in hunting sites. The more such correspondences found between the ethnographic and the archaeological data and the more specific attributes identified as being associated with a particular kind of feature, the stronger the case becomes for the analogical interpretation.

	Stage		Examples of associated technological innovations
CIVILIZATION			Alphabet and writing
BARBARISM	Upper		Iron tools
	Middle		Plant and animal domestication
	Lower		Pottery
SAVAGERY	Upper		Bow and arrow
	Middle		Fishing and fire
	Lower		Fruit and nut subsistence

Direction of unilinear evolution (arrow pointing up)

FIGURE 8.2

Lewis Henry Morgan's unilinear stages were used to equate past and present societies on a scale of evolutionary progress.

Abuse of Analogy

Before examining in more detail the different kinds of analogy and the ways they should be used, we should first understand some of the errors that have resulted from their improper use.

In the 19th century, when anthropology was dominated by the theory of unilinear cultural evolution (see Chapter 2), living primitive societies were often equated directly with the different stages of the proposed evolutionary sequence (Fig. 8.2). These stages were defined largely by technological attributes (Stone Age, Iron Age, and so on), and each stage was presumed to have its own corresponding developmental level of social system, political organization, and religious beliefs. By means of these combined technological, social, and ideological attributes, living societies were ranked with respect to their progress along the evolutionary scale.

Obviously, this kind of analogy is suspect: it is dominated by only one criterion—technology—and ignores other variables such as time and space. In linking the Australian Aborigines with the European Paleolithic, for instance, 19th-century anthropologists used an analogy that ignored a temporal separation of more than 10,000 years and a spatial separation of over 10,000 miles. Since the 19th century, anthropologists have compiled a great deal of information about all the varieties of human societies, including those using hunting and gathering as a means of subsistence. These studies show that while some regularities of social structure and cultural organization can be recognized, a single trait such as hunting cannot be used to predict the forms the rest of the culture will take. Yet this is essentially what the 19th-century unilinear evolutionists attempted to do.

The use of technological or other limited criteria to make wide-ranging analogies like those of the 19th-century unilinear cultural evolutionists is not reliable. However, simplistic analogies are not confined to the literature of the previous century. Similar careless equations between living cultures and those of the past may be found in some archaeological publications of the 20th century. Further, the general analogy between the hunters of the European Paleolithic and certain contemporary peoples still occurs—especially in popular accounts of the discovery of supposedly lost tribes who are usually described as "peoples from the Stone Age."

The obvious abuses of analogy in reconstructing the past have led to reactions, both by cultural anthropologists and by archaeologists, against the use of this method of reasoning. Much of the criticism of analogy has been concerned specifically with the uncritical use of ethnographic studies as analogs for archaeological interpretation. However, as we shall see below, the use of analogy in archaeology involves a wider range of analog sources, including historical accounts and modern experimental techniques.

Specific and General Analogy

It is important to distinguish between specific and general analogy. **Specific analogy** refers to particular comparisons within a single cultural tradition, while **general analogy** refers to broad comparisons that can be documented across many cultural traditions.

Specific analogy has rich potential for detailed interpretation of archaeological remains, but to use it, the archaeologist must defend its appropriateness on three grounds (which had been controlled in Binford's interpretation of the smudge-pits):

1. *Cultural continuity.* Specific analogies begin with continuity within a single cultural tradition. In the southwestern United States, for instance, there is considerable evidence that the contemporary Native American societies documented by ethnographic and historical accounts are the direct descendants, both culturally and biologically, of local prehistoric occupants (Fig. 8.3). This cultural link allows the archaeologist to draw frequent and reasonable analogies on the basis of living societies in order to interpret Southwestern prehistory.

2. *Comparability in environment.* Even where cultural continuity exists, environmental differences can alter links between past and present. Thus, an analog drawn from a society living in an environment different from that of the prehistoric society will be less reliable than one based on a society living in the same or similar environment.

3. *Similarity of cultural form.* Analogs must be based on observable similarities, which will usually be determined by the degree to which traditional behavior is maintained by the analog society. For example, in Southeast Asia, conservative highland tribal groups provide more likely analogs for local prehistoric reconstructions than do their urbanized neighbors in Bangkok.

General analogies can be applied in situations where specific analogies are unavailable. Because of the lack of cultural continuity, the problems in using

(a)

(b)

FIGURE 8.3

Cultural continuity, in the southwestern United States, for example, is an important criterion for using ethnographic studies as specific analogs for understanding ancient societies. The photographs above were taken around the turn of the century and show (a) an overall view of Oraibi Pueblo, Arizona, and (b) a room with equipment for preparing meals. Compare (b) with the mealing bin in Fig. 6.14. (Courtesy, Field Museum of Natural History, Chicago, (a) Neg# A185, (b) Neg# A246.)

169

living societies of hunters and gatherers as detailed analogs for Paleolithic groups have already been cited. Rather than throwing up their hands in dismay, however, archaeologists have developed better general analogies, each usually involving a narrow range of activities. Much of this has been accomplished through **actualistic studies,** where actual behavior can be tied to diagnostic material remains, regardless of the cultural setting. These studies range from observing modern trash-disposal patterns to examining how one group of hunters differs from another in consuming their prey. In all cases, the keys are rigorous specification both of the material traces of the past behavior and of the range of conditions under which certain kinds of behavior would be expected—and therefore might turn up in archaeological contexts.

Sources of Analogs

The analogs used in archaeological interpretation come from various sources: historical accounts and documents that describe societies in the past, ethnographic studies that describe present-day societies, and actualistic studies that attempt to duplicate conditions that existed in the past.

Historical sources include the full range of past records, studies written by professional historians, and descriptions made by casual observers such as travelers, merchants, soldiers, or missionaries. In the New World, much of our understanding of the pre-Columbian cultures of Mesoamerica and the Andes rests upon documents from the Spanish conquest of the 16th century (Fig. 8.4).

Ethnographic studies of living human societies are probably the most common source of archaeological analogs. Written by professional anthropologists, ethnographies are generally more focused and useful to the archaeologist than are other sources. However, professional ethnography is only about a century old, and most such work has been conducted among people influenced to some degree by European customs for far longer than that. Moreover, since ethnographers pursue their studies for their own interests, the data are often not presented in ways that relate behavior to material remains—that is, in ways that facilitate archaeological analogy. As we have said earlier, actualistic studies are undertaken by archaeologists to resolve precisely this dilemma, either through ethnoarchaeology or experimental archaeology.

Ethnoarchaeology refers to ethnographic research done by archaeologists so that the kinds of information needed to understand the past as well as the present will be recorded. Of particular importance are the correlations between activities and durable remains, which help researchers understand the ways materials enter the archaeological record and the kinds of behavior they reflect. For example, studies of the manufacture of stone tools and pottery reveal diagnostics for identifying workshops. William Longacre and James Ayres investigated a recently abandoned Apache wickiup (dwelling), recording all artifacts and features left behind. Using Apache ethnographic accounts for analogies, they interpreted their findings as the residence of a nuclear family typified by sexual division of labor, with female-associated activities predominating (Fig. 8.5). A recent trend in these studies has directed

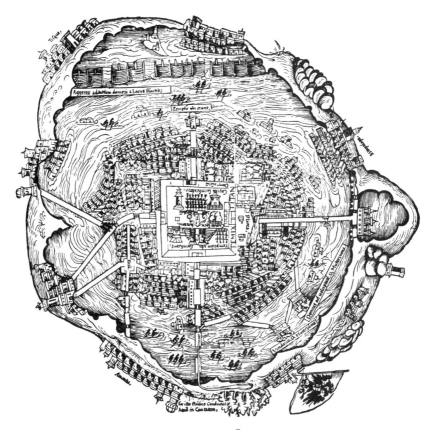

FIGURE 8.4

This 16th-century map of the Aztec capital of Tenochtitlán, Mexico, is illustrative of Spanish records that are used to complement the archaeological record of pre-Columbian societies. Although, in this case, spatial relationships are shown differently from those of modern maps, the document provides valuable information, such as means of access (causeways and canoes) to the city and planning of its central plaza. (By permission of the British Library.)

attention towards material diagnostics of behavior more likely to be otherwise invisible in the archaeological record, such as ideology or ethnicity.

Experimental archaeology is another aspect of actualistic studies done by archaeologists. Although experiments have a long history in archaeology, only recently have they begun to be used as a fundamental source for past reconstructions. Early examples often involved using actual archaeological materials or replicas, such as cutting tools and musical instruments, in an attempt to discover their ancient functions. Similar experiments continue, but in many cases experimental archaeology has been reoriented to provide analogs for a broader range of behavior—acquisition, manufacture, use, and disposal—associated with archaeological materials.

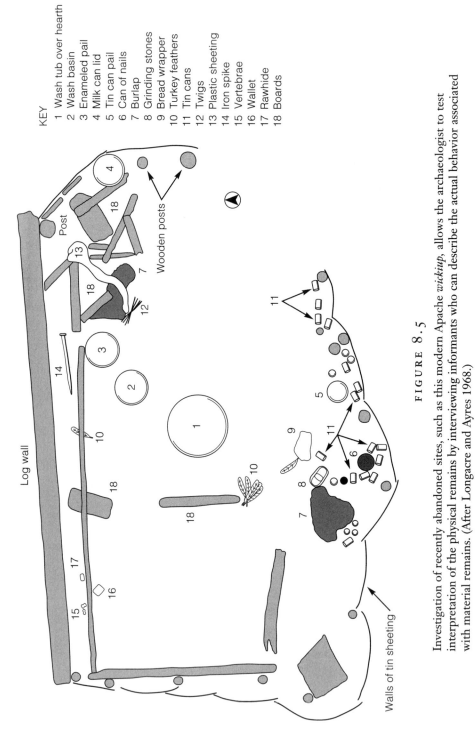

KEY

1 Wash tub over hearth
2 Wash basin
3 Enameled pail
4 Milk can lid
5 Tin can pail
6 Can of nails
7 Burlap
8 Grinding stones
9 Bread wrapper
10 Turkey feathers
11 Tin cans
12 Twigs
13 Plastic sheeting
14 Iron spike
15 Vertebrae
16 Wallet
17 Rawhide
18 Boards

Log wall

Post

Wooden posts

Walls of tin sheeting

FIGURE 8.5

Investigation of recently abandoned sites, such as this modern Apache *wickiup*, allows the archaeologist to test interpretation of the physical remains by interviewing informants who can describe the actual behavior associated with material remains. (After Longacre and Ayres 1968.)

Experimental work with stone artifacts is particularly well known. Don Crabtree and François Bordes were leaders in reconstructing the techniques used to manufacture ancient stone tools by experimental stone chipping designed to duplicate the archaeologically recovered forms. S. A. Semenov and Lawrence Keeley pioneered in studying the wear patterns produced on stone tools by various kinds of use (slicing, chopping, and so on) so that the functions of artifacts can be identified by analogy.

The most elaborate experimental studies involve reconstruction and maintenance of households and communities under past conditions. Archaeologists dealing with historically documented periods are in a better position to do experiments of this kind. Plimouth Plantation in Massachusetts and Colonial Pennsylvania Plantation in eastern Pennsylvania are examples of reconstituted colonial American communities (Fig. 8.6); in these experimental projects, crops are raised; food stored, processed, and cooked; buildings constructed; and tools manufactured and used all according to colonial customs. The experience provided by these cases is comparable to ethnoarchaeology, for the archaeologist has the opportunity to observe, participate in, and record the behavior associated with the material remains.

An important category of experimental archaeology involves study of what happens to archaeological materials upon disposal. These experiments consider the taphonomic and other transformational processes discussed in Chapter 4. Although these processes do not always involve human behavior, they are relevant to the interpretation of human behavior. For example, Glynn Isaac and his colleagues have sought to outline details that will help in distinguishing whether stone-tool scatters in riverbank locations are intact sites (use-related primary context) or just the cumulative effects of artifacts being washed downstream from their original deposition points (natural secondary context). To accomplish this, they systematically scattered groups of artifacts in the valley of a stream feeding into Lake Magadi, Kenya, returning annually to chart changes in artifact positions in these experimental analogs.

SPATIAL ORDER AND BEHAVIOR

The spatial distributions and associations of archaeological data are often directly observable; plotting finds on plans and maps, for example, is an essential part of data collection. But until the artifacts, ecofacts, and features are described, analyzed, and sorted in terms of time, archaeologists do not know which parts of these spatial distributions are remains of related activities. Past behavior cannot be reconstructed until the archaeologist knows whether bits of evidence go together in time or are from different periods. If they are from the same time span, they can give information about behavior and human interaction; if they are not, they allow the archaeologist to look at continuity and change in behavior through time.

FIGURE 8.6

The Colonial Pennsylvania Plantation is an example of experimental archaeology where past conditions and behavior are recreated to understand more fully what life was like in the past. (Courtesy of the Colonial Pennsylvania Plantation, Edgemont, Pa.)

In the following discussion, we will use the threefold division of culture commonly used by archaeologists in reconstructing ancient behavior:

1. **Technology** is the means by which human societies interact most directly with the natural environment. It consists of the set of techniques and the body of information that provide ways to procure raw materials and convert them into useful items, such as tools, food, and shelter. Because technology relates so closely to the natural environment, our discussion of technology will include the ways archaeologists reconstruct ancient environments.

2. **Social systems** assign roles and define relationships among people: kinship organization, political structure, exchange networks, and the like are all facets of the way people organize themselves and their social interactions. We will consider settlement patterns and evidence of exchange systems as examples of means for reconstructing ancient social systems.

3. **Ideology** encompasses the belief and value systems of a society—its attempts to explain its world. Religious beliefs come most readily to mind as examples of ideological systems, but art styles, writing, and other records also provide information about the ways human groups have codified their concepts about their world and existence.

The divisions among these three categories of human activity are not rigid. For example, exchange systems serve to move tools and raw materials, thus acting as part of the technological system, but also reflect (and affect) social relations. These categories simply represent broad distinctions among cultural behavior that relate people to their environment, to one another, and to ideas.

Technology

In Chapter 6, we discussed the technologies involved in the production and use of various kinds of artifacts. This information, focusing on the analysis of artifacts, enables the archaeologist to answer specific questions about how stone tools or pottery vessels were made and used. At this point, we need to expand the questions relating to technology to determine what means were available to a given group to relate or adapt to their environment. To do this, archaeologists ask specific research questions, such as, how were tools, facilities, and other products manufactured? or, was metallurgy practiced by the occupants of a given site or region? To answer these kinds of questions, they must ask another, what evidence indicates the presence of a given technology? An archaeologist usually forms a series of working hypotheses about the technologies employed by the prehistoric people being studied and tests these against the recovered evidence to answer the research questions.

Projectile points, for instance, are usually taken as evidence of hunting; discovery of these points in association with the bones of slaughtered animals, as in the Olsen-Chubbuck, Lindenmeier, or Folsom kill sites mentioned previously, clearly reveal aspects of the prehistoric subsistence technologies for these societies. Other hunting technologies, however, leave few artifacts. Trapping equipment, for example, is seldom preserved; the use of this kind of technology would have to be reconstructed from particular kinds of animal remains by analogy with modern trapping techniques and game used by inhabitants in the same area.

Remains of workshops provide extremely valuable technological evidence. Workshops are activity-specific clusters of artifacts, sometimes including specially constructed features such as kilns, that preserve a variety of details about manufacturing processes. There are as many kinds of workshop features as there are different manufacturing technologies. The elaborateness of the workshop facility often depends on the scale of the activity. For example, flint-knapping might be carried out by nonspecialized individual hunters with a few simple tools at a variety of locations over time; thus, a number of casual chipping stations might be found in a given area of occupation. Activities that require specialized individuals and facilities, however, such as iron metallurgy with its need for skilled labor and intense and controlled heat, are more likely to have readily identifiable areas set aside as workshops. In such a workshop, one would expect to find residues that reflect the manufacturing process, including raw materials, partially finished artifacts, mistakes (such as pottery vessels that cracked during firing), debris (such as stone debitage), and of course any special tools or features needed for production.

Technology mediates human interaction with the environment in many ways. People build shelters and make clothing to protect themselves from heat, cold, rain, wind, and snow. They make baskets to help in plant collecting, fashion spears and arrows to kill food animals, dig irrigation ditches to provide water for crops, and build roads to ease travel (such as the Sweetrack roadway discussed in Chapter 6). The precise techniques and equipment used for a given task in a given time and place depend on past accumulation of technological knowledge. But they also depend on the nature of the environment and the raw materials it supplies. The Inca of Peru, for example, built roads to unite their far-flung empire, often needing bridges to link segments of these roads. Where the rivers and other gaps were narrow, the bridges were made of stone and timber; where gaps were wider than those materials could span, however, they used plant fibers. The results were suspension bridges of stout rope, bridges so strong the Spanish could later cross them on horseback.

As we saw in Chapter 3, environment does not determine culture, but it provides a flexible framework within which every culture operates. Similarly, culture does not determine environment, but cultural values and technological capacity may serve to define the extent to which available resources are exploited. These principles are at the heart of one of the current theoretical frameworks in anthropology, cultural ecology.

Cultural ecology includes the interaction of people with both the natural and the cultural environment. Furthermore, the relation between technology and environment is itself complex and interactive. For example, an innovation in technology may redefine the nature of the exploitable environment: irrigation ditches can make gardens in the desert. The ecological questions asked by archaeologists center on which aspects of the range of environmental resources a prehistoric society exploited and which available resources it used. To answer these questions, archaeologists must reconstruct not only the techniques and equipment used by a past society, but also the nature of the environment that could be exploited by that society. In most research, the meeting ground for these approaches is the study of subsistence technology: what resources were available for food? which of these food resources were chosen and how were these obtained?

Archaeologists take two approaches to reconstruct ancient physical environments. The first is observation of the modern landscape, including topography and the range of biotic and mineral resources. The second is the collection of ecofacts. Such data give archaeologists evidence as to whether, and how, the available resources may have differed in ancient times. We have seen an example of this with the Star Carr study described in Chapter 6. Pollen studies have proven to be especially useful indicators of paleoenvironments. Combining these kinds of approaches, archaeologists attempt, usually in consultation with other specialists, to reconstruct the nature of the ancient environment in which the past society lived.

Examples of studies using both the collection of ecofacts and modern observation are easy to find. For instance, the Tehuacán Archaeological-Botanical Project defined its archaeological region for archaeological data collection to correspond to its resource area for modern environmental data collection. The overall goal of the project was to trace the development of agriculture in the New World. The Tehuacán Valley, in the Mexican state of Puebla, was chosen as the research location partly because it contained a number of dry caves that seemed to promise the climatic conditions under which maize and other domesticated plants would be preserved. At the same time, however, Richard MacNeish and his colleagues needed to determine the range of food resources available to the ancient residents of the Tehuacán Valley in order to outline the conditions under which they increasingly chose food production over food collection as their subsistence base. To get this information, the investigators surveyed the Tehuacán Valley and divided it into four microenvironmental zones, each with its own set of seasonally or perennially available resources. Combining this information with analysis of the ecofacts recovered from the region's archaeological sites, MacNeish and his coworkers were able to reconstruct the subsistence-related migrations of ancient human populations within the valley, postulating their movements in search of shifting food resources as the seasons passed. A few years later MacNeish applied the same approach to the Ayacucho Basin of Peru, defining the correlations between seasonal exploitation and different subsistence technologies (Fig. 8.7).

Social Systems

All societies define themselves and distinguish among their members by assigning various roles and statuses. The most fundamental distinctions are those based on age and sex differences, but most human groups organize social interaction along a number of other lines as well. Kinship studies, a well-known part of anthropological research, have revealed the great variety of ways people have developed for naming relatives, reckoning descent, governing what family members one lives with, and so on. Principles of social organization extend beyond consideration of family organization, however, to include such other things as the ways power is channeled (political organization) and who controls production and distribution of wealth and other resources (economic organization).

Much of the evidence of social structure recorded by ethnographers is intangible. Social, political, and economic categories, attitudes of respect, or kinship terms often leave little or no trace in the archaeological record. In recent years, however, archaeologists have tried to recognize how aspects of material remains might be clues to past social organization. In this section, we shall discuss two different approaches to reconstructing past social relationships and social structure—settlement archaeology and exchange systems.

Settlement archaeology is the study of the spatial distribution of ancient human activities and occupations, ranging from the differential location of activities within a one-room dwelling (see Fig. 8.5) to the arrangement of sites in a region (Fig. 8.7). Because they are concerned with locational information, settlement studies use features and sites as their principal data bases. Since the focus is on understanding the distribution of ancient activities, the archaeologist doing settlement studies needs locational information preserved by primary context, and features and sites retain such information intact. Artifacts and eco-

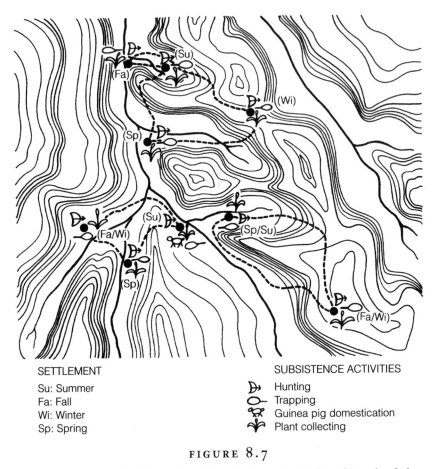

SETTLEMENT

Su: Summer
Fa: Fall
Wi: Winter
Sp: Spring

SUBSISTENCE ACTIVITIES

Hunting
Trapping
Guinea pig domestication
Plant collecting

FIGURE 8.7

Synthesis of archaeological data from the Ayacucho Valley of Peru has led to postulation that ancient populations moved seasonally among sites to exploit different subsistence resources. (After MacNeish, Patterson, and Browman 1975.)

facts are also considered when they are in primary context, especially when their arrangement reflects ancient activities (such as broken artifacts and debitage in a workshop).

Because they place sites and features in space, settlement studies have much potential relevance for examining ancient exploitation of the environment. This potential has certainly been recognized by archaeologists doing settlement research. In the Ayacucho Basin, for example, MacNeish and his colleagues not only examined ecofactual evidence of specific food use, they also looked at the distribution of occupational sites or base camps. The latter allowed them to reconstruct the seasonal cycle of shifting residence and food procurement (Fig. 8.7). In this section, however, we shall focus on how settlement archaeology can be used to reconstruct past social systems.

The assumption underlying settlement archaeology is that spatial patterns in the distribution of archaeological remains result from and reflect spatial patterns of ancient human behavior. Archaeologists analyze spatial patterns on three broad levels: (1) activities within a single structure or on a single occupation surface, such as a cave floor; (2) arrangements of activities and features within a settlement or site; and (3) distribution of sites within a region. We shall consider examples on each of these levels.

At the smallest level of human settlement, archaeologists reconstruct the spatial organization of activities within a single structure—a dwelling or some other kind of building—or a comparably limited space. Such a study can consist of identifying areas in which various activities were carried out, such as distinguishing food preparation areas from storage areas. Identifying what went on in this kind of archaeological space is inferred by analogy, comparing the archaeological remains with material remains of documented activities. For example, excavated remains of hearths, fire-blackened jars, and grinding stones would indicate a cooking area, based on ethnographic observations of activities associated with similar features and artifacts. At this smallest level of settlement analysis, then, the archaeologist attempts to understand how the prehistoric society divided up space into areas appropriate for particular activities.

At this microsettlement level, one of the most frequently studied kinds of feature is the dwelling. A number of scholars have examined the potential determinants for house form. Bruce Trigger's list of such factors includes subsistence strategy (whether the society is sedentary or mobile); climate; available building materials; family structure; wealth; incorporation of special activities, such as craft production; ideology; security; and style. Although a number of these factors are related to environmental variables, several reflect the social system of the culture being studied. For example, societies in which people live in extended families, with several generations of a family residing together, tend to have larger house structures than those in which the usual household units are nuclear families (parents plus children). In fact, study of households has been emphasized in recent archaeological research because these are fundamental organizational units of society.

The next level of settlement analysis is layout of the settlement itself. Here, the site is the unit of analysis, especially sites with evidence of residences (as opposed to kill sites, for example). At this level, archaeologists consider how individual microunits fit together to form larger social units; this allows them to examine aspects of prehistoric social systems from a number of perspectives.

Social stratification, for example, is frequently inferred partly on the basis of evidence from settlement analysis. At the Maya site of Tikal, Guatemala, archaeologists have found that houses are consistent in form throughout the site, but they range considerably in size, decoration, and the relative use of perishable versus stone construction materials. Larger, more substantial houses are assumed to have housed people who had more wealth or other means of controlling and acquiring goods and labor.

Aspects of social control can also be inferred from the regularity of settlement layouts. The site of Teotihuacán, Mexico, with its gridded streets and its orientation to the cardinal directions is a striking example of imposed planning, which implies the presence of a powerful elite class in society able to command and direct the placement of structures and facilities over the landscape. Ancient Chinese political centers were laid out according to a plan whose basis was partly religious, but whose execution required effective social control.

Social and political distinctions along with concerns with privacy or security can be detected archaeologically. For instance, settlement remains at the urban site of Chan Chan, in the Moche Valley of Peru, can be divided into three categories: small poorly constructed residences, intermediate residences, and monumental structures. The three categories reflect differences both of complexity and of regularity of arrangement; the monumental structures, a set of ten enclosures (Fig. 8.8), are the most complex and regular of all. The ways the three categories of residences relate—or were allowed to relate—in space reflect several aspects of Moche social organization. The small dwellings were segregated from the areas of intermediate residences, but the monumental compounds were the grandest and most exclusive of all. Although they encompassed great amounts of space, each had only one or two entrances, allowing its occupants to control strictly with whom they would interact. Each residence category can be equated with the social and status groups in Moche society. The ten compounds are interpreted as the exclusive and private royal residential complexes, the intermediate category as the residences of a distinct wealthy elite class, and the small category as the dwellings of the poorest commoners.

At the broadest level of settlement analysis, archaeologists consider the distribution of sites within a region. This can be approached in two ways. The first is to reconstruct the function of each component in the settlement system and then to look at the various ways in which all the components may have been organized into an interacting social network. The same settlement pattern can reflect a number of different systems of social relationships (Fig. 8.9). MacNeish's Ayacucho subsistence cycle is one example of a particular view of settlement systems. Two different analyses of Paleolithic sites in Europe having a stone-tool assemblage known as Mousterian demonstrate how intangibles like social systems can lead to divergent interpretations. These sites have been divided into a number of types based on differences in their Mousterian tools. François Bordes, a leader in delineating variation in Mousterian artifacts, argued that the different sites reflect occupations by contrasting social groups who used different styles of tool manufacture. Lewis and Sally Binford, however, used statistical analysis of some of the tool assemblages to contend that the variability represents, instead, different tasks being carried out from site to site. Their analysis led them to posit that some of the sites represent residential base camps, while others represent hunting/butchering or other work camps. The contrast in the kinds of social interaction implied by the two interpretations is clear. In one view, the different Mousterian sites represent distinct human social groups doing similar things in different ways; in the other, a single overall group was simply dividing up activities according to appropriate locales. This points out how all aspects of the settlement system must be examined in order to reconstruct the ancient social system.

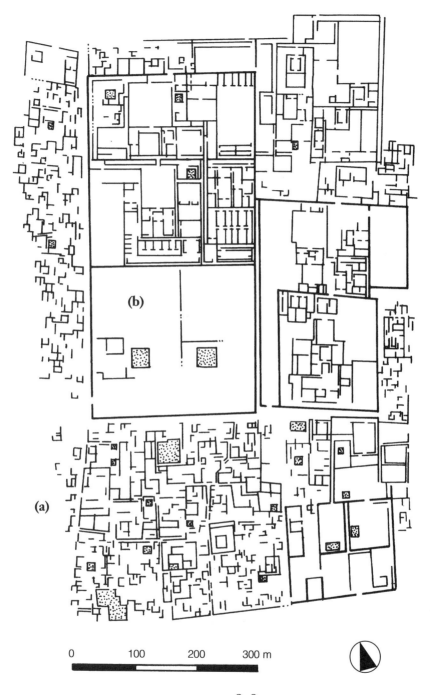

(b)

(a)

0   100   200   300 m

FIGURE 8.8

This portion of the map of Chan Chan, Peru, shows remains of (a) commoner
residential areas contrasting with (b) one of the ten royal walled enclosures
with restricted access from the outside. (After Moseley and Mackey 1974.)

181

OBSERVED SETTLEMENT PATTERN

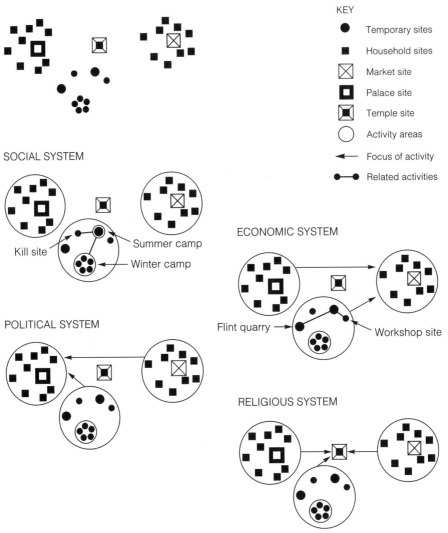

KEY

●   Temporary sites

■   Household sites

⊠   Market site

▣   Palace site

▣   Temple site

○   Activity areas

◄──   Focus of activity

●─●   Related activities

SOCIAL SYSTEM

Kill site

Summer camp

Winter camp

ECONOMIC SYSTEM

Flint quarry

Workshop site

POLITICAL SYSTEM

RELIGIOUS SYSTEM

FIGURE 8.9

A single settlement pattern may be the physical expression of a number of systems of social relations, each of which can be studied at several scales. For example, within the region, some households may live permanently in one place while others move seasonally from one place to another. Although the diverse people of the region may all be governed from a single political capital, it need not be located in the same place as the economic hub or the ritual center. (Redrawn from K. C. Chang, *Settlement Patterns in Archaeology*. © 1972 by The Benjamin/Cummings Publishing Company, Philippines copyright 1972 by The Benjamin/Cummings Publishing Company.)

The second way archaeologists study the distribution of sites is regional analysis, borrowed from economic geography. Many of the actual techniques refer more specifically to **locational analysis** and a particularly important example of these locational techniques called **central place theory**. Underlying this and similar techniques derived from economic geography is the assumption that efficiency and minimization of costs are among the most basic factors in spatial organization of human activities. For instance, an individual settlement will be located where a maximum number of resources can be exploited with the least effort; these resources will include not only aspects of the natural environment but also communication with neighboring groups. As the landscape fills with people, settlements will tend to space themselves evenly across it, and central places—settlements providing a wider variety of goods and services than their neighbors—will arise at regular intervals within the overall distribution. The most efficient pattern for spacing of communities is a hexagonal lattice. This is all in theory, of course; in practice, landscape variables such as steep topography or the presence of uninhabitable areas break up the predicted pattern. Still, a reasonably close approximation of the hexagonal-lattice pattern has been observed in a number of both modern and ancient situations, including Ian Hodder and Mark Hassall's study of Romano-British towns (Fig. 8.10).

A detailed example of settlement analysis is David Clarke's study of a small Iron Age settlement at Glastonbury, England. On the smallest level, many kinds of individual activity areas were defined based on cumulative workshop features that marked the locations of wool spinning, leather working, iron smelting, carpentry, weaving, milking, and animal husbandry. Distinct residential compounds were also identified (Fig. 8.11), each composed of several separate buildings. Individual dwellings were associated with distinct work and storage features; carpentry, metal working, and small corral areas seem to define male subdivisions of the compounds, while baking, spinning, and granary areas suggest female working and living areas.

Study of the Glastonbury site's layout gives an idea of the distribution of activities within the community, including social concerns about channelling traffic and protecting privacy: the settlement as a whole consisted of the seven residential compounds plus paths and intervening open spaces that connected them, an encircling palisade with guard houses at the entrances, and a small pier linking the east entry to the adjacent river. Distinctions among the seven Glastonbury compounds suggested wealth and status differences: the compound of the wealthiest residents was associated with a locally unique array of luxury and imported artifacts such as jewelry and fine pottery; the same compound (Fig. 8.11c) had apparently a long-standing importance, for it had provided the pivot around which the small community grew. Two neighbors also had sizable compounds, but lacked both wealth and higher status goods and facilities for the production of metal and other commodities, thus indicating something of the social hierarchy present even within such a small community.

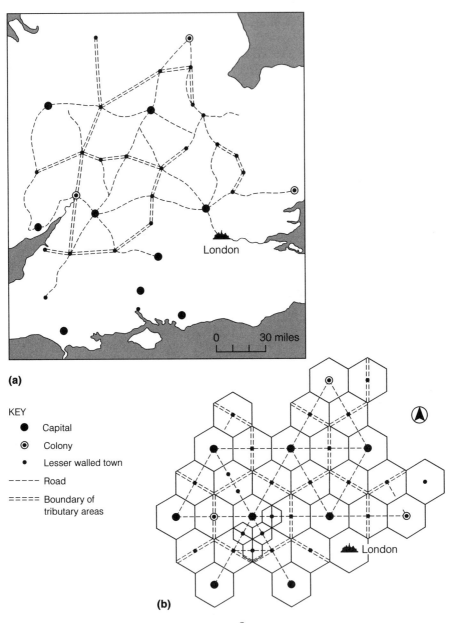

KEY

● Capital

◉ Colony

• Lesser walled town

----- Road

===== Boundary of
tributary areas

FIGURE 8.10

Romano-British settlement in the third century A.D.: (a) plotted on a conventional map, and (b) fitted to an *idealized* hexagonal lattice demonstrating central place theory. (After Hodder and Hassall 1971, by permission of McGraw Hill.)

On a more inclusive scale, Clarke described a series of three ever-larger regions beyond the site proper. The smallest of these regions, within a ten-mile radius of the site, embraced diverse economic resources such as pasture, sources of pottery clay or chipping stone, and fishing areas as well as neighboring settlements. The larger regions incorporated sites and resources up to 20 and 30 miles from Glastonbury, comprising areas within which the ancient residents of Glastonbury were less constantly involved, but which still contributed social, political, and economic settings important to their lives.

Another way that archaeologists can understand a past society is by studying evidence of its exchange system. **Exchange systems** are established so that people can acquire goods and services not normally available to them locally. Trading ventures and institutions arise to carry out cooperative and peaceful exchanges between two or more parties. Of course, there are other means to acquire nonlocal goods and services; foraging expeditions may be used to collect materials from distant sources, and raids or military conquest may plunder foreign lands for wealth and slaves.

The archaeologist may have difficulty in distinguishing trade goods from those acquired by other means, but the distinction is important for at least two reasons. First, the recognition of trade in the archaeological record leads to the reconstruction of past economic systems, and thus contributes to a fuller understanding of the organization of entire ancient societies. Second, since cooperative exchange between individuals and between societies provides a primary means for the transmission of new ideas, recognition of trade helps lead the archaeologist to an understanding of cultural change.

While human exchange systems involve the transfer of goods, services, and ideas, by necessity archaeologists deal directly only with the tangible products of trade, usually recovered as artifacts and ecofacts. These data are traditionally divided into two classes. The first category, utilitarian items, refers to food items; tools for acquiring, storing, and processing food; and other useful materials such as weapons or clothing. The second category, nonutilitarian items, includes the remainder of exchanged commodities, including gifts, ritual items, and status goods.

By considering such distinctions, the archaeologist attempts to reconstruct both the inventory of trade goods and the mechanism of exchange. The goal is to determine the sources, routes, destinations, and consumers of the trade goods. Such reconstructions are based on the archaeologist's ability to separate trade goods from local goods in the archaeological record and to amplify the understanding of ancient acquisition, manufacture, and use behavior (Fig. 8.12).

These data allow the archaeologist to reconstruct ancient trade and its accompanying social interaction by examining spatial patterning from several perspectives, including the presence or absence of certain trade items and quantitative patterns in their occurrence, such as distance decay plots (Fig. 8.13). Simple presence-absence plots show the distributions for one or more categories of traded artifacts and their identified raw-material sources, suggesting the spatial range and even the routes used in ancient trade systems.

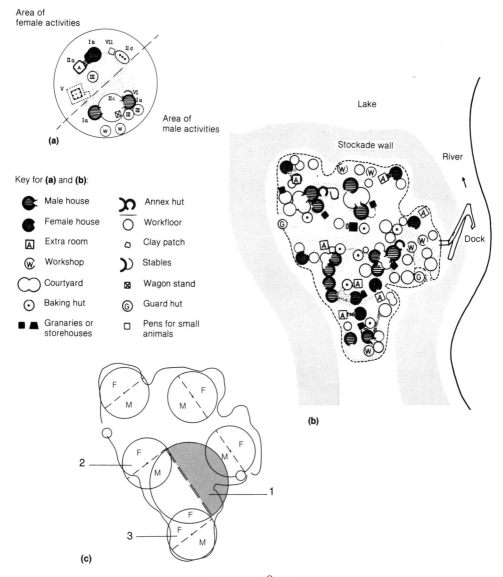

FIGURE 8.11

Iron Age Glastonbury illustrates several levels of settlement archaeology.
(a) An idealized household compound shows the kinds of activity areas
these contain. (b) The site of Glastonbury at the peak of its growth, showing the location of houses and other features. (c) A schematic version of
(b) identifies individual house compounds, each with male-associated (M)
and female-associated (F) areas. The large, partly shaded compound at the
lower right contains both the wealthiest (1) and the poorest house units (2
and 3) in the ancient community. (After Clarke 1972.)

(a)

(b)

FIGURE 8.12

Some nonlocal artifacts can be distinguished as imports because of their style. These two seals are both about 4000 years old and are similar in style. Each depicts a humped bull with a brief inscription above its back. Seal (a) comes from the Indus site of Mohenjo-daro, in Pakistan, where this style of seal is common and where stylistically related artifacts are also found. Seal (b) was discovered at Nippur, in Mesopotamia, where it is stylistically unusual, leading to the inference that it was imported. (Photo a courtesy of George Dales; photo b courtesy of McGuire Gibson.)

Ideological Systems

The final area of archaeological reconstruction, and certainly the most difficult to accomplish, deals with ideology. Ideological systems are the means by which human societies codify their beliefs about both the natural and supernatural worlds. Through ideology, people structure their ideas about the order of the universe, their place in that universe, and their relationships with each other and with things and beings around them. Ancient ideologies are preserved through symbols, which are their material expression. The difficulty in reconstructing ideologies lies not in discovering symbolic representations, but in recognizing them as such and in assigning them an appropriate meaning. For example, artifacts classed as ceremonial would appear to offer the kind of information needed to reconstruct ideologies; too often, however, that label is simply applied to artifacts whose function is unknown.

Archaeologists have traditionally given scant attention to ideology for two reasons. First, since the foundation of archaeology is material remains, it has often been assumed that the realm of ideas lies beyond the reach of archaeological inquiry. Second, since archaeology often emphasizes the processes of

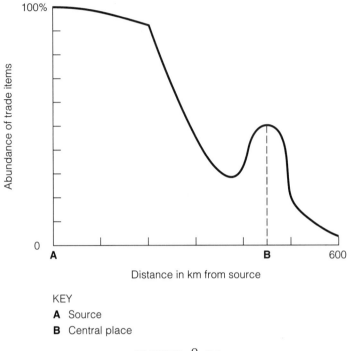

KEY
A Source
B Central place

FIGURE 8.13

The amount of an exchange item reaching a specific destination decreases with the distance of that destination from the source. But the rate of decrease is not completely constant, and the presence of redistribution centers in particular disrupts the distance decay curve. (After Renfrew 1975.)

culture change, ideology, especially religious ideology, has usually been ignored because it is considered a conservative force that resists change.

Thus, even in cases where this dimension of culture can be reconstructed archaeologically, ideologies are often seen as passive rather than causal forces in cultural change. It is often assumed that ideology can be safely disregarded because it is both difficult to deal with and not important to the concerns of archaeology. While the difficulty of inquiry into past ideologies is real, it has become clear that the assumption that ideology is unimportant is false. If ancient ideologies are ignored, our understanding of the past will remain woefully biased and incomplete.

The importance of research into this realm is attested by the expansion of archaeological interest in past ideological systems in recent years. This trend is closely linked to the development of contextual archaeology (see Chapter 3). We will briefly survey several areas of research into past ideologies, beginning with the core issue of recognizing and interpreting symbols.

FIGURE 8.14

A San rock art scene that was traditionally interpreted as people crossing a bridge but has been reinterpreted as a curing ritual based on ethnographic information. (After Lewis-Williams, in *Current Anthropology*, published by the University of Chicago Press, © 1986 by the Wenner-Gren Foundation for Anthropological Research.)

Symbol systems may be preserved in the material remains that archaeologists deal with every day. Symbols are things that stand for something else; the relationship between the symbol and what it stands for is arbitrary. Symbols are thus shorthand ways of conveying messages about often complex subjects. It is this arbitrariness and complexity that makes symbols both rewarding to study and difficult to interpret, especially in the archaeological record. Even when an interpretation seems obvious, there may be no way of testing this conclusion.

As an example, consider the rock art of southern Africa. The paintings come from areas once occupied by San hunter-gatherers, but the San of today have no surviving tradition of painting. Western analysts frequently interpret the pictures as representing life among the ancestral San, and the scene in Figure 8.14 is usually said to show people crossing a rope bridge. J. D. Lewis-Williams argues, however, that if we can step outside our own culture for a moment, and look from the perspective of San customs, the scene can be reinterpreted (and probably more accurately deciphered) as a curing ceremony like those known among the San today. Adopting this contextual perspective, the individuals depicted in the center of the scene have entered a trance; the lines above their heads represent their spirits leaving their bodies, while the dashed lines in front of one figure symbolize an active nosebleed (a frequent side effect

of trance). Other features of the painting likewise fit the trance-scene interpretation. The so-called bridge probably represents two curers facing each
other with outstretched arms, the exaggerated length and hairs of which correspond to sensations experienced in the trances. Whether or not these interpretations are completely correct in detail, they illustrate how easily misled we
may be in interpreting archaeological symbols unless we can consider them
within their own cultural context. Interpretation is possible, but it must be
done with caution.

One category of archaeological data most frequently subjected to symbolic interpretation involves burial practices, including mortuary goods. Much
attention has focused recently on funerary customs as indices of social organization: chiefs are frequently buried in areas separate from paupers, while grave
goods in individual interments are often a gauge of the kinds of possessions the
deceased had in life. John W. Hedges's study of Neolithic communal tombs in
the Orkney Islands of Scotland identified possible prehistoric social symbols
used by the ancient peoples of these islands. The best data came from the
Isbister tomb, used repeatedly for almost a thousand years (ca. 3200–2400 B.C.),
which contained more than 300 individuals and the bones of birds and other
animals. The animals are probably the result of offerings or mortuary feasting.
In contrast, almost all of the bird bones were not from edible species, but from
birds of prey, especially the white-tailed sea eagle. The presence of this species
in such numbers suggests that it had a symbolic meaning for the people who
buried their dead over the generations in this tomb. The distribution of various artifact styles suggested that Neolithic Orkney society was divided into a
number of distinct groups, each with its own chambered tombs. Other tombs
were associated with animal symbols different from the sea eagle. Hedges used
general analogy, relating these practices to the widespread human custom of
using animals as emblems to identify distinct social groups. Thus, the sea eagle
was interpreted as the emblem or symbol of the people who had buried their
dead in the Isbister tomb over four thousand years ago.

Writing systems provide the most regularized means of codifying symbols
(Fig. 8.15). With writing, archaeologists enter the realm of historical documentation, which allows far more complete and accurate interpretations of
ancient ideology. Writing systems were developed by many ancient societies all
over the world; some, like Minoan Linear A script, have not yet been deciphered. Maya hieroglyphic inscriptions have only in recent years been read
with any facility. The earliest writing in Southwest Asia dates to at least 3500
B.C., and people were carving inscriptions in stone in Mesoamerica by the first
millennium B.C. In both cases, the earliest records archaeologists have
unearthed pertain to counting—in the Middle East, to accounting records for
commercial transactions, and in Mesoamerica, to counts of time.

Interestingly, Alexander Marshack has proposed that the earliest known
notational records belong to a far earlier era. Marshack examined the scratches
and marks on a series of Upper Paleolithic bone artifacts, which had usually
been ignored by other scholars, but Marshack detected regularity in such characteristics as angle of nicking or spatial patterning of groups of marks. From

FIGURE 8.15

The earliest known written records are in cuneiform (wedge-shaped) characters, on clay tablets that first appeared in Southwest Asia in the fourth millennium B.C. (Courtesy of the University of Pennsylvania Museum.)

this he has argued that the marks represent the beginnings of notation—the precursors of writing. Marshack has further suggested that the subject of this Upper Paleolithic notation was time, the passage of lunar months, seasons, or other observable time periods. This theme raises an area of archaeological inquiry that has seen a great deal of investigation in recent years—**archaeoastronomy,** or the study of ancient astronomical knowledge from material remains. As noted in Chapter 6, a host of archaeological sites and features throughout the world have been identified as ancient astronomical observatories used to chart the cyclical movements of sun, moon, and other celestial bodies.

Archaeological features with astronomical associations are found throughout the world. In the Americas, astronomer Anthony Aveni and others have studied a variety of constructions in Mesoamerica to discover ancient astronomical alignments. At Cahokia, across the Mississippi from St. Louis, Warren Wittry has identified postholes from a series of large circles of wooden posts, dubbed woodhenges, dated to about A.D. 1000. These circles range from 240 to almost 500 feet in diameter, and may have served as observatories for tracking the seasonal movement of the sun. A variety of archaeoastronomical features identified in Chaco Canyon, New Mexico, have been dated to about the same time. Puebloan peoples of the area today still make daily observation of changes in the position of the sunrise, and a number of Chacoan sites may preserve earlier traces of this custom. Several unusual corner windows in the apartmentlike buildings at the site of Pueblo Bonito, for example, were probably used to observe sunrises (perhaps especially for the winter solstice). At sites located at the east and west ends of the canyon, the positions on the canyon rim that are best situated for observing winter solstice sunrise are marked by engraved sun symbols.

Worldviews represent how people of different cultures define and categorize their social and natural environment, including everything from their attitudes about raising children to burying their dead. Through symbols, some of these beliefs are expressed concretely. But, as we have already seen, there are numerous difficulties in interpreting symbols from the archaeological record.

The most reliable interpretations of symbols and worldviews, of course, can be made for situations in which ethnographic or historical records describe symbols and their meanings. As noted in Chapter 1, however, archaeology complements written texts in the kinds of data provided and balances the documentary bias toward affairs of only certain privileged social groups.

We have already mentioned the obvious difficulties in reconstructing ancient ideologies from material remains, which supported the assumption that these systems were unimportant in affecting the course of culture change. But this assumption has been successfully challenged by a series of studies combining archaeological and historical data that document the active role played by various ideological systems in the evolution of past societies. An excellent illustration is the rapid rise of the Mexica (or Aztec) nation of central Mexico in the 15th century, just prior to the Spanish conquest. The success achieved by the Mexica corresponds closely to a fundamental change in their worldview documented by both history and archaeology, as has been argued by Geoffrey Conrad and Arthur Demarest.

According to Conrad and Demarest, the change of Aztec fortunes was sparked by a reworking of their ideological system in the early 15th century. The ideological reforms were initiated by a few individuals within the ruling elite of Aztec society, and were directed toward creating a new and unified cult organized and controlled by the state. This cult combined economic, social, and religious systems and provided a strong motivation for military conquest. At its core, the cult created a new view of the universe and of the destiny of the Aztec people. According to this revised view, the sun (the Aztec patron deity and source of all life) was engaged in a daily struggle against destruction by the forces of darkness. Only by constantly feeding the sun with the source of its strength, the lives of human warriors, could the Aztecs save the universe from extinction. To support this new ideology and demonstrate that they were the chosen saviors of the universe, the Aztecs rewrote their history and altered their myths explaining the cosmos.

Since the essential food for the sun could only be secured by the taking of warrior captives and sacrificing them, Aztec society became perpetually mobilized towards conquest. Of course, the practical benefits from this military expansion included considerable wealth, for tribute was extracted from their vanquished enemies. But an essential motivation and key to the Aztecs' success as conquerors was ideological. Although both militarism and human sacrifice were practiced by all peoples of ancient Mexico, the Aztecs were unique in intensifying the scale of both to an unprecedented degree. Convinced that they were chosen to perpetuate the universe, the Aztec warriors fought with a fanatic zeal, believing that they could not fail. Facing this new military fanaticism dedicated to conquest and human sacrifice, many of the Aztecs' enemies lost their will to resist and succumbed in terror.

The Aztecs' belief in their destiny was reinforced by their initial successes, but soon these successes produced an internal crisis. The huge increases in wealth and power gained from conquest led to greater economic and social distinctions within Aztec society, which produced resentment and internal conflict. Moreover, fatal flaws in the new ideological system itself produced a more insidious crisis. The view of the universal struggle between sun and darkness assumed an infinite supply of enemy warriors, but the availability of this nourishment for the sun was soon threatened as the numbers of opponents diminished. The Aztecs compensated for this by, in effect, encouraging rebellions against their authority, since they did little to impose their control over conquered peoples. The uprisings that this policy produced gave the Aztecs new opportunities to capture additional warriors for sacrifice. But the consequences of inevitable defeats on the battlefield were more damaging to Aztec society. As the demands for human life and tribute mounted, determination to resist the Aztec terror increased. Eventually the Aztecs confronted enemies that could not be conquered, and, more troublesome, enemies that inflicted devastating defeats on their own armies. To the Aztecs, these events meant that their universe was threatened, since the sun was being weakened by fewer human sacrifices. Compounding this threat, each military disaster weakened the confidence and will of the entire society, for military failures challenged Aztec belief in their role as saviors of the universe. In sum, the ideology that led to a cycle of victories and confidence eventually yielded a cycle of defeats and demoralization.

Thus, Conrad and Demarest's interpretation illustrates both how a worldview can be reconstructed and how crucial ideology can be in the organization and motivation of human society. The Aztec ideological system guided and justified a military, economic, and political expansion that eventually dominated central Mexico. This development was due, in large measure, to a reformulated religious ideology created by a handful of their leaders. This is not to say that ideology should be viewed as the only or even the prime cause of culture change. Economic and other factors played a role in both the rise and decline of the Aztecs. But history is full of similar examples of ideologies that have made significant contributions to the direction and development of society, including the rise and fall of nations. Archaeologists must heed the lesson of these examples. They cannot ignore the role of ideology if they wish to reconstruct the past as fully as possible.

SUMMARY

Because past activities can never be directly observed, similarities between these data and the material correlates of living societies (either observed directly or recorded in historical or ethnographic accounts) are the basis for reconstructing the past. Reasoning by analogy has not always been correctly applied in archaeology, but use of logical guidelines can reduce or eliminate inaccuracies. For specific analogy, these guidelines are based on continuity of occupation, similarity of environmental setting, and comparability of cultural forms between the archaeological situation and the proposed analog. For general analogy, actualistic studies define links between particular behaviors and their material traces. The more analog links that can be established, using sources such as history, ethnography, and actualistic studies done by archaeologists, the more secure will be the proposed reconstruction.

Analogy is paired with examination of spatial order in archaeological data to reconstruct the varieties of ancient behavior. Human activities can be divided into three broad areas—technology, social systems, and ideology.

Technology refers to the behavior most closely related to the environment, best approached in archaeology through the concept of cultural ecology. This relationship is complex, for each environment provides a range of resources, and each culture defines, through capabilities and choices, which of these are actually used. As a result, understanding ancient technology requires study not only of cultural remains but also of the environment in which they were used.

Past social systems—the kinds of human organizations that channel human behavior—are reconstructed in various ways. Settlement archaeology relies on the spatial distribution of archaeological remains as reflections of the full range of human behavior, from single activity areas to households, sites, and entire regions. At this broader end of the scale, archaeologists study ancient exchange systems—the means used by human societies to procure nonlocal goods and services. These studies attempt to determine which artifacts or ecofacts are nonlocal and thus may reflect exchanges with other places. Reconstruction of these organizations rests on analogies drawn from ethnography, economics, geography, and other sources.

Ideological systems, the means used by human societies to codify their knowledge and beliefs, are the most difficult of human activities to approach archaeologically, since this kind of behavior is often marked by relatively fewer and more enigmatic material remains. Identification and study of symbols provide one approach, but while the archaeological record is full of such symbols, their proper interpretation is often difficult. Writing systems, when present, can provide the most direct evidence of ideological systems for, if deciphered, they allow reading of messages. Other notational forms, such as counts of astronomical or other events, also provide clues to ancient ideologies. Worldviews furnish the underlying concepts about the universe that guide individual behavior and the course of human societies. In order to provide the most complete reconstruction of the past possible, archaeology attempts to understand the roles played by technology, social systems, and ideology.

FOR FURTHER READING

ANALOGY

Binford 1967, 1978; Bordes 1968; Charleton 1981; Coles 1973; Crabtree 1972; Deetz 1977; Gould 1980; Keeley 1980; Lee and Devore 1968; Semenov 1964; Wauchope 1938

SPATIAL ORDER AND BEHAVIOR

Aveni 1982; Binford and Binford 1969; Bordes 1968; Chang 1972; Conrad and Demarest 1984; Ericson and Earle 1982; Hedges 1984; Hodder 1982; MacNeish et al. 1972; MacNeish, Patterson, and Browman 1975; Moseley and Mackey 1974

ADDITIONAL SOURCES

Andresen et al. 1981; Arnold 1985; Brain 1981; Butzer 1982; Clarke 1972b; Cowgill 1974; Hadingham 1984; Heggie 1982; Hodder and Hassall 1971; Hyslop 1984; Isaac 1984; Lewis-Williams 1986; Longacre and Ayres 1968; Marshack 1972; Netting 1977; Price and Brown 1985; Renfrew 1975, 1983; Topping 1978; Trigger 1968; Trinkaus 1987; Tuan 1977; Ucko 1969; Wilk and Rathje 1982; Willey 1953; Wittry 1977

Understanding the Past

IN THIS CHAPTER WE complete the final step in archaeological research—the reconstruction and interpretation of the past. We began this process in Chapters 7 and 8, where we considered how the analyses of different data categories (artifacts, ecofacts, and features) are combined across time and space to interpret those data. Those chapters involved interpretation in a descriptive sense—attempts to answer questions such as *what* happened in the past, *when* it happened, and *where* it happened. In this chapter, we turn to a more explanatory aspect that addresses the questions of *how* and *why* it happened.

To illustrate the differences, let us examine the cultures that successively occupied the Great Plains of the United States, each of which exploited a different aspect of the region's varied resources. The *what* of our understanding of the sequence is provided by the analysis of the archaeological and historical data pertaining to these cultures. The same sources describe *when* and *where* the cultures existed and *where* they lived within the Great Plains. But *how* did a new culture take the place of the old? And *why*?

The prehistoric occupants of the Plains were limited in their day-to-day mobility. The remains of stone weapons, campsites, bones of game animals, and plants tell us that those who hunted and gathered for their food exploited a wide variety of food sources (hunting small game, occasionally hunting large game, gathering wild plant foods, and so on) in small, localized groups. Some groups took up cultivation of maize (originally derived from Mexico) and other plants late in the first millennium A.D. In the 17th century, some adopted a new technology by hunting on horseback (the horses had been introduced by the Spanish) and thereby gained an increased mobility, speed, and transport capability that enabled them to specialize in the hunting of large game animals (bison). Because of this specialization, these groups proved vulnerable to outside invaders (Euro-American colonists) who had a different technology. This new technology included the repeating rifle, which was used to decimate the herds of bison and thereby destroy the subsistence base of the mobile Plains societies, and the plow, which allowed the invading settlers to harness a previously unexploited portion of the environment for extensive agriculture. What had been a land of hunters and horticulturalists, became a land of hunters, then a land of plow farmers. Of course, in the 20th century, a still-newer technology has led to the industrialized exploitation of yet another portion of this same environment—the vast deposits of fossil fuel and water located beneath the surface of the Plains.

It is easy to describe the what, when, and where of this simplified sequence of Great Plains cultures. But how and why did the changes take place? Some of the mechanisms of change—the "how"—are evident: adoption of ideas from other cultures, invasion, migration. Interpreting the reasons why the ideas took hold in the new culture, however, or why the mass movement of people took place (either peacefully or with violence)—is more difficult and controversial.

In this chapter we will discuss the principal models archaeologists have used to answer the questions of how and why things happened as they did. Our discussion of archaeological interpretation will follow the three approaches first introduced in Chapter 3, cultural history, cultural process, and contextual archaeology. Through the use of all three approaches, archaeologists meet the general goals of their research: to reconstruct, describe, and explain human behavior in the past.

CULTURAL HISTORY INTERPRETATION

In Chapter 3 we described the research goals and frameworks of cultural history archaeology. The temporal and spatial synthesis of the archaeological data produced by this approach provides the foundation for interpretation. The analogs used for cultural history interpretation usually presuppose a normative view of culture, describing idealized rules for how things should be done—how pottery should be made, what house forms were prescribed, and so on. These models are primarily descriptive, not explanatory, in that they identify and describe the elements and trends of cultural change, but these models do not attempt to describe the relationships among elements or identify the causes of change.

Because the cultural history approach emphasizes chronology and cultural change, most of the interpretive models used are diachronic, identifying and describing change in the archaeological record through time. A distinction can be made between those models that emphasize internal sources of change and those that focus on external stimuli (Fig. 9.1).

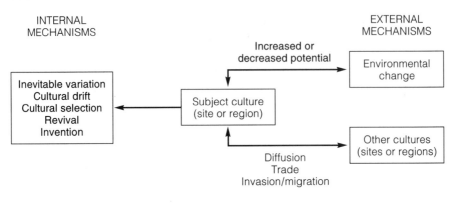

FIGURE 9.1

Cultural history interpretation is based on models that describe cultural change as proceeding from either internal or external mechanisms.

Internal cultural models describe mechanisms of change within a given culture. The most general of these mechanisms is **inevitable variation,** which follows the simple premise that all cultures inevitably change through time. One particular version is that all cultures experience growth and development analogous to that of a living organism; they grow, mature, and eventually die (the rise and fall of civilization). The inevitable variation model is so simplistic and general that it is of little use in archaeological interpretation: we do not increase our understanding by saying that Rome fell apart because it was destined to do so. Of greater benefit to archaeological interpretation are internal cultural models that identify specific variables with which to describe the mechanisms of cultural change.

How does this change come about? The human species is inquisitive and innovative. **Cultural invention** is the result of these human qualities; new ideas originate within a culture, either by accident or design. But to attribute to invention the appearance of a given trait in the archaeological record at a particular place, the archaeologist must demonstrate that the trait was not introduced from outside by trade or some other external mechanism. An example is the controversy over the early occurrence of bronze metallurgy in Southeast Asia. Proponents of an independent-invention model point out that cast bronze artifacts found in Thailand rival those of Southwest Asia in age. The counterargument is that Southwest Asia exhibits a full range of evidence for the local development of metallurgical technology, including evidence of workshops as well as evidence of gradually increasing sophistication in metalworking techniques. In order to establish that Southeast Asia was indeed an independent center for the invention of metallurgy, archaeological research is seeking equivalent evidence to that found in Southwest Asia, enabling archaeologists to document the local prototypes and developmental steps leading to an independent invention of bronze metallurgy.

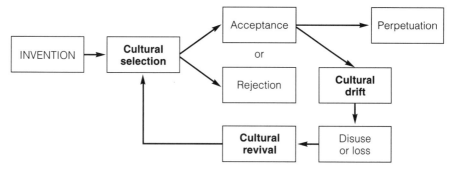

FIGURE 9.2

Internally induced cultural change is affected by the filtering mechanisms of cultural selection, cultural drift, and revival.

To contribute to cultural change, an invention must be accepted in a culture. Two general models, both founded on loose analogies to biological evolution, have been offered to describe mechanisms of acceptance, perpetuation, or rejection of new cultural traits (Fig. 9.2). The first, **cultural selection,** mirrors the biological concept of natural selection. According to this model, those cultural traits that are advantageous to members of a society are accepted or retained while those that are useless or actively harmful tend to be discarded. This tendency results in gradual and cumulative change through time. Selection can act on any cultural trait, whether technological, social, or ideological. Whether a given trait is advantageous or not depends ultimately upon whether it contributes to—or hinders—the survival and well-being of those who adopt it. For example, investment of power in a central authority figure may increase efficiency in food production, resolution of disputes, and management of interactions with neighboring societies. If such centralization of authority leads the society in question to prosper, centralization is advantageous and selection will favor its perpetuation. If, however, the society falls on hard times as a result of centralization—perhaps because of inept leadership—authority is likely to become more dispersed again.

Selection acts against innovative traits that are inconsistent with prevailing cultural values or norms. Generally speaking, technological inventions are more likely to be accepted than social or ideological ones because they are less likely to conflict with value systems. A new form of axe head, for instance, usually has an easier path to acceptance than does a change in the authority hierarchy or an innovative religious belief.

A related model, often labeled **cultural drift** (see Fig. 9.2), describes a mechanism complementary to that of cultural selection. Like selection, this process results in change through time, but it is a random process. Cultural traits are transmitted from one generation to the next by learning. Cultural drift results from the fact that cultural transmission is incomplete or imperfect; no individual ever learns all the information possessed by any other member of the society. Hence cultural changes through time have a random aspect. Sally Binford and others have suggested that cultural drift may be responsible for some of the variations in artifacts of early Paleolithic tool assemblages. That is, the accumulation of minor changes gives a superficial impression of deliberate stylistic innovation, but only after about a million years of development in these tool traditions can consistent styles be discerned.

Another source for cultural change is the **cultural revival** of elements that have fallen into disuse (Fig. 9.2). A number of stimuli may lead to the revival of old forms, including the chance rediscovery and reacceptance of old styles, reoccurrence of specific needs, and duplication of treasured heirlooms. One model relates revival to a coping response to stressful situations. Some kinds of stress elicit technological responses: for example, townspeople construct a fortification wall as a defense against siege. In other cases, societies deal with stress by social or ideological means. Cultural anthropologist Anthony F. C. Wallace developed a model that describes rapid and radical cultural change in the face of stress. This revitalization model refers to situations in which members of a society perceive their culture as falling apart, unable to provide them with an adequate standard of living. According to Wallace, a leader emerges who revives old symbols associated with earlier periods of well-being, squashes those identified with the stressful situation, inspires positive and prideful identification with the society, and promises renewed prosperity if people adhere to the new rules that are set down.

External cultural models describe change by the introduction of new customs from outside a particular society (Fig. 9.3). When a custom, such as that resulting from the acceptance of an invention, has become established within one society, its utility or prestige may allow it to spread far beyond its place of origin. The spread of new ideas and objects is a complex process. Various modes of dispersal are well documented by both history and ethnography; these are often used as models for cultural history interpretation. These include the spread of ideas (diffusion), the dispersal of material objects by exchange or trade, and the movement of human populations through migration or invasion and conquest.

Diffusion occurs under a variety of circumstances: any contact between individuals from different societies involves the potential transmission of new ideas from one culture to another. When a given society is exposed to a new idea, that idea may be accepted unchanged, reworked or modified to better fit the accepting culture, or completely rejected (governed by much the same factors that determine the fate of internal inventions).

The archaeological record contains numerous examples of ideas that have diffused over varying distances with varying degrees of acceptance. The pre-Columbian 260-day ritual calendar of Mesoamerica is found in a wide range of cultural contexts; although specific attributes such as day names vary from one society to the next, the essential unity of this calendrical system reflects a long-term exchange of ideas over a wide geographical area.

Diffusion is a well-documented mechanism of culture change in societies known from history and ethnography. Because diffusion is so common and

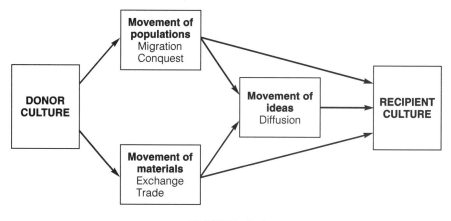

FIGURE 9.3

Externally induced cultural change includes the mechanisms of diffusion, trade, migration, invasion, and conquest.

because evidence of more specific mechanisms such as trade, migration, invasion, and invention is sometimes difficult to find, cultural history interpretations have relied heavily on this model. All too often, however, the concept is used uncritically, with *any* observed similarity between cultures attributed to diffusion. An extreme example of this kind of abuse is found in the diffusionist school of anthropology of the early 20th century, especially the branch that traced all world civilizations to roots in dynastic Egypt. Proponents such as Sir Grafton Elliot Smith argued that the observed distribution of widespread traits of civilization such as divine kingship and pyramid construction resulted from diffusion from a single Egyptian source. When applied in more plausible ways, however, the concept of diffusion rests on documenting how and why the cultures involved were in communication with each other.

Although diffusion is often an elusive mechanism, easy to invoke and difficult to substantiate, contact and communication via **trade** can frequently be demonstrated. This is because trade involves the exchange of material objects; the less perishable of these may be recovered by the archaeologist as artifacts and ecofacts, as discussed in Chapter 8. Once trade goods have been identified, archaeologists may be able to reconstruct ancient trade routes by plotting both the distribution of sources of material and the observed distribution of products from these sources. The important implication of trade distributions for cultural change is that archaeologists can use them to demonstrate contact between groups. When an obsidian trade route is reconstructed, for example, a minimal inference is that obsidian thus became available to people who could add tools made from that material to their cultural inventory. More broadly, however, the observed distribution of obsidian is concrete evidence of contact between groups, which potentially allowed the transmission of a much greater array of materials and ideas, some of which may leave no material trace in the archaeological record.

Another mechanism of culture change is the movement of populations, both as **migrations** and as aggressive **conquests.** Cultural history interpretations often cite these movements to account for evidence of widespread and rapid change. Emil W. Haury listed four conditions that must be met for an archaeologist to argue that migration has occurred:

1. A number of new cultural traits must appear suddenly, too many to be feasibly accounted for by diffusion, invention, or trade, and none having earlier local prototypes.
2. Some local materials should be modified in form, style, or function by the newcomers.
3. A source for the immigrant population must be identified—a homeland where the intrusive cultural elements have prototypes.
4. The artifacts used as indices of population movement must exist in the same form at the same time level in both the homeland and the newly adopted home.

As an example, Haury noted that new architectural styles, both sacred and secular, along with very specific ceramic attributes, appear suddenly in one particular sector of the prehistoric site of Point of Pines, Arizona. At the same time level, some distinctively "foreign" design elements are found on locally made pottery vessels, also recovered in this same sector. These findings supply the first two kinds of evidence needed to postulate a migration. Looking for a source for these cultural traits, he found the same elements in association at sites in northern Arizona on an equivalent time level. Finally, Haury noted that independent evidence points to a population decline in the proposed homeland at the appropriate time.

Migration can be contrasted with its more violent counterpart, conquest. This also involves population movements, but with presumably more drastic effects on the way of life of the recipient society. Elements cited as evidence of conquest include massive burning or other destruction of buildings in a settlement, usually accompanied by large-scale loss of human life (Fig. 9.4).

The change brought about by conquest may, of course, be the annihilation of the existing population, sometimes with no replacement by the intruders. In many cases, however, part of the original population survives and stays on, often under the political domination of the invaders. The invaders may bring in new cultural elements, but even historically documented conquests show up rather inconsistently in the archaeological record. A case in point is the Spanish conquest of the Americas in the 16th century. Both European and native chronicles of the period attest to the extent and severity of the changes wrought by the Spanish. Even so, archaeologists working in a number of the affected areas, including Mexico, Guatemala, and Peru, have sometimes had difficulty in identifying evidence of the Spanish arrival in the archaeological record. At some sites, European artifacts clearly appear, but local pottery and other traits often remain unchanged for long periods after the conquest. With

FIGURE 9.4

Evidence of cultural change through conquest can take dramatic forms.
This photograph shows human skeletal remains sprawled among the
remains of burned buildings in the walled palace compound of Hasanlu,
Iran, the result of the 9th century B.C. destruction of the city. (Courtesy of
Robert H. Dyson, Jr., and the Hasanlu Project, University of
Pennsylvania Museum.)

reference to Haury's criteria, then, archaeologists can positively identify some
prehistoric population movements, but the example just given argues rather
strongly that not all such movements—violent or peaceful—can be accurately
detected in the archaeological record.

Environmental change is used in cultural history interpretation as an
external factor (Fig. 9.1), independent of culture, that nonetheless may affect
the destiny of human society. This model describes rather general environmental sources of cultural change. In most cases, cultural history models of
culture and environment hold that each has the potential to modify the other
(Fig. 9.5). A dramatic example of the cultural impact of an environmental
change can be seen in the effects of the eruption of the volcano that formed

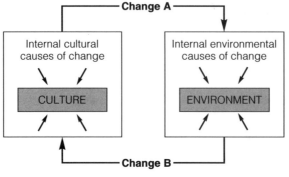

KEY
A Environmental change caused by cultural factors
B Cultural change caused by environmental factors

FIGURE 9.5

The cultural history approach stresses a simple interaction between culture and environment, based on the capability of each to modify the other (compare with Fig. 9.9).

Sunset Crater, near Flagstaff, Arizona, sometime in the middle of the 11th century A.D. The initial effect of the eruption was to drive away all residents in the approximately 800 square miles blanketed by the black volcanic ash. A century later, however, the area was resettled by a diverse population that apparently took advantage of the rich mulching action of the volcanic soil. By A.D. 1300, however, the environment had changed again: wind had converted the ash cover to shifting dunes, exposing the original hard clay soil. Once again, the human settlers moved away.

In contrast, culture also changes environment. A change in technology may redefine the environment by increasing or decreasing the range of exploitable resources. Agricultural overuse may exhaust local soils; the clearing of trees on hillsides may foster erosion, landslides, and ultimately—by increasing the load deposited in a streambed by runoff—flooding. Alteration of the natural environment by cultural activities is not an exclusively modern phenomenon; the alterations today may be far more catastrophic and extensive than before, but they are part of a long, global tradition of cultural impact on the natural world.

CULTURAL PROCESSUAL INTERPRETATION

The second major approach to reconstructing the past is by using processual interpretation. As we saw in Chapter 3, this approach is based on ecological and materialist views of culture and uses both systems and multilinear evolutionary

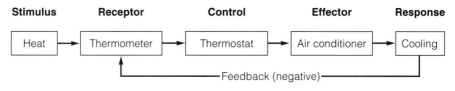

Stimulus	Receptor	Control	Effector	Response
Heat	Thermometer	Thermostat	Air conditioner	Cooling

Feedback (negative)

FIGURE 9.6

Diagram of a homeostatic temperature control system illustrating the operation of a closed system.

models to explain the past. Although the descriptive models discussed earlier are usually associated with cultural history reconstruction, they may also be applied in processual interpretations. As we have noted, cultural history models often generate hypotheses that are tested, modified, and advanced as explanations for prehistoric cultural processes. But just as some models are used more frequently in cultural history reconstructions, certain others are primarily associated with processual explanations.

Systems models recognize that an organization represents more than a simple sum of its parts; in fact, they emphasize the study of the relations between these parts. Two kinds of systems can be defined: open and closed. Closed systems receive no matter, energy, or information from other systems; all sources of change are internal. Open systems exchange matter, energy, and information with other systems; change can come either from within or from outside. Living organisms and sociocultural systems are open systems. In order to understand how systems operate, we will examine systems models that are often applied in cultural process interpretations.

Let us begin with a simple closed systems model. As an example, consider the components and relationships within a self-regulated temperature control system, such as those found within many modern buildings (Fig. 9.6). The components in the system are the air in the room or building, the thermometer, the thermostat, and the heater or air conditioner. In this case, a change in the air temperature acts as a stimulus that is detected by the thermometer and transmitted to the thermostat. When the temperature rises above a predetermined level, the thermostat triggers the air conditioner. The cooling response acts as **feedback** by stimulating the same interdependent components to shut down the air conditioner once the temperature has gone below the critical level.

This closed system illustrates how certain systems operate to maintain a stable condition, or steady state. When a specific change in one part of the system threatens the steady state, this stimulates a response from other component parts. When the steady state has been restored, a feedback loop shuts down the response. Feedback of this kind is **negative** in that it dampens or cuts off the system's response and thus maintains a condition of dynamic equilibrium in which the system's components are active, but the overall system is

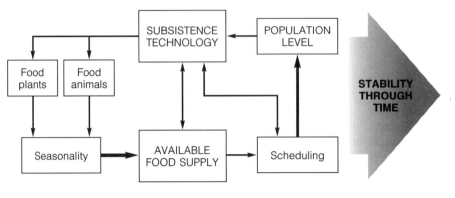

FIGURE 9.7

Simplified diagram of a system characterized by negative feedback mechanisms (→) that lead to population and cultural stability through time;
based on data from prehistoric Mesoamerica (ca. 8000–5000 B.C.). The
larger arrow at the right indicates the trajectory of the system as a whole.

stable and unchanging. Although they are useful for illustrating the operation
of systems, such models are applicable only to unchanging and stable aspects of
human societies.

Since archaeologists are more often concerned with cultural change, we must
also consider dynamic systems models that can account for cumulative systemic change. The most commonly applied model for this deals with **positive
feedback,** which stimulates change within the system. A good example of the
application of these concepts to an archaeological situation is Kent Flannery's
systems model for the development of food production in Mesoamerica. In
setting forth the model, Flannery first describes the food procurement system used by peoples of highland Mexico between about 8000 and 5000 B.C.
(Fig. 9.7). The components of this system were the people themselves, their
technology—including knowledge and equipment—for obtaining food, and
the plants and animals actually used for food.

People in the highland valleys lived in small groups, periodically coming
together into larger "macrobands" but not settling down in permanent villages.
The subsistence technology available to them included knowledge of edible
plants and animals that could be procured by gathering and hunting techniques, as well as the implements and facilities for procurement. Among the
food items actively used were cactus, avocado, white-tailed deer, rabbits, and so
on. Wild grasses related to maize were sometimes eaten but did not form a very
important part of the diet.

This food procurement system was regulated and maintained by negative
feedback acting through seasonality and scheduling. Seasonality refers to characteristics of the food resources themselves—some were available only during
one season or another. To gather enough food, the people had to go where it

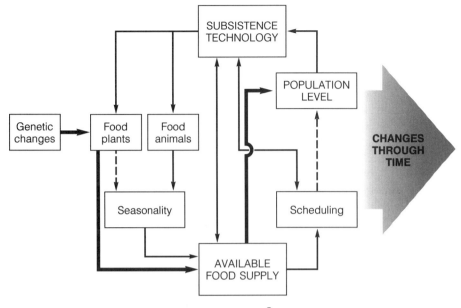

FIGURE 9.8

Simplified diagram of a system characterized by positive feedback
mechanisms (→) that both weaken the negative feedback mechanisms
in Fig. 9.7 and lead to population growth and cultural change stimulated
by genetic changes; based on data from prehistoric Mesoamerica (after
5000 B.C.).

was available. Periodic abundance of particular resources allowed people to
come together into temporary macrobands, but the seasons of lean resources
placed sharply defined limits on both total population and effective social
group size. Scheduling, the other negative feedback mechanism, refers to the
people's organizational response to seasonality. Seasonally scheduled population movement and diet diversity prevented exhaustion of resources by overex-
ploitation, but it also kept population levels low.

This stable system persisted for several thousand years. But according to
Flannery, sometime after 5000 B.C., genetic changes in some of the wild maize
stimulated a positive feedback system (Fig. 9.8). Improved traits of the maize,
such as larger cob size, induced people to reproduce the improved grass by
sowing. As a result, scheduling patterns were gradually altered. For instance,
planting and harvesting requirements increased the time spent in spring and
autumn camps, precisely where larger population gatherings had been feasible
before. The larger, more stable population groupings then invested more time
and labor in improving the quality and quantity of crop yield; this positive feedback continued to induce change in the subsistence system. For example, irrigation technology was developed to extend agriculture and settlement into

more arid zones. As Flannery says, the "positive feedback following these initial genetic changes caused one minor [sub]system to grow out of all proportion to the others, and eventually to change the whole ecosystem of the Southern Mexican Highlands."

Although some cultural systems may maintain a state of dynamic equilibrium for long periods of time, all cultures do change. Not all change involves growth, however. Sometimes positive feedback results in cultural loss or decline, and ultimately in dissolution of the system. The modern case of the Ik of East Africa, described by ethnographer Colin Turnbull, provides an example of such decline. Disruption of traditional behavior patterns by such factors as forced migration from preferred lands led to apathy, intragroup hostility, a devaluation of human life, and population decline. The result in this case is as dramatically bleak as Flannery's is dramatically positive. Most cases of cultural change are less extreme, as cultural systems are affected simultaneously by both growth and decline of subsystems within them in a gradual and cumulative course of change.

Cultural ecology models are a category of systems models that provide a more sophisticated understanding of the interaction between culture and environment than do cultural history models discussed previously. Whereas the cultural history approach often treated environment as a single entity, cultural ecology considers a given culture as interacting with an environmental system composed of three complex subsystems, the physical landscape, the biological environment, and the cultural environment, which refers to other adjacent human groups (Fig. 9.9).

For any given society, the sum of specific interactions contained within its overall cultural ecology describes the nature of the society's **cultural adaptation.** Each society adjusts itself or adapts to its environment primarily through its technological system, but these adaptations are reinforced through the social and ideological systems. The technological system interacts directly with all three components of the environment—physical, biological, and cultural— by providing, for instance, the tools and techniques required for securing shelter, food, and defense. The social system adapts by integrating and organizing society. The relationship described earlier between band organization and seasonality and scheduling in preagricultural highland Mexican societies is an example of social system adaptation to the biological environment. The ideological system is adaptive in that it reinforces the organization and integration of society by providing motivation, explanation, and confidence in the appropriateness of the technological and social adaptations.

Of course, the full set of interactions within such a complex system is difficult to study all at once. As a result, archaeologists often begin by isolating one or more of the subordinate systems directly involved in cultural adaptation. The technological system is the obvious focus of studies seeking to understand the adaptive process. Fortunately for the prehistoric archaeologist, not only is the technological subsystem a most obvious agent of cultural adaptation, but the remains of ancient technology are also usually the fullest part of the archaeological record. These technological data may be used to reconstruct a partic-

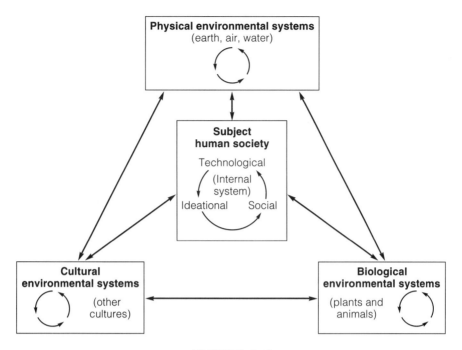

FIGURE 9.9

The cultural ecology system, illustrating the relationships between a given culture (the subject human society) and its environment, composed of physical, cultural, and biological subsystems (compare with Fig. 9.5).

ular aspect of the technological system, such as subsistence. Archaeologists then integrate their detailed models of different subsystems to create complex models of overall cultural adaptation, much as Flannery did in the example from Mexico described earlier.

Because of the mass of information involved in such models, computers are often used for information storage and processing. Computers also enable archaeologists to perform experimental manipulations of their models. After a hypothetical change is introduced in one component of a stable system, a **computer simulation** determines what kind of feedback would be induced by the original change. For example, Ezra Zubrow has used computer simulations to examine relationships among human population size and structure, biological resources of the environment, and settlement location in the prehistoric Southwestern United States. He finds that changing the characteristics of any of these system components produces different projected courses of population growth and decline.

In an analogy to biological adaptation, some archaeologists measure the effectiveness of cultural adaptation by the rate of population growth and resultant population size. In this sense, population growth and size are a measurable response to the overall cultural ecology system (see Fig. 9.9). With regard to population increase, some societies are characterized by one or more positive feedback mechanisms. For example, changes in the technological system may provide more efficient food production and storage capabilities, resulting in an increase in population. Changes in the social or ideational systems will follow to accommodate the population growth; these in turn may allow more efficient food distribution or expansion via conquest or colonization to open new areas for food production, resulting in still further population growth. This may place new stress on technology, which must respond with new changes to increase the food supply, and so forth. The result is an interrelated cycle of change and population growth, perhaps best illustrated by the phenomenon of recent world population growth.

However, successful adaptation (biological or cultural) can also be marked by stability of population size. Some societies maintain population stability by negative feedback mechanisms, including their own culturally acceptable population control methods (birth control, infanticide, warfare), migration, and social fissioning. Environmental mechanisms, including periodic famine or endemic disease, may also contribute to the maintenance of such systems.

Multilinear cultural evolutionary models constitute the final perspective of processual interpretation to be considered. These models combine the materialist view of culture and the adaptation concept of cultural ecology. In so doing, they view the evolution of culture as the cumulative changes in a system resulting from the continuous process of cultural adaptation over extensive periods of time. But how does the archaeologist reveal the causes of evolutionary change? Two schools of thought have emerged. The first emphasizes the identification of universal prime movers of cultural change; the second seeks multiple and variable causes.

The search for **prime movers** emphasizes the identification of a few specific, primary factors that underlie the process of cultural change and cultural evolution. It is based on the premise that the regularities and patterns in evolutionary change result from regularities of cause. Accordingly, this approach emphasizes the testing of broad hypotheses that seek the fundamental, far-reaching causes of all cultural change.

Population growth is often proposed as a fundamental cause of cultural change. This prime mover has been applied in various regions to explain the course of cultural evolution. For example, William T. Sanders and Barbara Price based their thesis for the development of pre-Columbian Mesoamerican culture through a succession of five evolutionary stages upon population growth and its effects upon two secondary factors, competition and cooperation (Fig. 9.10). Other prime movers, such as warfare or agriculture based on irrigation, have been proposed to explain evolutionary developments such as the rise of complex state societies.

The **multivariate strategy** attempts to delineate the basic processes of cultural change by focusing on specific subsystems most directly involved in each instance of cultural adaptation. In order to identify the focus of change, research of this kind may test hypotheses concerned, for example, with a variety of alternative subsistence modes or with the acquisition and distribution of critical natural resources. Since each instance of change is considered unique,

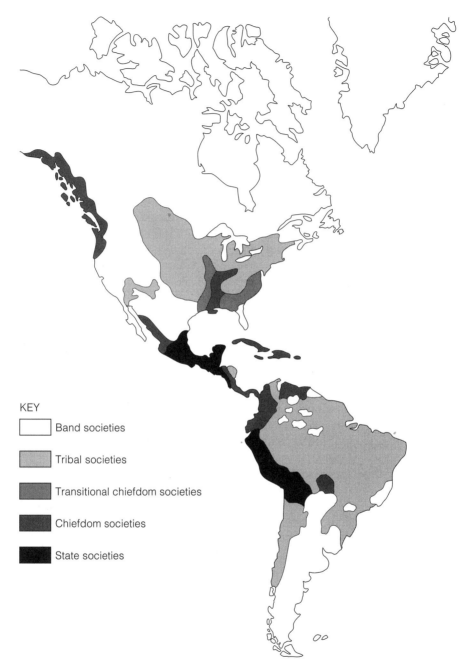

FIGURE 9.10

Map summarizing the distribution of New World societies in 1492, classified by organizational complexity according to one version of a multilinear
evolutionary model. (After Sanders and Price 1968, *Mesoamerica: The
Evolution of a Civilization.* Copyright McGraw Hill.)

this model holds that no single factor or small group of prime movers causes all cultural change. Cultural evolution, the overall product of change, is thus viewed within each society as the product of a unique series of adaptive adjustments of the sort that are a constant feature of all cultural systems. It is this perspective that gives this model of culture change its name—*multivariate*. Specific examples, such as Flannery's models for the transformation from hunting-and-gathering subsistence to food production, build upon this premise and call for substantial cumulative cultural changes over a sufficient period of time.

The multivariate concept of cultural evolution is usually based on cultural ecology and systems models. This approach requires that the archaeologist identify the components of, and understand the relationships among, the specific subsystems crucial to cultural adaptation. This is not an easy task, especially given the inherent limitations of archaeological data. The archaeologist must formulate and test a series of sophisticated hypotheses, using data that are often difficult to collect. As in the case of the transformation to food production in Mesoamerica described earlier in this chapter, such research may show that multivariate causes effectively explain fundamental cultural change.

CONTEXTUAL INTERPRETATION

Since contextual archaeology is still very much a developing approach, its interpretive frameworks are less well-defined. Contextual archaeology uses a cognitive culture concept (see Chapter 3), in which culture consists of the set of meanings each individual constructs and modifies in living and making sense of their lives. This emphasizes the active role of individual decision-making in cultural stability and change. The specific decisions, symbols, and societies of the past existed within their own distinct cultural contexts and should not be expected or assumed to mirror our own ideas and meanings. Contextual archaeologists attempt to reconstruct meaning in its own specific cultural context as the key to understanding the archaeological record.

For example, certain artifacts in the archaeological record represent gender distinctions. As we have seen, the meaning of gender-related or other kinds of patterning is an area of increasing emphasis in contextual archaeology, one often subject to alternative interpretations, depending on the kinds of models being applied to the data. To illustrate this, imagine finding clusters of cooking utensils near hearths and woodworking tools in a corner of a houseyard. This pattern would usually be explained as defining female and male activity areas, based on projecting our cultural expectations onto the archaeological record. Now assume that we have independent documentary evidence that this association between gender and activities is not correct for this society, and that both cooking and woodworking were in fact female activities. As a result, the meaning of the data patterning might be seen as reinforcing past concepts of femaleness within this society, while challenging those of our own society. In other words, the definition of these activity areas allows two different interpretations that define both occupational roles and gender concepts that when combined give a more complete meaning to the patterning in the archaeological record.

When dealing with cultural change, contextual interpretive models are dominated by internal change models. Some deal with some of the concepts we have already seen, such as diffusion and exchange. But they see the people of the past as active agents for change, rather than faceless and passive participants. Contextual models also treat variability at the level of individual decision-makers and symbol users, rather than focusing, as do processualists, on collective adaptations and variability between whole societies. In these ways, contextual interpretations both depart from and integrate models used by cultural historians and processual archaeologists.

Decision-making models are based on observed changes in the archaeological record that are interpreted as the accumulation of conscious decisions by individuals within a particular cultural context and worldview. These models address both very short-term fluctuations, and therefore are essentially synchronic, as well as longer time spans and culture change. Interpretation proceeds by identifying the nature of the settings in which decisions were made, the actors involved, and the meanings that those actors attached to those actions. This attempt to integrate small-scale and large-scale phenomena can be illustrated by two specific examples of active decision-making models, which also show how this approach differs from cultural history and processual approaches.

When Europeans arrived in eastern North America, many Native American groups were horticulturalists, and maize was the single most important food crop grown. As we know, maize was originally domesticated in highland Mexico; it reached the Eastern Woodlands by about A.D. 150–200 among societies that had by then practiced cultivation of local plants for well over 1500 years. Cultural historians would see the introduction of maize as a clear case of diffusion, the result of recognition of the value of this productive crop among receptive new societies. Processual archaeologists would see this development as an evolutionary process, in which people gradually modified available food plants within the local ecological system. But an interpretation by Patty Jo Watson and Mary C. Kennedy shows how considering the role of individual decision makers offers an expanded insight into this change. They point out that because maize was not native to the Eastern Woodlands, it required active care and tending, a deliberate decision to include and encourage this crop, rather than simply a passive or accidental acceptance of a new cultigen. This implies purposeful behavior on the part of ancient individuals, almost certainly women, highlighting the importance of women in promoting this cultural change. Watson and Kennedy do not claim that their view has been demonstrated, but it provides an alternative perspective on Eastern Woodland prehistory and suggestions (such as further study of native plant ecologies) for further research.

A more explicit decision-making model is illustrated by Ian Hodder's interpretation of the archaeological record of Neolithic Europe. In an evolutionary sense, he focuses on the same developmental transition as do Watson and Kennedy—the transition to sedentary, food-producing societies. He also emphasizes the role of individual decision makers in effecting changes in ancient life. In other ways, however, his approach is quite distinct, and represents a more thoroughly contextual orientation.

Hodder seeks to understand the form of the Neolithic European archaeological record and the ancient meanings it embodies. Instead of focusing on changes in plant or animal exploitation and their specific implications, he looks at the range of artifacts, ecofacts, and features from Neolithic Europe to identify widespread and long-term patterns in the forms of those data. For example, in central Europe, Hodder identifies consistent use of linear styles in house form (Fig. 9.11), pottery decoration, and, later, the shape of tombs. In these linear styles, space (whether in buildings or on vessel surfaces) is broken into distinct units or fields. Moreover, Hodder notes parallel changes over time in ceramic design motifs and the division of space within houses. Increasing emphasis was given to boundaries between spaces and overall complexity of design. In architecture, this was especially evident in the elaboration of house entrances, which tend to be where finds of decorated pottery concentrate. Hodder interprets these parallels as reflecting the cultural values that structured central European Neolithic society, in which boundaries and divisions became more important through time. The reason they did, Hodder concludes, is because people used them to distinguish the domesticated human domain from the wild surrounding world. By dramatizing house entrances, for example, and arranging the rooms within the building in a linear sequence, the occupants chose to stress increasing control over access by strangers, human or otherwise. The specific sequence of observable changes in house or ceramic style is, however, more gradual than abrupt because, while the individual builders and potters were actively reinterpreting symbols, they did so within the context of an established expressive system, in which their houses and vessels had to still be meaningful.

Hodder thus interprets the European Neolithic as a time of domestication of cultural forms generally, through the accumulation of individual, symbol-laden decisions in the creation and use of these cultural forms. Archaeologists have traditionally focused attention on the technological and economic side of the picture, on the Neolithic as the time of domestication of plants and animals. To Hodder, on the other hand, this was but one, relatively small reflection of changes in the overall cultural system.

The differences between this interpretation and cultural history or cultural processual interpretation are marked. Both the contextual approach and that of cultural history focus on style. Cultural history uses stylistic change to create time-space grids; for contextual archaeology, style allows inferring both the symbolic meaning behind the style and the manipulation of that meaning by its users. For processual archaeologists, on the other hand, we have seen that interpretation emphasizes the adaptive aspects of culture, usually by examining

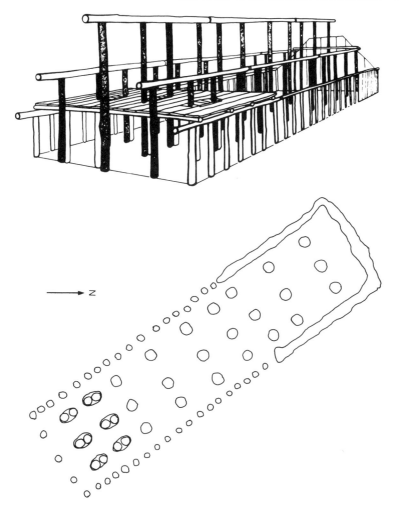

FIGURE 9.11

This reconstruction of the frame of a European Neolithic house (top), with its linear emphasis, is based on evidence from the ground plan (bottom) revealed by excavation. (After Lüning, in Hodder 1990.)

its most accessible parts—subsistence, technology, and (albeit indirectly) social organization—and seeks broad, crosscultural regularities. Contextual archaeology, however, looks to the structure and symbolic meaning behind cultural forms, and to do so, stays within the context of individual cultural traditions or sets of related traditions.

Different as these frameworks are, they are not incompatible. They are different ways of looking at the data, and they ask different questions of the archaeological record. But the emphasis is quite different. Where cultural history describes and cultural process seeks to explain, contextual archaeology seeks to understand the meanings inherent in the original past culture. Each approach provides working interpretations and each should be subjected to the kind of systematic examination we described in Chapter 2 that characterizes all pursuits of knowledge.

SUMMARY

The past is reconstructed from its material remains by synthesizing all analyzed data and interpreting these data in light of the various research questions. Interpretation attempts to describe what, when, and where the events of the past happened and to explain how and why they happened. Three complementary approaches are used: cultural history reconstructions set the foundation by identifying the what, when, and where; cultural process reconstructions follow (often using hypotheses generated from this descriptive reconstruction) to identify the how and why; and contextual approaches seek to understand the original meanings of culture at the level of the individual.

These approaches to archaeological interpretation are guided by several alternative views of culture. Cultural history reconstructions identify the events of the past based on temporal and spatial syntheses of data (time represented by the concept of tradition, space by the concept of horizon). Descriptive models based on the normative concept of culture are used to account for the similarities and differences observed in the data. Differences are usually emphasized and are seen as reflections of cultural change, ascribed to factors originating either inside (invention, selection, drift, and revival) or outside (diffusion, trade, migration, conquest, and environmental change) a particular culture.

Processual reconstruction is concerned with explaining the causes of cultural change based on testing a series of competing hypotheses. Explanatory models based on systems, ecological, or multilinear evolutionary concepts are most often used in such reconstructions. The systems and ecological perspectives emphasize reconstructions at one or more specific points in time, and seek causality from interactions within the system and of the system with its environment. The evolutionary perspective emphasizes reconstructions through time, seeking causality from the identification of single, universal (prime movers) or multiple (multivariate) factors.

The contextual approach offers a finer-grained interpretation, emphasizing the active role of individuals as decision makers and the meaning-laden context in which decisions are made. Meaning is viewed from the perspective of the culture under study, not the archaeologist's cultural viewpoint. While contextual interpretations are often based on synchronic models (or short-term fluctuations), they can have implications for evolutionary change as the cumulative sum of these decisions over time.

Finally, although archaeologists continue to debate the relative merits of the cultural history, cultural process, and contextual approaches, all three complement each other for developing the most complete and accurate understanding of the past. In confronting the complexities of the past, combining relevant aspects of all available approaches offers the most comprehensive research strategy for the archaeologist.

FOR FURTHER READING

CULTURAL HISTORY INTERPRETATION
Binford 1968; Flannery 1967, 1986; Haury 1958; Rouse 1962; Smith 1928; Willey and Phillips 1958; Willey and Sabloff 1980

CULTURAL PROCESS INTERPRETATION
Flannery 1967, 1968, 1972, 1986; Johnson and Earle 1987; Netting 1977; Sanders and Price 1968; Turnbull 1972; Willey and Sabloff 1980; Zubrow 1975

CONTEXTUAL INTERPRETATION
Gero and Conkey 1991; Gibbon 1989; Hodder 1982, 1989, 1991; Leone 1982; Pinsky and Wylie 1990; Preucel 1991; Watson and Kennedy 1991

ADDITIONAL SOURCES
Binford 1962, 1989; Childe 1954; Clarke 1972a; Conrad and Demarest 1984; Dunnell 1980, 1986; Meltzer, Fowler, and Sabloff 1986; Price and Brown 1985; Renfrew and Cherry 1986; Stark 1986; Steward 1955; Trigger 1984, 1989; Watson, LeBlanc, and Redman 1984; Wright 1986

Archaeology Today

ARCHAEOLOGY TODAY FACES A challenge to its very existence: the accelerating destruction of the remains of past societies. As we saw at the beginning of this book, the processes of transformation affect all forms of archaeological data, and among those processes is the impact of later societies. In recent decades, however, the toll of archaeological destruction has reached immense proportions. Critical information has already been lost forever, and many archaeologists fear that unless immediate action is taken, the bulk of the remains of most past societies will be completely destroyed in the near future (Fig. 10.1).

Archaeologists have attempted to stimulate public awareness and concern over the threats to archaeological remains throughout the world. This is especially apparent in the United States, where public awareness and governmental protective action concerning archaeology have traditionally lagged behind other nations. There are encouraging signs that this situation has changed. An important book by C. R. McGimsey, a leading advocate of public and governmental support for archaeology in the United States, reviewed the situation a generation ago and recommended future programs to be instituted on both state and federal levels. McGimsey's words are as appropriate today as when they were written:

> The next fifty years—some would say twenty-five—are going to be the most critical in the history of American archaeology. What is recovered, what is preserved, and how these goals are accomplished during this period will largely determine *for all time* the knowledge available to subsequent generations of Americans concerning their heritage from the past. . . . The next generation cannot study or preserve what already has been destroyed.
>
> (McGIMSEY 1972: 3)

218

FIGURE 10.1

A looted Maya tomb in northern Guatemala, strewn with shattered pottery, is mute testimony to the accelerating destruction of archaeological evidence throughout the world, one of archaeology's most difficult challenges. Tragically, in some areas of the world, most or all archaeological sites have been severely damaged by looting. (Photo by Ian Graham, Peabody Museum.)

The destruction of archaeological evidence has two sources. The most senseless is the looter who robs the remnants of ancient societies for artifacts or art that can be sold to collectors. On the other hand, there are the constant destructive effects from expanding societies all over the world. Everyday activities such as farming and construction, though not intended to obliterate archaeological information, nevertheless take their toll.

LOOTING AND ANTIQUITIES COLLECTING

Antiquities collecting is fueled by the **looting** of archaeological sites—the illicit and often illegal digging of sites by nonarchaeologists, who seek not information about the past but only objects with prestige or aesthetic or economic value. The weekend souvenir hunter does damage the archaeological record, but the biggest cause of the rapid acceleration of archaeological site destruction by looting is the voracious demand for ancient artifacts with commercial value. As long as collectors consider certain kinds of archaeological remains to be art worth collecting, the economics of supply and demand will lead to the plundering of sites to find such artifacts that have commercial value (Fig. 10.2). But plundering, of course, destroys all information about the archaeological association and context of these objects and usually physically destroys the rest of the archaeological record that lacks commercial value—the features, ecofacts, and artifacts associated with the rare objects worth money on the art market.

Most archaeologists recognize that the looting of sites can never be stopped completely. Under most circumstances, about all that can be done is to reduce the toll until it reaches less significant proportions. New laws that restrict domestic and international traffic in archaeological materials are needed, and present laws should be better enforced. International cooperation and standardization of import-export regulations would help, but customs laws alone cannot solve the problem.

The only effective way to reduce archaeological looting is to discourage the collector. If collectors no longer sought art from archaeological contexts, there would be no market for archaeological items and thus no incentive for the plundering of sites. Paintings, sculptures, or other works produced for the art market or art patrons are not at issue, for they were never part of the archaeological record. But the line must be drawn at any item that derives from an archaeological context, be it a Maya vase from a tomb or a Greek sculpture dragged from the bottom of the sea. Archaeological remains lose their scientific value when they have been ripped from their archaeological context. Archaeologists and all concerned people must therefore direct their efforts to preventing further destruction of the archaeological record and increase their efforts to preserve archaeological sites (Fig. 10.3).

Collectors are a diverse group of individuals and institutions. Only a few decades ago, most museums acquired at least some of the objects in their archaeological collections by purchase, and thus (directly or indirectly) encour-

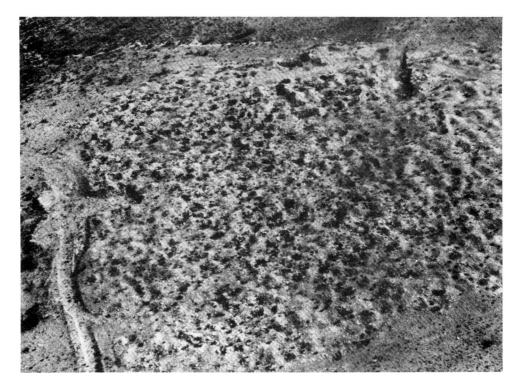

FIGURE 10.2

This aerial photograph shows Oldtown Village in New Mexico, one of the many sites of the prehistoric Mimbres culture that have been transformed by looters into cratered wastelands. Scenes like this are becoming all too common in many areas of the world, as collectors increase their demand for authentic archaeological specimens. (Photo after *The Mimbres People: Ancient Pueblo Painters of the American Southwest*, by Steven A. LeBlanc, © 1983 Thames and Hudson, Ltd.)

aged looting. Fortunately, that situation has changed: most anthropological museums have pledged to abide by international agreements prohibiting commercial dealings in archaeological materials. Unfortunately, many art museums with collections of so-called primitive art still purchase looted archaeological materials. Still, the individual collector remains the greatest problem, for although museum acquisitions often become public knowledge, purchases of archaeological materials by private individuals usually take place privately and remain secret. This does not mean that collectors are evil. Many may not even be aware of the destruction of knowledge that such collecting spawns. But they should be made aware that as long as they go on buying, looting will continue.

For example, in recent years the demand for painted pottery from archaeological sites in many areas of the world, such as Thailand and Guatemala, has reached such proportions that well-preserved specimens sell for tens, or even

(a)

FIGURE 10.3

Valuable archaeological evidence is often destroyed because it is sought by collectors and commands a high price on the art market. (a) Stela 1 from Jimbal, Guatemala, photographed shortly after its discovery in 1965. (b) Less than ten years later, looters had sawed off the top panel to steal the sculpted figures; in the process, they destroyed the head of the Maya ruler and the top of the hieroglyphic inscription. (Photo a courtesy of the Tikal Project, the University of Pennsylvania Museum; photo b courtesy of Joya Hairs.)

(b)

hundreds, of thousands of dollars apiece. These sums represent huge profits for the dealers at the end of the illegal supply pipeline; the plunderers who dig up these pots may receive little more than a few dollars for each pot they find. As a result of this demand, essentially every archaeological site in the plundered regions of Thailand or Guatemala has been damaged or utterly destroyed.

As we saw at the beginning of this book, the United States has problems in protecting its archaeological resources. Hundreds of Native American sites like Slack Farm (Chapter 1) have been destroyed by looters. Historical sites, such as Civil War battlefields, are also targets of looters, in this case collectors of military equipment and bullets. Shipwrecks are examples of historical sites often considered fair game for treasure hunters. This has allowed many shipwrecks with unique archaeological and historical value to be destroyed by treasure seekers. For example, in Florida the 1733 wreck of the *San Jose*, originally slated to become the world's first underwater shipwreck park, is now completely looted, all of its contents destroyed or scattered.

Unfortunately there are dozens of such cases of destruction for every example of what can happen with proper archaeological investigation. The positive results of such research are illustrated by the 1554 wreck of the *San Esteban*, excavated off the coast of Texas in 1973 under the sponsorship of the Texas State Antiquities Committee. The results of this effort include recovery of important new data on little-known 16th-century ship architecture and construction methods, conservation of the remains of the ship and its contents, and publication of the results in book, movie, and exhibition formats aimed at both public and professional audiences.

Hopefully the destruction of underwater sites such as the *San Jose* is a thing of the past. In 1988 Congress passed the Federal Abandoned Shipwreck Act. Many states have enacted laws protecting historic shipwrecks.

The demand for prized archaeological specimens has grown so much that collectors are turning to museum collections to satisfy their appetite for antiquities. Robberies of archaeological museums are becoming more commonplace. In 1985 several famous pre-Columbian artifacts were stolen from exhibits at the Museum of Anthropology in Mexico City. These objects are so well known that they could never be traded on the open market. Rather, thefts of this kind are often carried out by a few wealthy collectors who pay millions of dollars for antiquities that will have to remain hidden away indefinitely. In the Mexican case, fortunately, most of the stolen items were eventually recovered; otherwise the people of that nation would have lost a priceless portion of their national heritage.

The question still remains: how to discourage collectors from seeking and purchasing looted archaeological materials. Since the root of the problem is economic, the solution must be economic as well. One promising line of legal action, already implemented by some governments, involves changes in the inheritance laws so that individuals cannot bequeath archaeological collections to their heirs. Like legitimate art, most antiquities increase in value over time and thus represent an investment. But under this type of legislation, items defined as archaeological materials pass instead to the state. Many collectors may think twice about purchasing material that will ultimately be taken by the government.

The antiquities problem is as complex as it is urgent. In formulating antiquities legislation, politics and patronage often weigh more heavily than the security of archaeological materials. Archaeologists and other interested people must therefore fight to protect the past, or we shall lose it forever.

DESTRUCTION IN THE NAME OF PROGRESS

Vandalism and looting are serious problems, but well-intentioned activities can also be harmful. Although done in the name of progress, the opening of new lands to agriculture, construction of new roads and buildings, and creation of flood-control projects inevitably destroy countless remains of past human activity. Almost any action that affects the earth's surface is a threat to the archaeological record. Even under the best of circumstances, we can never answer all our questions about past cultural development, but as the physical remains continue to be obliterated, our ability to ask any new questions at all is drastically reduced.

Obviously, we cannot simply stop population growth and end new construction, so archaeological sites are going to continue to be destroyed. In the face of this fact, an increasing number of archaeologists are adopting a conservationist attitude toward cultural remains. This attitude involves a heightened emphasis on planning and a restructuring of the relative roles of excavation and survey in archaeological research. As we discussed in Chapter 4, archaeologists have a responsibility to the future, when greater resources and more sophisticated techniques may allow a more complete recovery of data. Therefore, unthreatened sites should never be completely excavated; a portion should always be left undisturbed for future archaeologists to investigate and efforts undertaken to ensure the preservation of those undisturbed remains. Even for sites threatened with imminent destruction, there has been a change of attitude. Traditionally, the archaeologist's response to such situations has been to excavate quickly and recover as much data as possible—sometimes literally one step ahead of construction crews. Now, however, with the invaluable assistance of a growing array of supportive legislation, archaeologists are more often able to take the time to assess the situation, reconnoiter the area concerned, and then, *if appropriate*, conduct excavations.

CULTURAL RESOURCE MANAGEMENT

Archaeologists have always responded to the threat of destruction, but until recently, the general public and governmental policy in most nations have shown little such concern. Fortunately, after years of neglect and destruction,

FIGURE 10.4

Archaeological remains are recognized national symbols for many countries, as well as providing huge revenues from tourists. One of the most famous examples is Teotihuacán, Mexico.

many countries have begun to enact firm protective legislation, based on the premise that the remains of the past, both historic and prehistoric, are a nonrenewable resource, like oil and other minerals, or a fragile resource, like rainforests.

The motives for such conservation efforts are both humanistic and scientific, but they also have a very practical basis. Knowledge of the past fosters self-esteem and national unity. It also fosters economic development. Tourism, founded at least in part upon a well-documented and spectacular past, is a multimillion dollar business in some nations. Sites such as Teotihuacán in Mexico, the Great Pyramids in Egypt, Machu Picchu in Peru, and Williamsburg in the United States not only serve as symbols of national heritage, but also attract millions of tourists every year (Fig. 10.4). In Egypt, the Aswan Dam salvage project, conducted in the 1960s, was organized by UNESCO to save the magnificent site of Abu Simbel (Fig. 10.5), one of the most visited sites in that country. The program also included work in less spectacular aspects of archaeology, such as locating prehistoric occupation sites that would otherwise have been lost.

In the United States, a series of federal laws dating back to 1906 have been enacted to conserve archaeological sites (Table 10.1). Until recently, however, other countries, including several in Europe and Latin America, were far ahead of the United States in providing legal protection for their archaeological resources. Fortunately, the last two decades have witnessed passage of an important series of laws which have helped the United States to catch up, although more protective measures are still needed.

TABLE 10.1

Major U.S. Federal Legislation
for the Protection of Archaeological Resources

Antiquities Act of 1906	Protects sites on federal lands
Historic Sites Act of 1935	Provides authority for designating National Historic Landmarks, and for archaeological survey before destruction by development programs
National Historic Preservation Act of 1966 (amended 1976 and 1980)	Strengthens protection of sites via the National Register; integrates state and local agencies into national program for site preservation
National Environmental Policy Act of 1969	Requires all federal agencies to specify impact of development programs on cultural resources
Archaeological Resources Protection Act of 1979	Provides criminal and civil penalties for looting or damaging sites on public and Native American lands
Convention on Cultural Property of 1982	Authorizes U.S. participation in 1970 UNESCO convention to prevent illegal international trade in cultural property
Cultural Property Act of 1983	Provides sanctions against U.S. import or export of illicit antiquities
Federal Abandoned Shipwreck Act of 1988	Removes sunken ships of archaeological interest from marine salvage jurisdiction; provides for protection under state jurisdiction
Federal Reburial and Repatriation Act of 1990	Specifies return of Native American remains and cultural property by U.S. museums to Native American groups

With continuing expansion in preservationist legislation, archaeologists have been needed in growing numbers to conduct the surveys and other work the new laws require. As a consequence, a new specialty has arisen within archaeology—**cultural resource management** (some call it simply CRM). As noted in Chapter 1, this specialty has become the fastest-developing area within American archaeology. Private CRM consulting firms now rival colleges and government agencies as employment places for professional archaeologists.

This development has not been without growing pains, which have stemmed chiefly from several related issues. First, the increase in both available funds and demand for archaeologists to conduct studies created some confusion in dealing with the unfamiliar complexities of the federal laws, regulations, and bureaucratic procedures, and a shortage of qualified archaeologists able to undertake the flood of new contracts. Second, archaeologists have had to re-

FIGURE IO.5

The spectacular remains of the temple of Abu Simbel were saved from
the rising waters behind the Aswan Dam by being cut apart, moved, and
reassembled on higher ground at a cost of over $40 million. (Courtesy of
David O'Connor.)

examine seriously the ethics and professional standards appropriate for this
kind of work, such as resolving competing priorities between preservation and
excavation.

A more promising effect has been the increasingly positive attitude of
archaeologists in general toward cultural resource management as an opportunity for creative research. As evidence of this, an expanding number of archaeologists are actively trying to coordinate with government officials, such as
heads of state historic preservation offices, to formulate broad regional
research goals and priorities. Though flexible, such plans increase the applica-
bility of data collected under CRM projects to questions of broader and more
general theoretical interest.

But CRM does not solve all the problems of archaeological destruction.
The laws providing for such work pertain only to sites on public land or those
threatened by government-sponsored projects. Many sites, however, especially in the eastern United States where far less land is under public control,
are on privately owned property. To preserve these sites, threatened just as
often by looting, construction development, or simple neglect, archaeologists
Mark Michel and Steven LeBlanc conceived of a private organization
modeled on the successful Nature Conservancy. Incorporated in 1979, the
Archaeological Conservancy seeks to identify archaeological sites worthy of

FIGURE 10.6

Oak Creek Pueblo, one of two important Sinagua culture ruins acquired
for preservation by the Archaeological Conservancy in 1985. This ruin is
located on Oak Creek in the Verde Valley of central Arizona and dates to
A.D. 1200–1450. At one time there were about forty Sinagua culture ruins
at the area, but most have been destroyed by looters and by development.
The Sinagua are thought to be ancestors of the modern Hopi. (Photo
courtesy of the Archaeological Conservancy.)

protection, secure their preservation through purchase or donation, and educate the public about the need to preserve our cultural heritage (Fig. 10.6).

Once a site has been secured, the Archaeological Conservancy ensures its
short-term protection, but eventually donates or sells it to institutions able to
undertake long-term conservation. For example, the Conservancy has donated
the Fort Craig site in New Mexico to the Bureau of Land Management, and
two other sites—Savage Cave in Kentucky and Powers Fort in Missouri—to
local universities as centers for both environmental and archaeological
research. As its resources grow, the Archaeological Conservancy promises to be
a major factor for the protection of archaeological sites in the United States.

Archaeologists cannot preserve or excavate all sites, and some sites have
more to tell us than others. Clearly, then, increased attention should be paid to
improving the means by which decisions are made between protection, immediate investigation, and sometimes-necessary sacrifice. The question is not
whether the past should be protected, but how best to protect it in the context
of a rapidly growing and changing world.

WORKING WITH ETHNIC GROUPS

Archaeologists are not alone in their concern about protecting cultural resources. A growing number of ethnic minorities and societies are actively pursuing the preservation of their traditions and heritage. There is some irony in this situation, since in several instances archaeologists have been a target of efforts to protect ethnic cultural resources. In some cases archaeologists have been accused of being unconcerned about the rights of native groups, and some native peoples have demanded return or reburial of excavated artifacts and human remains. A federal law enacted in 1990 provides for the repatriation of Native American materials in the United States and for a new national museum for Native Americans as part of the Smithsonian Institution in Washington, DC.

Because the heritages of some ethnic groups have been abused, in some cases archaeological research has been restricted or even prohibited. This should serve as a lesson for all archaeologists, so that in the future they recognize, respect, and heed the traditions of the ethnic groups they are studying. Obviously, if an archaeological site is known or suspected to be linked to a living ethnic group, the permission and cooperation of that community *must* be obtained before excavation. Cooperation can only lead to very real benefits for both archaeologists and the people involved, by adding new information about the cultural and biological heritage of the living descendants. For example, knowledge about ancient disease patterns can contribute to today's health care programs.

Both archaeologists and concerned ethnic groups recognize that the greatest agent of destruction of cultural resources is the looter motivated by monetary greed rather than knowledge of or respect for the past. The solution is already at hand; in many cases, archaeologists and ethnic groups have joined forces to protect cultural resources from looting and cooperated to increase our understanding of the past. Under such agreements, professional archaeologists, including a growing number of Native American archaeologists, conduct research to gain knowledge for both science and the living descendants of ancient societies. At the same time, this research must be designed to respect the concerns of the living descendants.

In cases of already excavated archaeological or human remains that are directly linked to living peoples, archaeologists have another obligation. As long as the scientific information gained from such remains is safeguarded and the final disposition of human remains is made in accordance with the law, archaeologists must ensure that the treatment of these finds is also consistent with the feelings and beliefs of the ethnic group involved. For example, if the living descendants do not object to public displays of excavated artifacts, an informative exhibit in a local museum might be appropriate. In other cases, descendants might prefer reburial of the remains after the scientific data are obtained.

THE RESPONSIBILITIES OF ARCHAEOLOGY

The archaeological profession has assumed certain responsibilities for the cultural resources that all peoples of the world have inherited from the past:

1. To preserve the world's archaeological resources.
2. To prevent the destruction of archaeological sites and resources. Toward this end it is unethical for archaeologists to maintain personal collections of archaeological materials or engage in any commercial activity—including purchase, sale, or evaluation—involving artifacts or other archaeological material.
3. To conduct their research consistent with the standards of archaeology and ensure that their research records and data are available for examination by qualified scholars.
4. To publish the results of their research, ensuring that all research reports are accurate and unbiased and are available to all who would benefit from such knowledge, including both professional and public audiences.
5. To respect the rights of the living descendants of the ancient populations that created the archaeological record.
6. To work toward future improvements and the continuity of the archaeological profession.

These ethical standards highlight the archaeologist's prime obligations— to protect and preserve the archaeological record, to conduct research to the highest standards, to share as widely as possible the information gained from that research, to respect the rights of people descended from those who created that record, to improve the field, and to educate new generations of archaeologists.

It is especially appropriate to close this introduction to archaeology by stressing the responsibilities that archaeologists have toward the future. Like all scientists, archaeologists must ensure that their research is accurate and unbiased and that its results are available to future generations of both scholars and the general public. The dissemination of valid archaeological information is crucial to make the public aware of the value of understanding our past and of the tragic loss of heritage caused by the wanton destruction of cultural resources.

Archaeological information is made available by a variety of means, ranging from public lectures and museum exhibits to the publication of both popular and scholarly articles and books. Most archaeologists recognize the obligation to make the results of their research available to their professional colleagues, but unfortunately not all see the need to provide this information to a more general audience. Because archaeologists are uniquely able to address the full range of the human past, they have an obligation to educate as many people as possible about the richness of our human heritage. The communication of archaeological information to the general public is not only an ethical responsibility but also wise policy, as it stimulates the recruitment of future archaeologists. Most importantly, perhaps, knowledge is the most powerful weapon against the destructive forces that threaten to rob all of us of our past cultural heritage.

SUMMARY

Archaeology today faces an unprecedented crisis from the rapidly increasing destruction of archaeological sites, which causes loss of the nonrenewable cultural resources of humankind. While some of this destruction will always occur as a result of the inescapable disturbances of modern activity, the greatest and most disturbing toll is taken by looting. Most of this intentional destruction is generated to supply an illicit world-wide market in antiquities. Although there is no easy solution to this destruction, success has been achieved by protective laws in the United States and in many other countries and by nongovernmental preservation initiatives such as the Archaeological Conservancy and the efforts of ethnic groups to protect their cultural heritage. These measures have fostered new attitudes about the past, giving rise to the field called cultural resource management—the mobilization of concerned individuals and organizations to protect and preserve the cultural heritage of all peoples. Archaeologists are central to this effort, for they have a professional responsibility to protect the record of the past, to work with concerned ethnic groups who wish to preserve their own heritage, and, through training and publication, to ensure that the knowledge acquired from their research is preserved and passed on to future generations.

FOR FURTHER READING

LOOTING AND ANTIQUITIES COLLECTING
   Bassett 1986; Coggins 1972; Fagan 1975, 1988; Giesecke 1987; LeBlanc 1983; McGimsey 1972; Wiseman 1984

DESTRUCTION IN THE NAME OF PROGRESS
   Davis 1972; Miller 1980; Wendorf 1973

CULTURAL RESOURCE MANAGEMENT
   Cleere 1984, 1989; Ford 1983; Lipe 1974, 1984; Michel 1981

WORKING WITH ETHNIC GROUPS
   Higgenbotham 1983; Layton 1989; McBryde 1985; Society for American Archaeology 1986; Talmadge 1982

THE RESPONSIBILITIES OF ARCHAEOLOGY
   Champe et al. 1961; Davis 1982; Fowler 1987; Green 1984; King 1983; McBryde 1985; Talmadge 1982

Glossary

Terms in italics are defined elsewhere in the glossary.

Absolute dating or **chronometric dating**   Determination of age using a specific time scale, as in years before present (*B.P.*) or according to a fixed calendar (compare with *relative dating*). (Chapter 7)

Acquisition   The first stage of *behavioral processes*, in which raw materials are procured (see *manufacture*, *use*, and *deposition*). (Chapter 4)

Actualistic studies   Detailed observations of the actual use of materials like those found in the *archaeological record* (*artifacts*, *ecofacts*, and *features*), used to produce reliable *general analogies* for *interpretation*. (Chapter 8)

Aerial reconnaissance   *Remote sensing* techniques carried out from the air (by balloon, airplane, satellite, and so on); includes direct observation, as well as recording by photographic, radar, or other images. (Chapter 5)

Alloy   A mixture of two or more metals, such as bronze (copper and tin), used in *metallurgy*. (Chapter 6)

Analogy   A process of reasoning in which similarity between two entities in some characteristics is taken to imply similarity in other characteristics as well; the basis of most archaeological *interpretation* (see *general analogy* and *specific analogy*). (Chapter 8)

Analysis   A stage in archaeological *research design* in which data are isolated, described, and structured, usually via typological *classification*, and chronological, functional, technological, and constituent determinations are made. (Chapter 4)

Annealing   Application of heat in the *manufacture* of *metal artifacts*. (Chapter 6)

Anthropology   The comprehensive study of the human species from biological, social, and cultural perspectives using both *synchronic* and *diachronic* views; in the United States, it comprises the subdisciplines of biological or physical anthropology, cultural anthropology, linguistic anthropology, and archaeology, usually including both *historical* and *prehistoric archaeology.* (Chapter 1)

Antiquarian   A nonprofessional who studies the past for its artistic or cultural value (compare with *archaeologist* and *looter).* (Chapter 2)

Arbitrary sample unit   A unit of archaeological investigation; a subdivision of the *data universe* with no cultural relevance, such as a *sample unit* defined by a site grid (compare with *nonarbitrary sample unit).* (Chapter 4)

Archaeoastronomy   Inference of ancient astronomical knowledge through study of astronomy-related aspects of the *archaeological record;* it combines perspectives of *archaeology* and astronomy. (Chapter 8)

Archaeological culture   The maximum grouping of all *assemblages* assumed to represent the sum of human activities carried out within a single ancient *culture.* (Chapter 5)

Archaeological record   The physical remains produced by past human activities, which are sought, recovered, studied, and interpreted by *archaeologists* to reconstruct the past (see also *artifact, ecofact, feature).* (Chapter 1)

Archaeologist   A professional scholar who studies the human past through its physical remains (compare with *antiquarian* and *looter).* (Chapter 1)

Archaeology   The study of the human past through material remains, with the aim of ordering and describing the events of the past and explaining their meaning. (Chapter 1)

Archaeomagnetic dating   Measurement of magnetic alignments within undisturbed *features,* such as hearths and kilns; comparison is then made to known schedules of past magnetic alignments within a region to yield an absolute age for the feature. (Chapter 7)

Artifact   A discrete and portable object in the archaeological record whose characteristics result wholly or in part from human activity; artifacts are individually assignable to *ceramic, lithic, metal, organic,* or other categories (see also *industry).* (Chapter 4)

Assemblage   A gross grouping of all *subassemblages* assumed to represent the sum of human activities carried out within an ancient community (see *archaeological culture).* (Chapter 5)

Association   Occurrence of an item of archaeological data adjacent to another and in or on the same *matrix.* (Chapter 4)

Attribute   The minimal characteristic used as a criterion for grouping artifacts into classes; includes *stylistic, form,* and *technological attributes* (see also *classification).* (Chapters 5)

Augering   A *subsurface detection* technique using a drill run by either human or machine power to determine the depth and characteristics of archaeological or natural deposits. (Chapter 5)

Battleship-shaped curve   A lens-shaped graph representing changes in artifact type frequencies through time, from origin to expanding popularity, decline, and finally disappearance. (Chapter 7)

Behavioral processes   Human activities, including *acquisition, manufacture, use,* and *deposition* behavior, that produce tangible archaeological remains (compare with *transformational processes).* (Chapter 4)

Blade   A long, thin, parallel-sided *flake* usually made from a cylindrical *core* (see *lithic technology).* (Chapter 6)

Bone chemistry   Several *relative dating* techniques applicable to bone material, including measurements of the depletion of nitrogen and the accumulation of fluorine and uranium. (Chapter 7)

B.P. Before present; used in age determinations; in calculating radiocarbon dates, *present* means 1950 (a fixed reference date). (Chapter 7)

Central place theory The theory that human settlements will space themselves evenly across a landscape depending on the availability of resources and communication routes and that these settlements will become differentiated, forming a hierarchy of controlling centers called *central places* (see *locational analysis*). (Chapter 8)

Ceramic artifacts *Artifacts* of fired clay belonging to *pottery*, figurine, or other ceramic *industries*. (Chapter 6)

Chronometric dating See *absolute dating*.

Classification The ordering of phenomena into groups (classes) based on the sharing of *attributes*. (Chapter 2)

Clearing excavations *Excavations* designed primarily to reveal the horizontal and, by inference, functional dimensions of archaeological *sites*—the extent, distribution, and patterning of archaeological data (compare with *penetrating excavations*). (Chapter 5)

Cold hammering A technique for making *metal artifacts* in which the metal is shaped by percussion without heating. (Chapter 6)

Computer simulation studies Reconstructions of the past based on *models* that describe ancient conditions and variables and then use computers to generate a sequence of events in order to compare the results against the known *archaeological record*, thus refining and testing *hypotheses* about the past. (Chapter 9)

Conjoining studies The refitting of fragments of artifacts and ecofacts to evaluate the integrity of an archaeological deposit; such studies allow definition of *cumulative features*, such as lithic debris scatters; they sometimes allow reconstruction of ancient *manufacture* and *use* behavior. (Chapter 5)

Conquest Aggressive movement of human groups from one area to another resulting in the subjugation of the native society. (Chapter 9)

Constructed feature A *feature* deliberately built to provide a setting for one or more activities, such as a house, storeroom, or burial chamber (compare with *cumulative feature*). (Chapter 6)

Context Characteristics of archaeological data that result from combined *behavioral* and *transformational processes*, which are evaluated by means of recorded *association*, *matrix*, and *provenience* (see *primary context* and *secondary context*). (Chapter 4)

Contextual interpretation Archaeological interpretation aimed at understanding the past by reconstructing the point of view of past people who produced the archaeological record. (Chapter 3)

Coprolites Preserved ancient feces, studied because they contain food residues that can be used to reconstruct ancient diet and subsistence activities. (Chapter 6)

Core A *lithic artifact* from which *flakes* are removed; it is used as a tool or a blank from which other tools are made (see *lithic technology*). (Chapter 6)

Coring A *subsurface detection* technique using a hollow metal tube driven into the ground to lift a column of earth for stratigraphic study. (Chapter 5)

Cultural adaptation The sum of the adjustments of a human society to its environment (see *cultural ecology*). (Chapter 9)

Cultural drift Gradual cultural change due to the imperfect transmission of information between generations; it is analogous to genetic drift in biology. (Chapter 9)

Cultural ecology The study of the dynamic interaction between human society and its environment, which views *culture* as the primary adaptive mechanism in the relationship. (Chapter 9)

Cultural evolution The theory that human societies change via a process analogous to the evolution of biological species (see *unilinear cultural evolution* and *multilinear cultural evolution*). (Chapter 2)

Cultural history interpretation Archaeological *interpretation* based on temporal and spatial syntheses of data and the application of general descriptive *models* usually derived from a normative view of *culture*. (Chapter 3)

Cultural invention The origin of new cultural forms within a society whether by accident or design. (Chapter 9)

Cultural process interpretation Archaeological *interpretation* aimed at delineating the interactions and changes in cultural *systems* by the application of both descriptive and explanatory *models* based on ecological and materialist views of *culture*. (Chapter 3)

Cultural resource management (CRM) The conservation and selective investigation of prehistoric and historic remains; specifically, the development of ways and means, including legislation, to safeguard the past. (Chapters 1 and 10)

Cultural revival Reuse of abandoned cultural elements. (Chapter 9)

Cultural selection The process that leads to differential retention of cultural traits, which increases a society's potential for successful *cultural adaptation* while eliminating maladaptive traits. (Chapter 9)

Culture The concept that both underlies and unites the discipline of *anthropology* and, in its various definitions, acts as a central *model* by which archaeological data are interpreted; a definition suited to archaeology sees culture as the cumulative resource of human society that provides the means for nongenetic adaptation to the environment by regulating behavior in three areas—*technology, social systems,* and *ideology*. (Chapter 1)

Culture area A spatial unit defined by *ethnographically* observed cultural similarities within a given geographical area; used archaeologically to define spatial limits to *archaeological cultures* (see also *time-space grids*). (Chapter 3)

Cumulative feature A *feature* without evidence of deliberate construction but which results instead from accretion, as a *midden,* or subtraction, as a quarry (compare with *constructed feature*). (Chapter 6)

Data acquisition A stage in archaeological *research design* in which data are gathered, normally by *reconnaissance, surface survey,* and *excavation*. (Chapter 4)

Data processing A stage in archaeological *research design* usually involving, in the case of *artifacts,* cleaning, conserving, labeling, inventorying, and cataloging. (Chapter 4)

Data universe A defined area of archaeological investigation, often a *region* or *site,* bounded in time and space. (Chapter 4)

Dendrochronology The study of tree-ring growth patterns, which are linked to develop a continuous chronological sequence. (Chapter 7)

Deposition The last stage of *behavioral processes,* in which *artifacts* are discarded (see *acquisition, manufacture,* and *use*). (Chapter 4)

Diachronic Pertaining to phenomena as they occur or change over a period of time; a chronological perspective (compare with *synchronic*). (Chapter 1)

Diffusion Transmission of ideas from one culture to another. (Chapter 9)

Direct dating Determination of the age of archaeological data by analysis of the *artifact, ecofact,* or *feature* itself (compare with *indirect dating*). (Chapter 7)

Direct percussion   A technique used for the manufacture of chipped stone *artifacts* in which *flakes* are produced by striking a *core* with a hammerstone or striking the core against a fixed stone or anvil (compare with *indirect percussion* and *pressure flaking*). (Chapter 6)

Ecofact   Nonartifactual evidence from the past that has cultural relevance; the category includes both inorganic and organic objects. (Chapter 4)

Ethnoarchaeology   *Ethnographic* studies designed to aid archaeological *interpretation*, such as descriptions of *behavioral processes;* especially the ways material items enter the *archaeological record* (see *analogy*). (Chapter 8)

Ethnocentrism   An observational bias in which other societies are evaluated by standards relevant to the observer's *culture*. (Chapters 2 and 9)

Ethnography   The description of contemporary cultures; part of the subdiscipline of cultural *anthropology*. (Chapter 1)

Ethnology   The comparative study of contemporary cultures; part of the subdiscipline of cultural *anthropology*. (Chapter 1)

Excavation   A method of *data acquisition* in which *matrix* is removed to discover and retrieve archaeological data from beneath the ground, which reveals the three-dimensional structure of the data and matrix, both vertically (see *penetrating excavations*) and horizontally (see *clearing excavations*). (Chapters 5)

Exchange systems   Systems for trade or transfer of goods, services, and ideas between individuals and societies. (Chapter 8)

Experimental archaeology   Studies designed to aid archaeological *interpretation* by attempting to duplicate *behavioral processes* experimentally under carefully controlled conditions (see *analogy*). (Chapter 8)

Explanation   The end product of scientific research; in *archaeology* this refers to determining what happened in the past, and when, where, how, and why it happened (see *interpretation*). (Chapter 1)

Feature   A nonportable archaeological remain, one that cannot be recovered from its *matrix* without destroying its integrity (see *constructed feature* and *cumulative feature*). (Chapter 4)

Feedback   A response to a stimulus that acts within a *system* (see *negative feedback* and *positive feedback*). (Chapter 9)

Flake   A *lithic artifact* detached from a *core*, either as waste or as a tool (see *lithic technology*). (Chapter 6)

Form   The physical characteristics—arrangement, composition, size, and shape—of any component of a *culture* or cultural *system;* in archaeological research, the first objective is to describe and analyze the physical *attributes* (form) of data to determine distributions in time and space (see *function*). (Chapter 1)

Form attributes   *Attributes* based on the physical characteristics of an *artifact*, including overall shape, the shape of parts, and measurable dimensions; leads to form *classification*. (Chapter 5)

Form types   Classes of *artifacts* based on *form attributes*. (Chapter 5)

Formulation   The first stage in archaeological *research design*; involves definition of the research problem and goals, background investigations, and feasibility studies. (Chapter 4)

Frequency seriation   A *relative dating* technique in which artifacts or other archaeological data are chronologically ordered by ranking their relative frequencies to con-
form with *battleship-shaped curves* (see *seriation*). (Chapter 7)

Function   The purpose or use of a component of a *culture* or of a cultural *system;* the
second goal of archaeological research is analysis of data and their relationships to
determine function and thus reconstruct ancient behavior (see *form*). (Chapter 1)

General analogy   An *analogy* used in archaeological *interpretation* based on broad and
generalized comparisons that are documented across many cultural *traditions* (see *actualistic studies*). (Chapter 8)

Geochronology   Determining age by studying the *association* of archaeological data
with geological formations. (Chapter 7)

Glaze   A specialized *slip* applied to *pottery,* that produces an impermeable and glassy
surface when fired at high temperatures (see *vitrification*). (Chapter 6)

Ground reconnaissance   The traditional method for the discovery of archaeological
sites in which the area is visually inspected from ground level. (Chapter 5)

Ground survey   A *surface survey* technique using direct observation to gather archaeological data present on the ground surface; includes mapping and surface collection.
(Chapter 5)

Ground truth   Determination of the causes of patterns revealed by *remote sensing,*
such as by examining, on the ground, features identified by aerial photography.
(Chapter 5)

Half-life   The period required for one-half of a radioactive isotope to decay and form
a stable element; this decay rate, expressed as a statistical constant for each isotope with
a specified range of error, provides the measurement scale for *radiometric dating.*
(Chapter 7)

Historical archaeology   That area of *archaeology* concerned with literate societies and
often allied with *history*. In the United States, both historical archaeology and *prehistoric
archaeology* are usually considered part of *anthropology*. (Chapter 1)

History   The study of the past through written records, which are compared, judged
for accuracy, placed in chronological sequence, and interpreted in light of preceding,
contemporary, and subsequent events. (Chapter 1)

Horizon   Cross-cultural regularities at one point in time; the spatial baseline of the
New World *cultural history interpretation* synthesis proposed by Willey and Phillips
(1958) (compare with *tradition*). (Chapter 3)

Horizontal stratigraphy   Chronological sequences based on successive horizontal
displacements, such as sequential beach terraces; analogous to *stratigraphy*. (Chapter 7)

Hypothesis   A proposition, often derived from a broader generalization or law, which
postulates relationships between two or more variables based on specified assumptions
and which makes predictions that are tested by further research. (Chapter 1)

Ideology   One of three components of *culture;* the knowledge or beliefs used by
human societies to understand and cope with their existence (see also *technology* and
social systems). (Chapter 8)

Implementation   The second stage in archaeological *research design,* which involves
obtaining permits, raising funds, and making logistical arrangements. (Chapter 4)

Indirect dating Determining the age of archaeological data by using its *association* with a *matrix* or object of known age (compare *direct dating*). (Chapter 7)

Indirect percussion A technique used to manufacture chipped stone artifacts in which *flakes* are produced by striking a punch, usually made of wood or bone, placed against a *core* (compare with *direct percussion* and *pressure flaking*). (Chapter 6)

Industry A category of *artifacts* defined by shared material and *technology*, such as the chipped stone or *pottery* industries. (Chapter 6)

Inevitable variation The premise that all cultures vary and change through time without specific cause; a general and unsatisfactory descriptive *model* sometimes implied in *cultural history interpretation*. (Chapter 9)

Interpretation A stage in archaeological *research design* involving the synthesis of results of data *analysis* and the *explanation* of their meaning in order to reconstruct the past. (Chapter 4)

Law of superposition The principle that the sequence of observable *strata* from bottom to top reflects the order of deposition from earliest to latest (see *stratigraphy*). (Chapter 5)

Lithic technology *Artifacts* made from stone, including the chipped stone and ground stone *industries*. (Chapter 6)

Locational analysis Techniques from geography used to study locations of human settlement and to infer the determinants of these locations (see *central place theory*). (Chapter 8)

Looter An individual who plunders archaeological *sites* to find *artifacts* of commercial value, at the same time destroying the evidence that archaeologists rely on to understand the past (compare with *antiquarian* and *archaeologist*). (Chapters 1 and 10)

Magnetometer A device used in subsurface detection that measures minor variations in the earth's magnetic field, which may reveal archaeological *features* as magnetic anomalies. (Chapter 5)

Manufacture The second stage of *behavioral processes*, in which raw materials are modified to produce *artifacts* (see *acquisition*, *use*, and *deposition*). (Chapter 4)

Matrix The physical medium that surrounds, holds, or supports archaeological data. (Chapter 4)

Metallurgy The group of *industries* involved in extracting metals from ore and using them to make artifacts; includes the copper, bronze, and iron industries. (Chapter 6)

Metate A common New World term for ground stone basins used to process grains (see also *quern*). (Chapter 6)

Midden An accumulation of debris resulting from human disposal and removed from areas of *manufacture* and *use*; may result from either one-time refuse disposal or long-term disposal resulting in *stratification*. (Chapter 4)

Migration Movement of human populations from one area to another, usually resulting in cultural contact. (Chapter 9)

Model A theoretical scheme constructed to understand a specific set of data or phenomena; descriptive models deal with the form and structure of phenomena, while explanatory models seek underlying causes for phenomena; models may also be *diachronic* or *synchronic*. (Chapters 1 and 2)

Multilinear cultural evolution   A theory of *cultural evolution* that sees each society pursuing an individual evolutionary career shaped by accumulated specific *cultural adaptations*, rather than seeing all societies as pursuing the same course (compare with *unilinear cultural evolution*). (Chapters 2 and 9)

Multiple working hypotheses   The simultaneous testing of alternative *hypotheses* to minimize bias and maximize the chances of finding the best available choice. (Chapter 3)

Multivariate strategy   A class of *models* of *multilinear cultural evolution* that sees major cultural changes as the result of multiple, relatively small adaptive adjustments (compare with *prime movers*). (Chapter 9)

Natural secondary context   A *secondary context* resulting from natural *transformational processes* such as erosion or animal and plant activity (compare with *use-related secondary context*). (Chapter 4)

Negative feedback   A response to changing conditions that acts to dampen or stop a *system's* reaction. (Chapter 9)

Nonarbitrary sample unit   A unit of archaeological investigation; a subdivision of the *data universe* with cultural relevance, such as rooms or houses (compare with *arbitrary sample unit*). (Chapter 4)

Norms   Rules that govern behavior in a particular society. (Chapter 3)

Obsidian hydration   Adsorption of water on exposed surfaces of obsidian; if the local hydration rate is known and constant, this phenomenon can be used as an *absolute dating* technique through measurement of the thickness of the hydration layer. (Chapter 7)

Organic artifacts   *Artifacts* made of organic materials, including products of the wood, bone, horn, fiber, ivory, or hide *industries*. (Chapter 6)

Penetrating excavations   *Excavations* designed primarily to reveal the vertical, temporal dimensions of archaeological deposits—the depth, sequence, and composition of buried data (compare with *clearing excavations*). (Chapter 5)

Period   A broad and general chronological unit defined for a *site* or *region* based on combined data, such as sets of contemporary *artifact* types (see also *time-space grid*). (Chapter 3)

Phytoliths   Microscopic silica bodies that form in living plants and provide a durable floral *ecofact* that allows the identification of plant remains in archaeological deposits. (Chapter 6)

Population   The aggregate of all *sample units* within a *data universe*. (Chapter 4)

Positive feedback   A response to changing conditions that acts to stimulate further reactions within a *system*. (Chapter 9)

Potassium-argon dating   A *radiometric dating* technique based on the *half-life* of the radioactive isotope of potassium (^{40}K) that decays to form argon (^{40}Ar). (Chapter 7)

Pottery   A class of *ceramic artifacts* in which clay is formed into containers by hand, in molds, or using a potter's wheel, often decorated, and fired. (Chapter 6)

Prehistoric archaeology   The area of *archaeology* concerned with preliterate or nonliterate societies. In the United States, both prehistoric archaeology and *historical archaeology* are considered a part of *anthropology*. (Chapter 1)

Pressure flaking   A technique for manufacturing chipped stone *artifacts* in which *flakes* or *blades* are produced by applying pressure against a *core* with a punch usually made of wood or bone (compare with *direct percussion* and *indirect percussion*). (Chapter 6)

Primary context   The condition that results when *provenience*, *association*, and *matrix* have not been disturbed since the original *deposition* of archaeological data (compare with *secondary context*). (Chapter 4)

Prime movers   Factors crucial to stimulating major cultural change; they are emphasized in some *models* of *multilinear cultural evolution* (compare with *multivariate strategy*). (Chapter 9)

Processual archaeology   See *cultural process interpretation.*

Provenience or **provenance**   The three-dimensional location of archaeological data within or on the *matrix* at the time of discovery. (Chapter 4)

Pseudoarchaeology   Use of real or imagined archaeological evidence to justify non-scientific accounts about the past. (Chapter 1)

Publication   The final stage of archaeological *research design*, providing reports of the data and *interpretations* resulting from archaeological research. (Chapter 4)

Quern   A common Old World term for ground stone basins used to process grains (see also *metate*). (Chapter 6)

Radar   An instrument used in *subsurface detection* that records differential reflection of radar pulses from buried *strata* and *features.* (Chapter 5)

Radiocarbon dating   A *radiometric dating* technique based on measuring the decay of the radioactive isotope of carbon (^{14}C) to stable nitrogen (^{14}N). (Chapter 7)

Radiometric dating   A variety of *absolute dating* techniques based on the transformation of unstable radioactive isotopes into stable elements (see *potassium-argon dating* and *radiocarbon dating*). (Chapter 7)

Reconnaissance   A method of *data acquisition* in which archaeological remains are systematically identified, including both discovery and plotting of their location; it is often conducted along with *surface survey.* (Chapter 5)

Region   A geographically defined area containing a series of interrelated human communities sharing a single cultural-ecological *system.* (Chapter 4)

Relative dating   Determining chronological sequence without reference to a fixed time scale (compare with *absolute dating*). (Chapter 7)

Remote sensing   *Reconnaissance* and *surface survey* methods involving aerial or subsurface detection of archaeological data. (Chapter 5)

Research design   A systematic plan to coordinate archaeological research to ensure the efficient use of resources and to guide the research according to the *scientific method* (see *formulation, implementation, data acquisition, data processing, analysis, interpretation,* and *publication*). (Chapter 4)

Resistivity detector   An instrument used in *subsurface detection* that measures differences in the conductivity of electrical current and thus may identify archaeological *features.* (Chapter 5)

Retouch   A technique of chipped stone *artifact manufacture* in which *pressure flaking* is used to remove small steep *flakes* to modify the edges of flake tools. (Chapter 6)

Sample data acquisition Investigation of only a portion of the *sample units* in a *population* using either probabilistic or nonprobabilistic sampling (compare with *total data acquisition*). (Chapter 4)

Sample unit The basic unit of archaeological investigation; a subdivision of the *data universe*, defined by either arbitrary or nonarbitrary criteria (see *arbitrary sample units* and *nonarbitrary sample units*). (Chapter 4)

Science The systematic pursuit of knowledge about natural phenomena (in contrast to the nonnatural or supernatural) by a continually self-correcting method of testing and refining the conclusions resulting from observation (see *scientific method*). (Chapter 9)

Scientific method The operational means of *science*, by which natural phenomena are observed and conclusions drawn. (Chapter 1)

Secondary context The condition where *provenience*, *association*, and *matrix* have been wholly or partially altered by *transformational processes* after original *deposition* of archaeological data (compare with *primary context*). (Chapter 4)

Sequence comparison A relative dating technique based on the presence of similar sequences of artifacts at two or more sites. (Chapter 7)

Seriation Techniques used to order materials in a *relative dating* sequence in such a way that adjacent items in the series are more similar to each other than to items farther apart in the series (see *frequency seriation* and *stylistic seriation*). (Chapter 7)

Settlement archaeology The study of the spatial distribution of ancient activities, from remains of single activity areas to those of entire *regions*. (Chapter 8)

Shovel testing A *subsurface detection* technique using either posthole diggers or shovels to make a rapid determination of the density and distribution of archaeological remains. (Chapter 5)

Site A spatial clustering of archaeological data, comprising *artifacts*, *ecofacts*, and *features* in any combination. (Chapter 4)

Slip A solution of clay and water applied to *pottery* to provide color and a smooth and uniform surface (see also *glaze*). (Chapter 6)

Smelting Application of heat to ores to extract metals prior to the manufacture of metal artifacts (see *metallurgy*). (Chapter 6)

Social systems One of the three basic components of *culture*; the means by which human societies organize themselves and their interactions with other societies (see also *technology* and *ideology*). (Chapter 8)

Specific analogy An *analogy* used in archaeological *interpretation* based on specific comparisons that are documented within a single cultural *tradition*. (Chapter 8)

Strata The definable layers of archaeological *matrix* or *features* revealed by *excavation* (see *stratification*). (Chapters 2 and 5)

Stratification Multiple *strata* whose order of deposition reflects the *law of superposition* (see *stratigraphy*). (Chapter 5)

Stratigraphy The archaeological evaluation of the significance of *stratification* to determine the temporal sequence of data within stratified deposits by using both the *law of superposition* and *context* evaluations; also a *relative dating* technique. (Chapters 2, 5, and 7)

Stylistic attributes *Attributes* defined by the surface characteristics of *artifacts*—color, texture, decoration, and so forth—leading to stylistic *classifications*. (Chapter 5)

Stylistic seriation A *relative dating* technique in which *artifacts* or other data are ordered chronologically according to stylistic similarities (see *seriation*). (Chapter 7)

Stylistic types   *Artifact* classes based on *stylistic attributes*. (Chapter 5)

Subassemblage   A grouping of *artifact* classes based on *form* and *function* that is assumed to represent a single occupational group within an ancient community (see *assemblage* and *archaeological culture*). (Chapter 5)

Subsurface detection   *Remote sensing* techniques of area below ground carried out at ground level; includes *auguring, coring, shovel testing*, and use of a *magnetometer, resistivity detector, radar*, and similar means. (Chapter 5)

Surface survey   A method of *data acquisition* in which data are gathered and evaluated from the surface of archaeological *sites*, usually by mapping of *features* and surface collection of *artifacts* and *ecofacts*. (Chapter 5)

Synchronic   Pertaining to phenomena at one point in time; a concurrent perspective (compare with *diachronic*). (Chapter 1)

System   An organization that functions through the interdependence of its parts. (Chapters 3 and 8)

Taphonomy   Study of the *transformational processes* affecting organic ecofacts after the death of the original organisms. (Chapter 4)

Technological attributes   *Attributes* related to the characteristics of raw materials and *manufacturing* methods; leads to technological *classifications*. (Chapter 5)

Technological types   *Artifact* classes based on *technological attributes*. (Chapter 5)

Technology   One of the three basic components of *culture*; the means used by human societies to interact directly with and adapt to the environment (see *ideology* and *social systems*). (Chapter 8)

Temper   A nonplastic substance (such as sand) added to clay prior to *pottery manufacture* to reduce shrinkage and breakage during drying and firing. (Chapter 6)

Three-age technological sequence   A traditional *diachronic model* describing the sequence of technological *periods* in the Old World, each period characterized by predominant use of stone, bronze, or iron tools. (Chapter 2)

Time-space grids   A synthesis of temporal and spatial distributions of data used in *cultural history interpretation* based on *period* sequences within *culture areas*. (Chapter 3)

Total data acquisition   Investigation of all *sample units* in a *population* (compare with *sample data acquisition*). (Chapter 4)

Trade   Transmission of material objects from one society to another; a descriptive cultural *model* used in *cultural history interpretation* (see *exchange systems*). (Chapter 9)

Tradition   Cultural continuity through time; the temporal basis of the New World *cultural history interpretation* synthesis proposed by Willey and Phillips (1958) (compare with *horizon*). (Chapter 3)

Transformational processes   Conditions and events that affect archaeological data from the time of *deposition* to the time of recovery (compare with *behavioral processes*; see also *taphonomy*). (Chapter 4)

Transposed primary context   *Primary context* resulting from waste disposal leading to *midden* formation (compare with *use-related primary context*). (Chapter 4)

Type   A class of data defined by a consistent clustering of *attributes* (see *classification*). (Chapter 5)

Unilinear cultural evolution   A 19th-century version of *cultural evolution* holding that all human societies change according to a single fixed evolutionary course, passing through the same stages, described as savagery, barbarism, and civilization by Lewis Henry Morgan (compare *multilinear cultural evolution*). (Chapter 2)

Use The third stage of *behavioral processes*, in which *artifacts* are utilized (see *acquisition*, *manufacture*, and *deposition*). (Chapter 4)

Use-related primary context A *primary context* resulting from abandonment of materials during either *manufacture* or *use* (compare with *transposed primary context*). (Chapter 4)

Use-related secondary context A *secondary context* resulting from disturbance by human activity after original *deposition* of materials (compare with *natural secondary context*). (Chapter 4)

Vitrification Melting and fusion of glassy minerals within clay during high-temperature firing of *pottery* (above 1000° C), resulting in loss of porosity. (Chapter 6)

 Bibliography

Note: This brief bibliography is designed to introduce the student to the vast literature on archaeology and the human past. The works listed include books and articles, both recent publications and classics. A fuller bibliography can be found in *Archaeology: Discovering Our Past*, 2nd ed. (Sharer and Ashmore, 1993). Of course, we would also recommend that the interested reader explore libraries for other works, including new books and issues of magazines and journals. In general, periodicals such as *Archaeology, National Geographic, Natural History, Scientific American,* and *Smithsonian* publish articles for the broadest audience. Such journals as *American Antiquity, American Scientist, Journal of Field Archaeology, Nature,* or *Science* are more technical in content and language.

Agurcia Fasquelle, R. 1986. Snakes, jaguars, and outlaws: Some comments on Central American archaeology. In *Research and Reflections in Archaeology and History. Essays in Honor of Doris Stone*, ed. E. W. Andrews V, pp. 1–9. New Orleans: Middle American Research Institute, Tulane University.

Aiken, M. J. 1985. *Thermoluminescence Dating.* Orlando: Academic Press.

———. 1990. *Science-Based Dating in Archaeology.* London: Longman.

Alexander, J. 1970. *The Directing of Archaeological Excavations.* London: John Baker.

Allen, K. M. S., S. W. Green, and E. B. W. Zubrow, eds. 1990. *Interpreting Space: GIS and Archaeology.* London: Taylor & Francis.

Alva, W. 1990. New tomb of royal splendor. *National Geographic Magazine* 177 (6): 2–15.

Ammerman, A. J. 1981. Surveys and archaeological research. *Annual Review of Anthropology* 10: 63–88.

Andresen, J. M., B. F. Byrd, M. D. Elson, R. H. McGuire, R. G. Mendoza, E. Staski, and J. P. White. 1981. The deer hunters: Star Carr reconsidered. *World Archaeology* 13: 31–46.

Arden, H. 1989. Who owns our past? *National Geographic Magazine* 175 (3): 376–392.

Arnold, D. 1985. *Ceramic Theory and Cultural Process.* Cambridge: Cambridge University Press.

Aveni, A. F., ed. 1982. *Archaeoastronomy in the New World*. Cambridge: Cambridge University Press.

Baillie, M. G. L. 1982. *Tree-Ring Dating and Archaeology*. Chicago: University of Chicago Press.

Bannister, B. 1970. Dendrochronology. In *Science in Archaeology*, 2nd ed., ed. D. Brothwell and E. S. Higgs, pp. 191–205. New York: Praeger.

Bass, G. F. 1966. *Archaeology Under Water*. London: Thames & Hudson.

Bass, W. M. 1986. *Human Osteology: A Laboratory and Field Manual of the Human Skeleton*. Columbia, Mo.: Missouri Archaeological Society.

Bassett, C. A. 1986. The culture thieves. *Science 86* 7 (6): 22–29.

Behrensmeyer, A. K., and A. P. Hill, eds. 1980. *Fossils in the Making: Vertebrate Taphonomy and Paleoecology*. Chicago: University of Chicago Press.

Benson, E. P., ed. 1979. *Pre-Columbian Metallurgy of South America*. Washington, D.C.: Dumbarton Oaks.

Binford, L. R. 1962. Archaeology as anthropology. *American Antiquity* 28: 217–225.

———. 1964. A consideration of archaeological research design. *American Antiquity* 29: 425–441.

———. 1967. Smudge pits and hide smoking: The use of analogy in archaeological reasoning. *American Antiquity* 32: 1–12.

———. 1972. *An Archeological Perspective*. New York: Seminar Press.

———. 1978. *Nunamiut Ethnoarchaeology*. New York: Academic Press.

———. 1981. *Bones: Ancient Men and Modern Myths*. New York: Academic Press.

———. 1982. The archaeology of place. *Journal of Anthropological Archaeology* 1: 5–31.

———. 1983a. *In Pursuit of the Past: Decoding the Archaeological Record*. New York: Thames & Hudson.

———. 1983b. *Working at Archaeology*. New York: Academic Press.

———. 1989. *Debating Archaeology*. San Diego: Academic Press.

Binford, L. R., and S. R. Binford. 1969. Stone tools and human behavior. *Scientific American* 220 (4): 70–84.

Binford, S. R. 1968. Ethnographic data and understanding the Pleistocene. In *Man the Hunter*, ed. R. B. Lee and I. DeVore, pp. 274–275. Chicago: Aldine.

Biscott, J. L., and R. J. Rosenbauer. 1981. Uranium series dating of human skeletal remains from the Del Mar and Sunnyvale sites, California. *Science* 213: 1003–1006.

Bordaz, J. 1970. *Tools of the Old and New Stone Age*. Garden City, N.Y.: Natural History Press.

Bordes, F. 1968. *The Old Stone Age*. New York: McGraw-Hill.

Bordes, F., and D. de Sonneville-Bordes. 1970. The significance of variability in Paleolithic assemblages. *World Archaeology* 2: 61–73.

Brain, C. K. 1981. *The Hunters or the Hunted? An Introduction to African Cave Taphonomy*. Chicago: University of Chicago Press.

Brew, J. O. 1968. *One Hundred Years of Anthropology*. Cambridge: Harvard University Press.

Brothwell, D. R. 1981. *Digging Up Bones*. 3rd ed. Ithaca, N.Y.: Cornell University Press.

Bunn, H. T. 1981. Archaeological evidence for meat-eating by Plio-Pleistocene hominids from Koobi Fora and Olduvai Gorge. *Nature* 291: 574–577.

Bunn, H. T., J. W. K. Harris, G. Isaac, Z. Kaufulu, E. Kroll, K. Schick, N. Toth, and A. K. Behrensmeyer. 1980. FxJj50: An early Pleistocene site in northern Kenya. *World Archaeology* 12: 109–136.

Butzer, K. W. 1982. *Archaeology as Human Ecology: Method and Theory for a Contextual Approach*. New York: Cambridge University Press.

Cahan, D., L. H. Keeley, and F. L. Van Noten. 1979. Stone tools, toolkits, and human behavior in prehistory. *Current Anthropology* 20: 661–683.

Champe, J. L., D. S. Byers, C. Evans, A. K. Guthe, H. W. Hamilton, E. B. Jelks, C. W. Meighan, S. Olafson, G. I. Quimby, W. Smith, and F. Wendorf. 1961. Four statements for archaeology. *American Antiquity* 27: 137–138.

Champion, S. 1980. *A Dictionary of Terms and Techniques in Archaeology.* Oxford: Phaidon Press.

Chang, K. C. 1972. *Settlement Patterns in Archaeology.* Modules in Anthropology, no. 24. Reading, Mass.: Addison-Wesley.

Chapman, R., I. Kinnes, and K. Randsborg, eds. 1981. *The Archaeology of Death.* Cambridge: Cambridge University Press.

Charleton, T. H. 1981. Archaeology, ethnohistory, and ethnology: Interpretive interfaces. In *Advances in Archaeological Method and Theory*, vol. 4, ed. Michael B. Schiffer, pp. 129–176. New York: Academic Press.

Childe, V. G. 1954. *What Happened in History.* Rev. ed. Harmondsworth, England: Penguin.

Chippindale, C. 1986. Stonehenge astronomy: Anatomy of a modern myth. *Archaeology* 39 (1): 48–52.

Christenson, A. L., ed. 1989. *Tracing Archaeology's Past: The Historiography of Archaeology.* Carbondale: Southern Illinois University Press.

Clark, J. G. D. [1954] 1971. *Excavations at Star Carr.* Reprint. Cambridge: Cambridge University Press.

Clarke, D. L., ed. 1972a. *Models in Archaeology.* London: Methuen.

———. 1972b. A provisional model of an Iron Age society. In *Models in Archaeology*, ed. D. L. Clarke, pp. 801–869. London: Methuen.

Cleere, H., ed. 1984. *Approaches to the Archaeological Heritage: A Comparative Study of World Cultural Resource Management Systems.* Cambridge: Cambridge University Press.

———, ed. 1989. *Archaeological Heritage Management in the Modern World.* London: Unwin Hyman.

Coggins, C. C. 1972. Archaeology and the art market. *Science* 175: 263–266.

Coles, B., and J. M. Coles. 1986. *Sweet Track to Glastonbury: The Somerset Levels in Prehistory.* New York: Thames & Hudson.

Coles, J. M. 1973. *Archaeology by Experiment.* New York: Scribner's.

———. 1984. *The Archaeology of Wetlands.* Edinburgh: Edinburgh University Press.

———. 1989. The world's oldest road. *Scientific American* 261 (5): 100–106.

Conrad, G. W., and A. A. Demarest. 1984. *Religion and Empire: The Dynamics of Aztec and Inca Expansionism.* Cambridge: Cambridge University Press.

Cottrell, A. 1981. *The First Emperor of China, the Greatest Archaeological Find of Our Time.* New York: Holt, Rinehart and Winston.

Cowgill, G. L. 1974. Quantitative studies of urbanism at Teotihuacán. In *Mesoamerican Archaeology: New Approaches*, ed. N. Hammond, pp. 363–397. Austin: University of Texas Press.

Crabtree, D. E. 1972. *An Introduction to Flintworking: Part I. An Introduction to the Technology of Stone Tools.* Occasional Papers no. 28. Pocatello: Idaho State University.

Cronyn, J. M. 1990. *The Elements of Archaeological Conservation.* London: Routledge.

Daniel, G. 1967. *The Origins and Growth of Archaeology.* Baltimore: Penguin.

———. 1981. *A Short History of Archaeology.* London: Thames & Hudson.

Daniel, G., and C. Chippindale, eds. 1989. *The Pastmasters: Eleven Modern Pioneers of Archaeology.* London: Thames & Hudson.

Davis, E. L. 1975. The "exposed archaeology" of China Lake, California. *American Antiquity* 40: 39–53.

Davis, H. A. 1972. The crisis in American archaeology. *Science* 175: 267–272.

———. 1982. Professionalism in archaeology. *American Antiquity* 47: 158–162.

Deetz, J. F. 1967. *Invitation to Archaeology*. Garden City: Natural History Press.

————. 1977. *In Small Things Forgotten: The Archaeology of Early American Life*. Garden City: Doubleday/Anchor.

Deetz, J. F., and E. Dethlefsen. 1967. Death's head, cherub, urn and willow. *Natural History* 76 (3): 28–37.

DeNiro, M. J. 1987. Stable isotopy and archaeology. *American Scientist* 75: 182–191.

Dillon, B., ed. 1985. *Student's Guide to Archaeological Illustrating*. Rev. ed. Archaeological Research Tools 1. Los Angeles: UCLA Institute of Archaeology.

————. 1989. *Practical Archaeology: Field and Laboratory Techniques and Archaeological Logistics*. Revised ed. Archaeological Research Tools 2. Los Angeles: UCLA Institute of Archaeology.

Dimbleby, G. W. 1985. *The Palynology of Archaeological Sites*. Orlando: Academic Press.

Dorrell, P. G. 1989. *Photography in Archaeology and Conservation*. Cambridge: Cambridge University Press.

Dunnell, R. C. 1980. Evolutionary theory and archaeology. In *Advances in Archaeological Method and Theory*, vol. 3, ed. M. B. Schiffer, pp. 35–99. New York: Academic Press.

————. 1982. Science, social science, and common sense: The agonizing dilemma of modern archaeology. *Journal of Anthropological Research* 38: 1–25.

————. 1986. Five decades of American archaeology. In *American Archaeology Past and Future: A Celebration of the Society for American Archaeology 1935–1985*, ed. D. J. Meltzer, D. D. Fowler, and J. A. Sabloff, pp. 23–49. Washington, D.C.: Smithsonian Institution Press.

Ebert, J. I. 1984. Remote sensing applications in archaeology. In *Advances in Archaeological Method and Theory*, vol. 7, ed. Michael B. Schiffer, pp. 293–362. Orlando: Academic Press.

Elachi, C. 1982. Radar images of the earth from space. *Scientific American* 247 (6): 54–61.

Ericson, J. E., and T. K. Earle, eds. 1982. *Contexts for Prehistoric Exchange*. New York: Academic Press.

Estes, J. E., J. R. Jensen, and L. R. Tinney. 1977. The use of historical photography for mapping archaeological sites. *Journal of Field Archaeology* 4: 441–447.

Fagan, B. M. 1975. *The Rape of the Nile*. New York: Scribner's.

————. 1978. *Quest for the Past: Great Discoveries in Archaeology*. New York: Scribner's.

————. 1985. *The Adventure of Archaeology*. Washington, D.C.: National Geographic Society.

————. 1988. Black day at Slack Farm. *Archaeology* 41 (8): 15–16, 73.

Falk, L., ed. 1991. *Historical Archaeology in Global Perspective*. Washington, D.C.: Smithsonian Institution Press.

Farnsworth, P., J. E. Brady, M. J. DeNiro, and R. S. MacNeish. 1985. A re-evaluation of the isotopic and archaeological reconstructions of diet in the Tehuacán Valley. *American Antiquity* 50: 102–116.

Feder, K. L. 1990. *Frauds, Myths, and Mysteries: Science and Pseudoscience in Archaeology*. Mountain View, Calif.: Mayfield Publishing Company.

Fish, S. K., and S. A. Kowalewski, eds. 1990. *The Archaeology of Regions: A Case for Full-Coverage Survey*. Washington, D.C.: Smithsonian Institution Press.

Flannery, K. V. 1967. Culture history vs. cultural process: A debate in American archaeology. *Scientific American* 217 (2): 119–122.

————. 1968. Archeological systems theory and early Mesoamerica. In *Anthropological Archeology in the Americas*, ed. B. J. Meggers, pp. 67–87. Washington, D.C.: Anthropological Society of Washington.

————. 1972. The cultural evolution of civilizations. *Annual Review of Ecology and Systematics* 2: 399–426.

————, ed. 1976. *The Early Mesoamerican Village*. New York: Academic Press.

—. 1986. A visit to the master. In *Guila Naquitz, Archaic Foraging and Early Agriculture in Oaxaca, Mexico*, ed. K. V. Flannery, pp. 511–519. Orlando: Academic Press.

Ford, J. A. 1954. The type concept revisited. *American Anthropologist* 56: 42–53.

Ford, R. I. 1983. The Archaeological Conservancy, Inc.: The goal is site preservation. *American Archaeology* 3: 221–224.

Fowler, D. D. 1987. Uses of the past: Archaeology in the service of the state. *American Antiquity* 52: 229–248.

Friedman, I., and F. W. Trembour. 1983. Obsidian hydration dating update. *American Antiquity* 48: 544–547.

Frink, D. S. 1984. Artifact behavior within the plow zone. *Journal of Field Archaeology* 11: 356–363.

Gathercole, P., and D. Lowenthal, eds. 1989. *The Politics of the Past*. London: Unwin Hyman.

Gero, J. M. 1991. Genderlithics: Woman's roles in stone tool production. In *Engendering Archaeology: Women and Prehistory*, ed. J. M. Gero and M. W. Conkey, pp. 163–193. Oxford: Basil Blackwell.

Gero, J. M., and M. W. Conkey, eds. 1991. *Engendering Archaeology: Women and Prehistory*. Oxford: Basil Blackwell.

Gibbon, G. 1984. *Anthropological Archaeology*. New York: Columbia University Press.

—. 1989. *Explanation in Archaeology*. Oxford: Basil Blackwell.

Giddings, J. L. 1967. *Ancient Men of the Arctic*. New York: Knopf.

Giesecke, A. G. 1987. The Abandoned Shipwreck Bill: Protecting our threatened cultural heritage. *Archaeology* 40 (4): 50–53.

Gilbert, R. I., Jr., and J. H. Mielke, eds. 1985. *The Analysis of Prehistoric Diets*. Orlando: Academic Press.

Gladfelter, B. G. 1981. Developments and directions in geoarchaeology. In *Advances in Archaeological Method and Theory*, vol. 4, ed. M. B. Schiffer, pp. 343–364. New York: Academic Press.

Glassie, H. 1975. *Folk Housing in Middle Virginia: A Structural Analysis of Historic Artifacts*. Knoxville: University of Tennessee Press.

Glob, P. V. 1969. *The Bog People: Iron-Age Man Preserved*. Trans. R. Bruce-Mitford. Ithaca, N.Y.: Cornell University Press.

Gould, R. A. 1980. *Living Archaeology*. Cambridge: Cambridge University Press.

Gould, S. J. 1985. *The Flamingo's Smile*. New York: Norton.

—. 1986. Evolution and the triumph of homology, or why history matters. *American Scientist* 74: 60–69.

Green, E. L., ed. 1984. *Ethics and Values in Archaeology*. New York: Free Press.

Hadingham, E. 1984. *Early Man and the Cosmos*. New York: Walker.

Hall, R. L. 1977. An anthropomorphic perspective for eastern United States prehistory. *American Antiquity* 42: 499–518.

Hamilton, S. L., and R. Woodward. 1984. A sunken 17th-century city: Port Royal, Jamaica. *Archaeology* 37 (1): 38–45.

Harris, E. C. 1989. *Principles of Archaeological Stratigraphy*. 2nd ed. London: Academic Press.

Harris, M. 1968. *The Rise of Anthropological Theory: A History of Theories of Culture*. New York: Crowell.

Hart, D., ed. 1983. *Disease in Ancient Man*. Agincourt, Ontario: Irwin.

Hassan, F. A. 1981. *Demographic Archaeology*. New York: Academic Press.

Haury, E. W. 1958. Evidence from Point of Pines for a prehistoric migration from northern Arizona. In *Migrations in New World Culture History*, ed. R. H. Thompson, pp. 1–6. Social Science Bulletin, no. 27. Tucson: University of Arizona.

Haviland, W. A. 1967. Stature at Tikal, Guatemala: Implications for ancient demography and social organization. *American Antiquity* 32: 316–325.

———. 1985. *Anthropology*, 4th ed. New York: Holt, Rinehart and Winston.

Hawkins, G. S. 1965. *Stonehenge Decoded.* New York: Doubleday.

Hedges, J. W. 1984. *Tomb of the Eagles: Death and Life in a Stone Age Tribe.* New York: New Amsterdam.

Hedges, R. E. M., and J. A. J. Gowlett. 1986. Radiocarbon dating by accelerator mass spectrometry. *Scientific American* 254 (1): 101–107.

Heggie, D. C., ed. 1982. *Archaeoastronomy in the Old World.* Cambridge: Cambridge University Press.

Hester, T. A., R. F. Heizer, and J. A. Graham, eds. 1975. *Field Methods in Archaeology*, 6th ed. Palo Alto, Calif.: Mayfield Publishing Company.

Higgenbotham, C. D. 1983. Native Americans versus archaeologists: The legal issues. *American Indian Law Review* 10: 91–115.

Hill, J. N. 1970. *Broken K Pueblo: Prehistoric Social Organization in the American Southwest.* Anthropological Paper no. 18. Tucson: University of Arizona Press.

Hill, J. N., and R. K. Evans. 1972. A model for classification and typology. In *Models in Archaeology*, ed. D. L. Clarke, pp. 231–273. London: Methuen.

Hodder, I., ed. 1982. *Symbolic and Structural Archaeology.* Cambridge: Cambridge University Press.

———. 1989. *The Meaning of Things: Material Culture and Symbolic Expression.* London: Unwin Hyman.

———. 1990. *The Domestication of Europe: Structure and Contingency in Neolithic Societies.* Oxford: Basil Blackwell.

———. 1991. *Reading the Past: Current Approaches to Interpretation in Archaeology.* 2nd ed. Cambridge: Cambridge University Press.

Hodder, I., and M. Hassal. 1971. The non-random spacing of Romano-British walled towns. *Man* 6: 391–407.

Hoving, T. 1978. *Tutankhamun: The Untold Story.* New York: Simon and Schuster.

Hyslop, J. 1984. *The Inca Road System.* Orlando: Academic Press.

Isaac, G. L. 1984. The archaeology of human origins: Studies of the Lower Pleistocene in East Africa 1971–1981. In *Advances in World Archaeology*, ed. F. Wendorf and A. E. Close, pp. 1–87. Orlando: Academic Press.

Isbell, W. H. 1978. The prehistoric ground drawings of Peru. *Scientific American* 239 (4): 140–153.

Jackson, T. L. 1991. Pounding acorn: Woman's production as social and economic focus. In *Engendering Archaeology: Women and Prehistory*, ed. J. M. Gero and M. W. Conkey, pp. 301–325. Oxford: Basil Blackwell.

Johnson, A. W., and T. Earle. 1987. *The Evolution of Human Societies: From Foraging Group to Agrarian State.* Stanford: Stanford University Press.

Johnstone, P. 1980. *The Sea-Craft of Prehistory.* Cambridge: Harvard University Press.

Joukowsky, M. 1980. *A Complete Manual of Field Archaeology.* Englewood Cliffs, N.J.: Prentice-Hall.

Jovanovic, B., 1980. The origins of copper mining in Europe. *Scientific American* 242 (5): 152–167.

Keeley, L. H. 1980. *Experimental Determination of Stone Tool Uses: A Microwear Analysis.* Chicago: University of Chicago Press.

Kelley, J. H., and M. P. Hanen. 1988. *Archaeology and the Methodology of Science.* Albuquerque: University of New Mexico Press.

Kenworthy, M. A., E. M. King, M. E. Ruwell, and T. Van Houten. 1985. *Preserving Field Records: Archival Techniques for Archaeologists and Anthropologists.* Philadelphia: University Museum, University of Pennsylvania.

Kidder, A. V. (1924) 1962. *An Introduction to the Study of Southwestern Archaeology.* Reprint with introduction, Southwestern archaeology today, by I. Rouse. New Haven: Yale University Press.

King, M. E. 1978. Analytical methods and prehistoric textiles. *American Antiquity* 43: 89–96.

King, T. F. 1983. Professional responsibility in public archaeology. *Annual Review of Anthropology* 12: 143–164.

Klein, R. G., and K. Cruz-Uribe. 1984. *The Analysis of Animal Bones from Archaeological Sites.* Chicago: University of Chicago Press.

Kolata, A. 1987. Tiwanaku and its hinterland. *Archaeology* 40 (1): 36–41.

Layton, R., ed. 1989a. *Conflict in the Archaeology of Living Traditions.* London: Unwin Hyman.

———, ed. 1989b. *Who Needs the Past? Indigenous Values and Archaeology.* London: Unwin Hyman.

LeBlanc, S. A. 1983. *The Mimbres People: Ancient Pueblo Painters of the American Southwest.* New York: Thames & Hudson.

Lechtman, H. 1984. Pre-Columbian surface metallurgy. *Scientific American* 250 (6): 56–63.

Lee, R. B., and I. DeVore, eds. 1968. *Man the Hunter.* Chicago: Aldine.

Leone, M. P. 1982. Some opinions about recovering mind. *American Antiquity* 47: 742–760.

Levin, A. M. 1986. Excavation photography: A day on a dig. *Archaeology* 39 (1): 34–39.

Lewis–Williams, J. D. 1986. Cognitive and optical illusions in San rock art research. *Current Anthropology* 27: 171–178.

Limp, W. F. 1974. Water separation and flotation processes. *Journal of Field Archaeology* 1: 337–342.

Lipe, W. D. 1974. A conservation model for American archaeology. *The Kiva* 39: 213–245.

———. 1984. Value and meaning in cultural resources. In *Approaches to the Archaeological Heritage: A Comparative Study of World Cultural Resource Management Systems,* ed. H. Cleere, pp. 1–11. Cambridge: Cambridge University Press.

Longacre, W. A., and J. E. Ayres. 1968. Archeological lessons from an Apache wickiup. In *New Perspectives in Archaeology,* ed. S. R. Binford and L. R. Binford, pp. 151–159. Chicago: Aldine.

Loy, T. H. 1983. Prehistoric blood residues: Detection on tool surfaces and identification of species of origin. *Science* 220: 1269–1271.

McBryde, I., ed. 1985. *Who Owns the Past?* Melbourne: Oxford University Press.

McGimsey, C. R., III. 1972. *Public Archeology.* New York: Seminar Press.

McKusick, M. 1984. Psychic archaeology from Atlantis to Oz. *Archaeology* 37 (6): 48–52.

MacNeish, R. S., M. L. Fowler, A. G. Cook, F. A. Peterson, A. Nelken-Terner, and J. A. Neely. 1972. *Excavations and Reconnaissance: The Prehistory of the Tehuacán Valley,* vol. 5. Austin: University of Texas Press.

MacNeish, R. S., T. C. Patterson, and D. L. Browman. 1975. *The Central Peruvian Interaction Sphere.* Andover, Mass.: Phillips Academy.

Madden, R., J. D. Muhly, and T. S. Wheeler. 1977. How the Iron Age began. *Scientific American* 237 (4): 122–131.

Marshack, A. 1972. Upper Paleolithic notation and symbol. *Science* 178: 817–827.

Meltzer, D. J., D. D. Fowler, and J. A. Sabloff, eds. 1986. *American Archaeology Past and Future: A Celebration of the Society for American Archaeology 1935–1985.* Washington, D. C.: Smithsonian Institution Press.

Michael, H. N. 1985. Correcting radiocarbon dates with tree ring dates at MASCA. *University Museum Newsletter* (University of Pennsylvania) 23 (3): 1–2.

Michel, M. 1981. Preserving America's prehistoric heritage. *Archaeology* 34 (2): 61–63.

Michels, J. W. 1973. *Dating Methods in Archaeology.* New York: Academic Press.

Miller, D. 1980. Archaeology and development. *Current Anthropology* 21: 709–726.

Moseley, M. E. 1975. Prehistoric principles of labor organization in the Moche valley, Peru. *American Antiquity* 40: 190–196.

Moseley, M. E., and C. J. Mackey. 1974. *Twenty-four Architectural Plans of Chan Chan, Peru: Structure and Form at the Capital of Chimor.* Cambridge: Harvard University, Peabody Museum Press.

Mueller, J. W., ed. 1975. *Sampling in Archaeology.* Tucson: University of Arizona Press.

Netting, R. M. 1977. *Cultural Ecology.* Menlo Park, Calif.: Cummings.

Noël Hume, I. 1969. *Historical Archaeology.* New York: Knopf.

———. 1979. *Martin's Hundred: The Discovery of a Lost Colonial Virginia Settlement.* New York: Knopf.

Numbers, R. L. 1982. Creationism in 20th-century America. *Science* 218: 538–544.

Oakley, K. P. 1956. *Man the Tool-Maker.* 3rd ed. London: British Museum.

———. 1970. Analytical methods of dating bones. In *Science in Archaeology,* 2nd ed., ed. D. Brothwell and E. S. Higgs, pp. 35–45. New York: Praeger.

Olsen, S. J. 1964. *Mammal Remains from Archaeological Sites.* Papers of the Peabody Museum 56. Cambridge: Harvard University.

Orme, B., ed. 1982. *Problems in Case Studies in Archaeological Dating.* Atlantic Highlands, N.J.: Humanities Press.

Orton, C. 1980. *Mathematics in Archaeology.* Cambridge: Cambridge University Press.

Paddayya, K. 1990. *The New Archaeology and Aftermath: A View from Outside the Anglo-American World.* Pune, India: Ravish Publishers.

Parrington, M. 1983. Remote sensing. *Annual Review of Anthropology* 12: 105–124.

Pearce, S. M. 1990. *Archaeological Curatorship.* Washington, D.C.: Smithsonian Institution Press.

Petrie, W. M. F. 1901. *Diospolis Parva.* Memoir no. 20. London: Egyptian Exploration Fund.

Pinsky, V., and A. Wylie, eds. 1990. *Critical Traditions in Contemporary Archaeology.* Cambridge: Cambridge University Press.

Plog, S., F. Plog, and W. Wait. 1978. Decision making in modern surveys. In *Advances in Archaeological Method and Theory,* vol. 1, ed. M. B. Schiffer, pp. 282–421. New York: Academic Press.

Potts, R., and P. Shipman. 1981. Cutmarks made by stone tools on bones from Olduvai Gorge, Tanzania. *Nature* 291: 577–580.

Price, T. D., and J. A. Brown, eds. 1985. *Prehistoric Hunter-Gatherers: The Emergence of Cultural Complexity.* Orlando: Academic Press.

Preucel, R. W., ed. 1991. *Processual and Postprocessual Archaeologies: Multiple Ways of Knowing the Past.* Center for Archaeological Investigations, Occasional Papers 16. Carbondale: Southern Illinois University.

Pulak, C., and D. A. Frey. 1985. The search for a Bronze Age shipwreck. *Archaeology* 38 (4): 18–24.

Rapp, G., Jr., and J. A. Gifford, eds. 1985. *Archaeological Geology.* New Haven: Yale University Press.

Rathje, W. L. 1978. The ancient astronaut myth. *Archaeology* 31 (1): 4–7.

Redman, C. L., and P. J. Watson. 1970. Systemic, intensive surface collection. *American Antiquity.* 35: 279–291.

Renfrew, C. 1971. Carbon 14 and the prehistory of Europe. *Scientific American* 225 (4): 63–72.

———. 1973. *Before Civilization: The Radiocarbon Revolution and Prehistoric Europe.* New York: Knopf.

———. 1975. Trade as action at a distance: Questions of integration and communication. In *Ancient Civilization and Trade,* ed. J. A. Sabloff and C. C. Lamberg-Karlovsky, pp. 3–59.

School of American Research. Albuquerque: University of New Mexico Press.

————. 1983. The social archaeology of megalithic monuments. *Scientific American* 249 (5): 152–163.

Renfrew, C., and J. F. Cherry, eds. 1986. *Peer Polity Interaction and Socio-Political Change.* Cambridge: Cambridge University Press.

Rice, P. M. 1987. *Pottery Analysis: A Sourcebook.* Chicago: University of Chicago Press.

Rouse, I. 1962. Introduction to revised edition. In *An Introduction to Southwestern Archaeology* [orig. 1924], by A. V. Kidder. New Haven: Yale University Press.

Rovner, I. 1983. Plant opal phytolith analysis: Major advances in archaeobotanical research. In *Advances in Archaeological Method and Theory*, vol. 6, ed. M. B. Schiffer, pp. 225–266. New York: Academic Press.

Sabloff, J. A. 1975. *Ceramics: Excavations at Seibal*, no. 2. Memoirs of the Peabody Museum of Archaeology and Ethnology, vol. 13. Cambridge: Harvard University, Peabody Museum.

————. 1982. Introduction. In *Archaeology: Myth and Reality: Readings from Scientific American*, ed. J. A. Sabloff, pp. 1–26. San Francisco: Freeman.

Salmon, M. 1982. *Philosophy and Archaeology.* New York: Academic Press.

Sanders, W. T., and B. J. Price. 1968. *Mesoamerica: The Evolution of a Civilization.* New York: Random House.

Schiffer, M. B. 1976. *Behavioral Archaeology.* New York: Academic Press.

————. 1987. *Formation Processes of the Archaeological Record.* Albuquerque: University of New Mexico Press.

Schliemann, H. [1881] 1968. *Ilios, the City and Country of the Trojans.* Reissue. New York: Benjamin Blom.

Schortman, E., P. Urban, W. Ashmore, and J. Benyo. 1986. Interregional interaction in the southeast Maya periphery: The Santa Bárbara Archaeological Project 1983–1984 seasons. *Journal of Field Archaeology* 13: 259–272.

Schuyler, R. L., ed. 1978. *Historical Archaeology: A Guide to Substantive and Theoretical Contributions.* Farmingdale, N.Y.: Baywood.

Semenov, S. A. 1964. *Prehistoric Technology.* New York: Barnes & Noble.

Shanks, M., and C. Tilley. 1987. *Re-Constructing Archaeology.* Cambridge: Cambridge University Press.

Sharer, R. J. 1994. *The Ancient Maya.* 5th ed. Stanford: Stanford University Press.

Sharer, R. J., and W. Ashmore. 1993. *Archaeology: Discovering Our Past.* 2nd ed. Mountain View, Calif.: Mayfield Publishing Company.

Shennan, S. J., ed. 1988. *Quantifying Archaeology.* San Diego: Academic Press.

Smith, G. E. 1928. *In the Beginning: The Origin of Civilization.* New York: Morrow.

Smith, G. S., and J. E. Ehrenhard, eds. 1991. *Protecting the Past.* Boca Raton: CRC Press.

Society for American Archaeology. 1986. Statement concerning the treatment of human remains. *Bulletin of the Society for American Archaeology* 4 (3): 7–8.

Society of Professional Archeologists. 1978. Qualifications for recognition as a professional archeologist. *SOPADOPA: Newsletter of the Society of Professional Archeologists* 2 (no. 3).

South, S. A. 1977. *Method and Theory in Historical Archaeology.* New York: Academic Press.

Spaulding, A. C. 1953. Statistical techniques for the discovery of artifact types. *American Antiquity* 18: 305–313.

Stark, B. L. 1986. Origins of food production in the New World. In *American Archaeology Past and Future: A Celebration of the Society for American Archaeology 1935–1985*, ed. D. J. Meltzer, D. D. Fowler, and J. A. Sabloff, pp. 277–321. Washington, D.C.: Smithsonian Institution Press.

Stein, J. K., and W. R. Farrand, eds. 1985. *Archaeological Sediments in Context.* Orono, Maine: Center for the Study of Early Man.

Steward, J. H. 1955. *Theory of Culture Change*. Urbana: University of Illinois Press.

Stone, P., and R. MacKenzie, eds. 1989. *The Excluded Past: Archaeology in Education*. London: Unwin Hyman.

Stuart, G. E. 1976. *Your Career in Archaeology*. Washington, D.C.: Society for American Archaeology.

Talmadge, V. A. 1982. The violation of sepulture: Is it legal to excavate human burials? *Archaeology* 35 (6): 44–49.

Taylor, R. E., and I. Longworth, eds. 1975. Dating: New methods and new results. *World Archaeology* 7 (no. 2).

Taylor, W. W. (1948) 1967. *A Study of Archaeology*. American Anthropological Association Memoir 69. Reprint. Carbondale: Southern Illinois University Press.

Thomas, D. H. 1973. An empirical test for Steward's model of Great Basin settlement patterns. *American Antiquity* 38: 155–176.

Topping, A. 1978. China's incredible find. *National Geographic Magazine* 153: 440–459.

Torrence, R., ed. 1989. *Time, Energy and Stone Tools*. Cambridge: Cambridge University Press.

Toth, N. 1987. The first technology. *Scientific American* 256 (4): 112–121.

Trigger, B. G. 1968. The determinants of settlement patterns. In *Settlement Archaeology*, ed. K. C. Chang, pp. 53–78. Palo Alto: National Press.

———. 1970. Aims in prehistoric archaeology. *Antiquity* 44: 26–37.

———. 1984. Archaeology at the crossroads: What's new? *Annual Review of Anthropology* 13: 275–300.

———. 1989. *A History of Archaeological Thought*. Cambridge: Cambridge University Press.

Trinkaus, K. M., ed. 1987. *Polities and Partitions: Human Boundaries and the Growth of Complex Societies*. Tempe, Ariz.: Anthropological Research Papers.

Tuan, Y. 1977. *Space and Place: The Perspective of Experience*. Minneapolis: University of Minnesota Press.

Turnbull, C. 1972. *The Mountain People*. New York: Simon and Schuster.

Tylor, E. B. 1871. *Primitive Culture*. London: Murray.

Ubelaker, D. H. 1989. *Human Skeletal Remains: Excavation, Analysis, Interpretation*. 2nd ed. Manuals on Archaeology. Washington, D.C.: Taraxacum.

Ucko, P. J. 1969. Ethnography and archaeological interpretation of funerary remains. *World Archaeology* 1: 262–280.

van der Merwe, N. J. 1982. Carbon isotopes, photosynthesis, and archaeology. *American Scientist* 70: 596–606.

van der Merwe, N. J., and P. Avery. 1982. Pathways to steel. *American Scientist* 70: 146–155.

Van Noten, F., D. Cahan, and L. Keeley. 1980. A Paleolithic campsite in Belgium. *Scientific American* 242 (4): 48–55.

Veit, U. 1989. Ethnic concepts in German prehistory: A case study on the relationship between cultural identity and archaeological objectivity. In *Archaeological Approaches to Cultural Identity*, ed. S. Shennan, pp. 35–56. London: Unwin Hyman.

Villa, P. 1982. Conjoinable pieces and site formation processes. *American Antiquity* 47: 276–290.

Watson, P. J., and M. C. Kennedy. 1991. The development of horticulture in the Eastern Woodlands of North America: Woman's role. In *Engendering Archaeology: Women and Prehistory*, ed. J. M. Gero and M. W. Conkey, pp. 255–275. Oxford: Basil Blackwell.

Watson, P. J., S. A. LeBlanc, and C. L. Redman. 1984. *Archaeological Explanation: The Scientific Method in Archaeology*. New York: Columbia University Press.

Wauchope, R. 1938. *Modern Maya Houses*. Carnegie Institution of Washington Publication 502. Washington, D.C.

———. 1962. *Lost Tribes and Sunken Continents*. Chicago: University of Chicago Press.

Wendorf, F. 1973. "Rescue" archaeology along the Nile. In *In Search of Man: Readings in Archaeology*, ed. E. L. Green, pp. 39–42. Boston: Little, Brown.

Wertime, T., and S. Wertime, eds. 1982. *Early Pyrotechnology*. Washington, D.C.: Smithsonian Institution Press.

Whallon, R., and J. A. Brown, eds. 1982. *Essays on Archaeological Typology*. Evanston, Ill.: Center for American Archeology Press.

Wheat, J. B. 1972. *The Olsen-Chubbuck Site: A Paleo-Indian bison kill*. Society for American Archaeology Memoir no. 26. Washington, D.C.

Wheeler, M. 1954. *Archaeology from the Earth*. Harmondsworth, England: Penguin.

White, P. 1974. *The Past Is Human*. New York: Taplinger.

White, T. D. 1990. *Human Osteology*. San Diego: Academic Press.

Wilk, R. R., and W. L. Rathje, eds. 1982. Archaeology of the household: Building a prehistory of domestic life. *American Behavioral Scientist* 25 (no. 6).

Willey, G. R. 1953. *Prehistoric Settlement Patterns in the Virú Valley, Peru*. Bureau of American Ethnology, Bulletin 155. Washington, D.C.: Smithsonian Institution.

———, ed. 1974. *Archaeological Researches in Retrospect*. Cambridge, Mass.: Winthrop.

Willey, G. R., and P. Phillips. 1958. *Method and Theory in American Archaeology*. Chicago: University of Chicago Press.

Willey, G. R., and J. A. Sabloff. 1980. *A History of American Archaeology*. 2nd ed. San Francisco: Freeman.

Williams, S. 1991. *Fantastic Archaeology: The Wild Side of North American Prehistory*. Philadelphia: University of Pennsylvania Press.

Wilson, J. 1982. *The Passionate Amateur's Guide to Archaeology in the United States*. New York: Collier.

Wing, E. S., and A. R. Brown. 1980. *Paleonutrition: Method and Theory in Prehistoric Foodways*. New York: Academic Press.

Wiseman, J. R. 1984. Scholarship and provenience in the study of artifacts. *Journal of Field Archaeology* 11: 67–77.

———. 1985. Odds and ends: Multimedia documentation in archaeology. *Journal of Field Archaeology* 12: 389.

Wittry, W. L. 1977. The American Woodhenge. In *Explorations in Cahokia Archaeology*, ed. M. L. Fowler, pp. 43–48. Illinois Archaeological Survey Bulletin 7. Urbana: University of Illinois.

Wolfman, D. 1984. Geomagnetic dating methods in archaeology. In *Advances in Archaeological Method and Theory*, vol. 7, ed. M. B. Schiffer, pp. 363–458. Orlando: Academic Press.

Wood, M. 1985. *In Search of the Trojan War*. New York: Facts on File Publications.

Woolley, C. L. 1934. *Ur Excavations*. Vol. II: *The Royal Cemetery*. Oxford and Philadelphia: British Museum and University Museum, University of Pennsylvania.

Wright, H. T. 1986. The evolution of civilizations. In *American Archaeology Past and Future: A Celebration of the Society for American Archaeology 1935–1985*, ed. D. J. Meltzer, D. D. Fowler, and J. A. Sabloff, pp. 323–365. Washington, D.C.: Smithsonian Institution Press.

Zeuner, F. E. 1958. *Dating the Past: An Introduction to Geochronology*. London: Methuen.

Zubrow, E. 1975. *Prehistoric Carrying Capacity: A Model*. Menlo Park, California: Cummings.

Index

Absolute dating, 145, 151, 153–155, table 7.1
Abu Simbel (Egypt), 255, fig. 10.5
Acquisition
    as behavioral stage, 61, 66, 67, figs. 4.6, 4.7
    from experiments, 171
    in trade, 185
    of raw materials, 117–118, 128–129, 141–142
    See also Behavioral process
Acquisition of data. *See* Data acquisition
Acrotiri (Greece), 135
Actualistic studies, 170
Aerial photos, 82, 83–84, 89, 90, figs. 5.4, 5.5
Aerial radar images, 84, 90
Aerial reconnaissance, 82, 83–85, fig. 5.5
Alloy, 124–125
Alluvium, 65, 96, 150
Altar de Sacrificios (Guatemala), fig. 6.13
Amateurs, 23–24, 30
American Anthropological Association (AAA), 20
Analogy, 119, 122, 123–124, 164–172, 179, figs. 8.1–8.6
Analysis. *See* Data analysis
Annealing, 124, 127
Anthropological models, 32–34
Anthropology, 15–17, 32–34, 167, 170
Antiquarians, 24–30

Antiquities market, 65, 220. *See also* Art market
Arbitrary sample units, 71–72, fig. 4.14
Archaeoastronomy, 191–192
Archaeological Conservancy, 227–228, fig. 10.6
Archaeological conservation
    of artifacts, 107, figs. 4.16, 5.22
    in data processing, 104, 107, fig. 5.22
    of sites, 223, 225–228, 230–231
Archaeological culture, 111, fig. 5.24
Archaeological data. *See* Data
Archaeological Institute of America (AIA), 20, table 1.1
Archaeological legislation, 220, 223–224, 225–226, 229, table 10.1
Archaeological method
    in contextual archaeology, 48, 49, 53
    in cultural history, 36–41, 48
    in cultural process, 43–47, 48
    in data acquisition, 79–111
    in sampling, 70–75
    and science, 10–12
    and theory, 10, 17
Archaeological projects, 75–76, 79, 80, 87, 176–177, 185, fig. 4.16
Archaeological record
    approaches to, 35, 42, 45, 50, 53
    creation of, 61–70

257